W9-CLH-585

The saying goes, "When all you have is a hammer, everything looks like a nail." For far too long apologetics has been a hammer that attempted to strike every false teaching and cultic movement the same way in every community. *Urban Apologetics* is a much-needed, multifaceted tool kit that offers an interdisciplinary approach to promoting biblical faithfulness and gospel fluency. You will find that it utilizes history, sociology, theology, philosophy, and ethics, giving us the screwdrivers, scissors, pliers, wrenches, and hammers needed to repair broken faith in urban communities. As an urban apologist in New York City, the birthplace of many of the ideologies covered in this seminal work, I plan on carrying this tool kit with me wherever I am called to give an answer for the faith within me, and I encourage you to do the same.

—*Pastor Rasool Berry,* Bridge Church, New York City

Eric Mason and team have captured, in one sitting, the rumblings of the cultural winds that threaten to knock down the pillars of our truth that are lost in retweets and likes and memes. Mason's pen is a testament that orthodoxy and swag can coexist like Christ and the most current colloquialisms. This book shouts loud to our times! Jesus is real! No cap.

—*Kirk Franklin,* award-winning gospel artist

As its title suggests, *Urban Apologetics* is about the defense of the faith and, more particularly, a contextualized defense of the faith. It addresses serious threats to the truth of the gospel within the Black community that are mostly unfamiliar to believers outside that community. The contributors are expert analysts who serve readers well with insightful, intelligent commentary and strategy. But the book is so much more. The editor wisely anticipates that many readers will first need to understand *why* so many in the Black community reject the gospel in favor of some truly bizarre belief systems. The common denominator is dismissal of, and reaction to, whiteness. *Urban Apologetics* helps outsiders comprehend what the problem of whiteness means and how it is a genuine impediment for so many to embrace the gospel of Christ. Only after understanding how Western history, culture, and Christianity have contributed to the power of this obstacle can one understand why so many people in the Black community are attracted to belief systems that seem so peculiar to outsiders. *Urban Apologetics* simultaneously informs and provokes, inspires and saddens, educates and chastises, all with an irenic tone from brothers and sisters in Christ that will stir believers within and without the Black community to spiritual solidarity under Jesus our king and brother.

—*Dr. Michael S. Heiser,* executive director, Awakening School of Theology and Ministry, Jacksonville, FL, bestselling author of *The Unseen Realm,* cohost of *The Naked Bible Podcast*

It is my privilege to endorse this very timely and important work, full of information and insight. In contrast to historically false claims that Christianity is a white religion or irrelevant to justice, this work articulates the real story based on real facts from African and African American Christian history. It also invites the church to communicate that message. If you care about communicating to the rising generation, this book is worth your time.

—*Dr. Craig S. Keener,* F. M. and Ada Thompson Professor
of Biblical Studies, Asbury Theological Seminary

The urban context of America warrants a fresh and fiery apologetic. With this text, Dr. Mason delivers! The contributors provide the reader with ample tools to cast down numerous obstacles to the faith. Moreover, this book transforms defenders of the faith to be holistic disciples in their cities. For far too long, our communities have awaited a book like this. At last, it is here!

—*Pastor Cam Triggs,* Grace Alive

In a social climate where genuine Christianity is increasingly seen as irrelevant and impotent, false religions proliferate and entice in every area of culture. The authors of *Urban Apologetics* unpack how false religions exploit Western Christianity's errors to target African American communities; their essays simultaneously celebrate the power of the Holy Spirit to expose all falsehoods and point souls home to Christ. *Urban Apologetics* shows the reader how God transforms persuasive ideological arguments into gospel opportunities, proclaiming Christ's victory over sin, error, and human insufficiency—for his glory and fame.

—*K. A. Ellis,* director, the Edmiston Center for the Study of the Bible and Ethnicity

Eric Mason's team of philosophers and theologians has created apologia for a community whose heterodox teachings have been misunderstood and ignored by traditional theological resources. Speaking to those who have whitewashed or "consciousness community" educations, *Urban Apologetics* reveals the racial biases—evangelical and secular—that have been baptized as truth and masqueraded as the only right readings of history, theology, and Scripture. Within these pages is a corrective needed to help defend the hope all believers hold while also embracing the human dignity of all persons in the body of Christ. This is a *tolle lege* call to any who have a heart that longs for the salvation of the spiritually lost within the African American community. It is a masterful work that lays bare the weaknesses of the Black religious identity cults for those tempted to find hope and power in their teachings.

—*Eric C. Redmond,* PhD, professor of Bible, Moody Bible Institute, Chicago, associate
pastor of preaching, teaching, and care, Calvary Memorial Church, Oak Park, Illinois

Seldom is there a bridge built between the prophetic, the pastoral, and the personal. Such is the case in this work under the oversight of Dr. Eric Mason. The reader senses and experiences the divinely intended connection between the pulpit, the pew, and the prophetic with in this rare work produced out of the contextual hermeneutic of the reality of the westernized urban community.

—*Kenneth C. Ulmer,* DMin, PhD, trustee, the King's University, author of *Walls Can Fall*, senior pastor, Faithful Central Bible Church, Los Angeles, presiding bishop, Macedonia International Bible Fellowship

Black Christians—in schools and prisons, on the streets and on the internet—are under siege, consistently questioned about their faith in Jesus Christ, aggressively told that Christianity is a tool of white supremacy and incompatible with a healthy black identity. That's why *Urban Apologetics* is a godsend, a book that is fully equipped to demolish the myth that "Christianity is the white man's religion" once and for all. Through scholarship that is irrefutable and writing that is engaging and understandable to laymen and academics alike, this work is a must-read for anyone interested in reaching people of African descent with the gospel.

—*Chris Broussard,* founder and president, the K.I.N.G. Movement, internationally known sports broadcaster

Dr. Eric Mason has assembled a brilliant group of male and female marketplace scholars who have symphonically brought together historical accuracy and biblical truth to dispel destructive myths. These myths, if left unaddressed, will continue to do damage in our culture today and for years to come. This book clarifies our past while at the same time providing insight for engaging the present. *Urban Apologetics* is one of those rare books that will become a baton to be handed to men and women who are serious about global gospel transformation.

—*Pastor James White,* executive VP of organizational relations at the YMCA

A much-needed resource for those doing ministry in the urban context, and a great tool to debunk false narratives about the Christian faith.

—*Lisa Fields,* founder and president of the Jude 3 Project

URBAN
APOLOGETICS

URBAN

APOLOGETICS

RESTORING BLACK DIGNITY WITH THE GOSPEL

ERIC MASON

General Editor

ZONDERVAN
REFLECTIVE

ZONDERVAN REFLECTIVE

Urban Apologetics
Copyright © 2021 by Eric Mason

Requests for information should be addressed to:
Zondervan, *3900 Sparks Dr. SE, Grand Rapids, Michigan 49546*

Zondervan titles may be purchased in bulk for educational, business, fundraising, or sales promotional use. For information, please email SpecialMarkets@Zondervan.com.

ISBN 978-0-310-10476-6 (audio)

Library of Congress Cataloging-in-Publication Data

Names: Mason, Eric, (Eric M.) editor.
Title: Urban apologetics : restoring Black dignity with the gospel / Eric Mason, general editor.
Description: Grand Rapids : Zondervan, 2021. | Includes index.
Identifiers: LCCN 2020036122 (print) | LCCN 2020036123 (ebook) | ISBN 9780310100942
    (hardcover) | ISBN 9780310100959 (ebook)
Subjects: LCSH: African Americans--Religion. | African American churches. | African American
    women--Conduct of life. | Church work with African Americans.
Classification: LCC BR563.N4 U725 2021 (print) | LCC BR563.N4 (ebook) | DDC 239/.9--dc23
LC record available at https://lccn.loc.gov/2020036122 LC ebook record available at https://lccn
    .loc.gov/2020036123

Cover design: Micah Kandros Design
Cover photos: © Blackday; Mimage Photography / Shutterstock
Interior design: Kait Lamphere

CONTENTS

Part 3: Tools for Urban Apologetics

CONTRIBUTORS

Vince Bantu is the ohene (president) of the Meachum School of Haymanot and assistant professor of church history and Black church studies at Fuller Theological Seminary. Bantu is the author of the books *A Multitude of All Peoples* and *Gospel Haymanot* as well as a katabi (editor) of the *Haymanot Journal*.

Adam Coleman is the founder and president of Tru-ID Apologetics Ministries. Tru-ID Apologetics Ministries specializes in providing training opportunities for Christians to learn how to defend the Christian Faith with evidence and reason.

Jerome Gay Jr. is the founding and teaching pastor of Vision Church. He's married to Crystal Gay, and they have two lovely children, Jamari Christina Gay and Jerome Jordan Gay III. Jerome has a bachelor's degree from Saint Augustine's University in Broadcasting and a master's degree in theology and ethics from Southeastern Baptist Theological Seminary. He is the author of *Renewal: Grace and Redemption in the Story of Ruth* and *The Whitewashing of Christianity: A Hidden Pastor, a Hurtful Present and a Hopeful Future.*

Tiffany Gill, PhD, is a college professor, historian, and a nationally recognized researcher and scholar of African American history. She currently lives in Philadelphia where she serves as a deacon and a member of the SALT Women's Ministry Leadership Team at Epiphany Fellowship.

Doug Logan is an associate director for Acts 29 and has been in urban ministry for nearly twenty-five years. He serves as the president of Grimké Seminary, founded On the Block Collective, and is the author of *On the Block: Developing a Biblical Picture for Missional Engagement.*

Sarita T. Lyons, JD, PhD, is a psychotherapist specializing in clinical and forensic psychology, and she is on staff at Epiphany Fellowship Church as the director of community life and women's ministry. She serves the local and corporate church through speaking, bible teaching, and consulting on leadership, ministry to women, and the intersection of faith, mental health, and justice. She and her husband Mark have four children.

Eric Mason, DMin, is the founder and lead pastor of Epiphany Fellowship in Philadelphia, as well as the founder and president of Thriving, an urban resource organization committed to developing leaders for ministry in the urban context. He has authored four books: *Manhood Restored, Beat God to the Punch, Unleashed*, and *Woke Church.*

Zion McGregor serves as the minister of apologetics at Bethlehem Baptist Church in Mansfield, Texas.

Damon Richardson, a native of Queens, New York, was raised in Clearwater, Florida, where he grew up in a Muslim household under the teaching of the Nation of Islam. He became a born again believer of Jesus Christ at the age of sixteen and over the last thirty years, he has planted and pastored three churches, traveled itinerantly teaching the Bible, and equipped Christians globally to defend the Christian faith. Damon is married and he and his wife have three sons and one daughter.

Brandon Washington is the pastor of preaching at the Embassy Church in Denver, Colorado. He is a graduate of Denver Seminary where he studied systematic theology, apologetics, and ethics.

Blake Wilson is lead pastor of Crossover Bible Fellowship in Houston, Texas. He also serves as president of Houston Area Pastors: United We Stand and is an executive board member for Houston Church Planters Network. He has an MA in Christian education from Dallas Theological Seminary. He and his wife, Dr. Ronique Wilson, have two children, Reagan Faith Abrielle Wilson and Robert Chance Priest Wilson.

INTRODUCTION

Eric Mason

I became a Christian on the campus of Bowie State University, a histori-
cally Black college, in the early 1990s. During that time, being Black and
Christian was to many African Americans an oxymoron. Hip-hop culture had
popularized Nation of Islam teachings, Five-Percent Nation teachings, and
Pan-Africanism—influences that are still felt to this day. As a new Christian,
I constantly had to give an answer for my faith. I'd spend hours talking and
engaging in evangelism with people of differing ideologies. Books like *Stolen
Legacy*,[1] *Destruction of Black Civilization*,[2] *The World's Sixteen Crucified
Saviors*,[3] *African Holistic Health*,[4] *Message to the Blackman in America*,[5]
Black Men, Obsolete, Single, Dangerous?[6] and many others shaped African
Americans' mindset towards Christianity. John Henrik Clarke, Chancellor
Williams, Yosef Ben-Jochannan, Cheikh Anta Diop, and a host of others played
a vital role in shaping conscious Black thinking in the Black community.

The internet has also given legs to false ideologies in the Black community
in ways we have never seen before. From Sa Neter TV to the Hebrew Israelite
Unity Camp videos to the *Hidden Colors* documentary, the internet is home
to a blitz of information that has indoctrinated thousands of multiclass Blacks
throughout the western hemisphere.

The Black community has experienced a cyclical confusion over knowledge
of self. Every twenty to thirty years, Blacks go through a so-called awakening—an awareness of our need to go back and find our roots. As a Black
individual, I agree that we have been the most pillaged people in the history of
humanity; yet I want us to be educated in truth, not to be intellectually molested
by revisionist falsehood. For years I have been searching for a one-stop shop
to introduce people to what I call "urban apologetics." There are Facebook
groups, personal pages, and YouTube channels on this topic, and while they
are helpful tools, they cannot take the place of the in-depth treatment this book
seeks to provide.

The Black church used to be a central hub for Black life, but that is no longer true. The decentralization of Black life from the Black church has created one of the strongest cultural shifts that African Americans have seen in the last fifty years. The ideologies represented by digital and written resources like the ones mentioned above bear part of the blame. For one hundred years, these falsehoods have grown, and there hasn't been a strong and holistic evangelism and apologetics effort in the Black community to counteract the pseudo scholars of groups like the Hebrew Israelites, Moorish Scientists, Egyptian (Kemetic) spiritualists, and practitioners of African mysticism.

In this resource we will discuss several different groups, many of which are known by different names. At times, we will summarize these groups with the collective phrase "the Black Consciousness Community" or simply the "conscious community." Included in this collective group we include the Moorish Science Temple, the Nation of Islam, Kemetics, Kemetic spirituality, Kemetic Scientists, African mystics, Yoruba spirituality, Africa spirituality, Pan-Africanist, and Black Nationalists. This collective conscious community does not always consider the Hebrew Israelites as a part of their community, although there are strands of the conscious community that have relationships with the Hebrew Israelites because of their common disdain for Christianity. Keep in mind as you read through these chapters that none of the groups are monolithic, and several have overlapping identities. For the most part, those who engage in urban apologetics see the conscious community as a somewhat nebulous group having no clear rubric beyond a Black ethnocentrism and a view that white people (as a group) are fundamentally flawed. Different chapters in this book will provide introductions to and summaries of some of the above groups, explain what they believe, and suggest how urban apologists might respond.

On the college campus I attended and in many of the cities where I've lived, I didn't realize that the work I was doing was a form of apologetics for a Black, urban culture. Even the Christian hip-hop of the late '90s and early 2000s was an attempt to engage in urban apologetics. To meet the need for useful Christian apologetic thinking for an urban audience, I started Thriving, an organization that provides resources for people engaging in ministry in cities and locations where urban culture exists.

Thriving exists to equip urban missionaries for comprehensive global urban ministry through, for, and from the local church. We are biblically based, theologically rich, historically rooted, Christ-centered, Spirit-guided, justice-oriented, missiologically driven, and tailored to the needs of people of color in our efforts to proclaim and practice the multifaceted wisdom of God for the underserved areas of cities. We want to promote the growth of scholarly practitioners for underserved urban environments by training leaders to have a robust love for Jesus and people (1 Chron. 12:32; Mic. 6:8; Matt. 23:23; Acts 2:47; 4:31; Col 1:16; 4:2–6; 2 Tim. 2:15). Our focus is to connect with underserved communities to help provide robust theological acumen from the Scriptures that creatively and contextually prepare God's people for service while at the same time focusing on Jesus. We want to equip and support those dedicated to urban ministry to grow outstanding character, competence, commitment, and compatibility so that they can better serve their city and the local church. Through functional events, media, and online tools, we will work to equip leaders to serve well and to multiply, growing and developing more and more leaders for the building up of Christ's kingdom.

I'm excited for you to get your hands on this resource, and we have some top-notch contributors. In Part 1 of the book, we explore the context for engaging in urban apologetics. Chapter 1 looks at why it is essential that Black dignity engage whiteness on some level. Then, in chapter 2, Pastor Jerome Gay continues the discussion by looking at how Christianity is seen as the white man's religion in the conscious community and among Blacks in general. Pastor Jerome will answer the lie by arguing that Christianity is for all people (Blacks included). In chapter 3, I will further define what we mean by urban apologetics, pointing out the problem of neglecting it and suggesting a better understanding of its biblical, theological, and contextual purpose. For chapter 4, I've asked Dr. Gill to provide a history of how the Black church in America has engaged in apologetics in the past. To finish out the first section, Zion McGregor explains a crisis found in many Black churches today. Many older Black churches are struggling to transition to the new missiological landscape, and this affects the younger generations that have grown up in the church and in communities where these churches exist. Rev. McGregor will help the Black church to chart a new path toward answering the urgent questions of this generation.

Part two of the book looks at several religious and ethnic identity groups. Chapter 6 begins with an introduction to the Nation of Islam. Although they are not as influential as they were from the 1960's through the 1990's, no other group within the conscious community has had as much influence on Black sociological thinking as the Nation of Islam. Each sect within the conscious community (save the Moorish Science Temple) owes a great debt to the Nation of Islam for the way in which they think about identity and connection.

Although they aren't new, one of the groups that has grown in popularity in recent years is the Hebrew Israelites. In chapter 7, I explore the varying beliefs and philosophies of this group, including the popular belief that African Americans are really descended from the Israelites and are of non-African descent. My primary concern in this chapter is with the theological framework of one of the major sects of the Hebrew Israelites and those who are influenced by their theological beliefs. In this chapter I will engage several of their key beliefs with Scripture and point readers to the gospel.

In chapter 8, Dr. Vince Bantu will provide us with a broad view of African history that helps us to defuse the underlying arguments of African spirituality and Kemetic philosophy. Many of the anti-Christian beliefs held by these groups are borrowed from white liberal Christian scholarship and fail to engage the history of the Christian faith. Much of what you find in this movement is little more than confirmation bias.

Most of the groups mentioned above are dominated by men, and in many instances Black women have been treated unkindly by men, both Black and white. Yet Black women have been the backbone of the Black community for generations. Today, many millennial and Gen Z Black women are being influenced by feminist and womanist movements, and the Black conscious community is giving women more influence. In chapter 9, Dr. Sarita T. Lyons contends that the Black conscious community and feminism are both "lifeless lifeboats," that cannot rescue Black women. She charts a biblical path for Black women navigating questions about Christianity and biblical femininity.

If the Christian church is going to be effective in reaching the men that dominate the groups mentioned in this book, it needs to cast a compelling vision of what it looks like to be a Christian man and what the gospel says to men. We must paint a biblical and historical picture of the true Jesus, and in chapter 10, I give several practical steps for doing so.

Finally, we end part 2 with a look at Black atheism. Celebrities like D. L. Hugely and many members of the conscious community mix atheism with ethnocentricity. In chapter 11, Adam Coleman examines the components of the new Black atheism and where this worldview comes from. Adam will help us better understand how to respond to this significant surge of atheism in the Black community.

In part 3, we seek to offer some practical tools for engaging in urban apologetics. Chapter 12, by Pastor Brandon Washington, looks at the dominant worldviews and philosophies typically present in urban cultures. This chapter gives you the mental "lay of the land," along with suggestions for using the gospel to engage people in an urban setting.

Most of the chapters in this book deal with verbal apologetic engagement, yet in most urban contexts, outreach that includes acts of service to the community are just as needed. Service opportunities provide gospel engagement and create common ground with the community; in chapter 13, Doug Logan stirs our hearts for the task of "outreach" apologetics.

At the core of much of what we are discussing is the need for biblical literacy. In chapter 14, Pastor Blake Wilson covers the need to know your Bible, offering pastoral counsel on how to know a fake by knowing the real thing. Knowing the Bible and having intimacy with the Most High are irreplaceable tools for engaging apologetically.

And in chapter 15, I conclude by reminding us of the larger spiritual context in which we engage these apologetic questions and concerns. The Bible teaches that we don't wrestle against flesh and blood; while we utilize arguments, rebuttals, and historical facts, these are not enough if we lack God's armor and fail to pray for the Spirit of God to be at work. We must not think for one minute that our good works alone are sufficient to win over hearts and minds. Urban apologetics is spiritual warfare, a supernatural work that requires us to depend on the LORD.

My hope is that we will eventually see millions of African Americans saved and our church communities purged of the pseudo nonsense of the conscious community and other false religious and ethnocentric groups. I want people to see and experience Jesus's supremacy in every area of life. "For from him and through him and for him are all things. To him be the glory forever! Amen" (Rom. 11:36).

PART I

THE CONTEXT FOR

URBAN APOLOGETICS

CHAPTER 1

RESTORING BLACK DIGNITY

Eric Mason

THIS CHAPTER introduces the pressing need to recover the biblical concept of dignity for Blacks. While much work remains to be done, this chapter provides four examples of specific ways we can work to reintroduce the value of Black dignity.

The show *A Different World*, which ran from 1987–1993, was one of the most highly rated shows of its time and remains heavily syndicated. This show offered viewers of all ethnicities a sneak peek into the life of students at a historically Black college (hereafter HBCU). More significantly, the show tackled deep issues that Black college students often face, like drugs, rape, white supremacy, AIDS, economics, careers, and history. For many African Americans, *A Different World* was our show. It dealt with our issues and was willing to take risks to give voice to Blacks in America without adopting a blaxploitation format.

A Different World played a role in communicating Black dignity in a way that still rings true to many of us today. By including characters who were not from the "hood" or from single parent homes, it sought to show that African Americans aren't monolithic. Black college enrollment increased exponentially during the time of this show. I participated in this trend, going to Bowie State University, which is the third oldest HBCU in the country and a college that began in a Black church.

This show's role in restoring African American dignity is important because dignity has historically been stripped from African Americans. As a people we were unbiblically kidnapped[1] and sold unwillingly into slavery by Europeans, carried across the blue chasm, raped, left for dead, or thrown overboard to become shark food. Once on shore, we were sold again—often while naked or scantily clothed. We were introduced to the land of the free as broken, reeking, undignified persons and considered subhuman, belonging to everyone *but* the living God.

Our dignity has lingered in a state of confusion for generations in this country as we've faced constant harassment, false theologies, white supremacy, syncretistic evangelicalism, and civic suppression. Our dignity has been molested from every side: misuse of the Bible and civic commendation, the Curse of Ham, the Thirteenth Amendment, the KKK, the criminalization of Black boys, underfunded education, redlined housing, unjust gentrification, horrendous food, drugs, guns—the list goes on. From the time of slavery to today, our country has created a perfect storm to annihilate Black people. The traumatic effects of white supremacy and the traumatization of Blacks generationally have made it difficult for Blacks to assimilate into white culture and have led many to develop coping mechanisms to make sense of the mad experience called the "United States of America."

AFRICAN INFLUENCE IN THE EARLY CHURCH

Black students are always shocked to learn that many of the early Christian church fathers were African. Tertullian, Augustine, Athanasius, Cyprian, Origen, and others were all from North Africa, and while they were not all necessarily dark skinned, they were probably not white. Athanasius bore the nickname "Black Dwarf" (although the author who claims this has not provided a citation).[2] As Oden writes of Athanasius:

> Christians living before Athanasius were long settled in the middle Nile as far south as Oxyrhynchus and the Fayyum. Athanasius, according to his own statement, came from an environment of very modest means, not from a foreign elite. As a child he was noticed playing on the beach by Alexander, the bishop of Alexandria, and virtually adopted as if an orphan, according to an early tradition. This leaves entirely mute the genetics of the great leader, but there are many indications that he kept close and active ties with middle Nile ethnics of many varieties who spoke proto-Coptic or cognate Nilotic-based languages. When he was forced into exile, he sought refuge in the desert areas far away from the cosmopolitan, Greek-speaking urban ban ethos of Alexandria.[3]

More than likely many of these church fathers had variations in skin colors— yet when I look at illustrations of them in books and commentaries, they are usually portrayed as white men.

Most of us assume "Latin" means "Roman" and assume that anyone writing in Latin was white. Biblical scholars like Adolf von Harnack and many others carried along these fallacies without any opposition, and the picture of the early church fathers as white men continues to exist in much of global academia.[4] Scholar Thomas Oden indicates that this was intentional:

> If the writings of Philo, Synesius, Victor of Vita and Shenute of Atripe had all been written in France, they would be called European. But they were not. They were written in Africa. So why shouldn't they be called African? There is a prejudice at work here: suspect anything of intellectual value that comes from the African continent as having some sort of secret European origin.
>
> What convincing argument can be set forth to deny their Africanness? How black were the Christians of North Africa? Black enough, if blackness is understood in terms of intergenerational suffering and oppression.[5]

Generally speaking, the more central the figure is to the history of Christian history and theological development, the greater the temptation has been for European historians and theologians to ignore that person's ethnicity. Historians like to paint history in their own image.

Ignoring details like these have contributed to the whitewashing of history. This is just one of many ways that white people have been misleading the church. The pen of Christian history has been placed in white hands. In my own experience, for as much as I loved my theological education, the contributions of those who were not white Europeans were largely neglected. Not only was there miseducation but also brash ignorance. For example, a seminary student once asked his professor, "What have Blacks contributed to theology and Christian history?" In response, the professor joked, "You all can really sing!" This was a professor who had been in the classroom for almost four decades. Needless to say, this comment did little to help. It only further contributed to the student's pain of being educated by the descendants of his ancestor's oppressors.

Many professors will only grudgingly admit that many of those who shaped western philosophy, rhetoric, exegesis, apologetics, missionary efforts, and our doctrinal understandings were people of color. We must recover and highlight this fact. I encourage you to say this right now, out loud to yourself: "Most of the pioneers of early Christian formation were not whites, but people of color."

Our desire in this book is not to repaint history Black, however. Rather, we want to be people of integrity and truth, as Scripture calls us to be:

> Lord, who can dwell in your tent? . . . The one who lives blamelessly, practices righteousness, and acknowledges the truth in his heart. (Ps. 15:1, 2 CSB)

Whoever speaks the truth declares what is right, but a false witness speaks deceit. (Prov. 12:17 CSB)

A truthful witness rescues lives, but one who utters lies is deceitful. (Prov. 14:25 CSB)

BLACK DIGNITY THROUGHOUT AMERICAN HISTORY

With the end of slavery in the United States, many Blacks were searching for an ethnic identity. Much of what they saw and experienced of Christianity was culturally white. African American church leaders faced the hard work of decontextualizing the culturally captive components of Christianity into their raw form and then properly recontextualizing them for the Blacks in this country. Because our African-ness had been tortured out of us, and some had even grown to despise it, there was a daunting tension inherent in being Black in a white country. Black American Christians struggled to understand who we are as human beings. The Bible is clear that we were made to be creators of culture (Gen. 1:28), yet since the ancient boundaries of our land, language, and culture had all been removed, we found ourselves in a deep state of confusion.

American culture trains us to have an imperialist's view of other cultures (i.e. "we are the best") while simultaneously acting like America has none of its own cultural shortcomings or biases. Our brown siblings are ostracized if they struggle with English; Asians are mocked for their stereotypical academic intelligence; while Africans are viewed as bush people. We aren't trained in America to allow people to express their culture; this suppression of culture was compounded for freed slaves, contributing to their confusion over who they are. Because God is the one who made our ethnicities, they matter and need to be redeemed. If you are unclear about your ethnicity, you will find yourself confused over what about you needs redeeming.

The Black church is the cultural innovation of Black people in America. Because Blacks were rejected by whites, we created our own traditions so that we could possess a sense of indigenous culture—something of our own. Yet many Blacks view the Black church as an African expression of a white man's religion, a mixture of what was remembered from the African culture of our homeland and adaptations from white, American Christianity. Others, like Bishop Mason, founder of the Church of God in Christ, tried to contextualize various cultural expressions from Africa and redeem them for the Black church worship experience. Although some would still argue that the Black church is a European expression of Christianity, the Church of God in Christ's founder clearly sought something different.

> [Bishop] Mason especially insisted upon the centrality of personal inner transformation without shedding distinctive African cultural expressions. Mainline black churches saw adherence to African worldviews and religious folk culture associated with rural life or Slave Religion, which reflected a low cultural standing. Rising middle-class educated blacks seeking assimilation in the majority white culture preferred European worldviews shaped by the Enlightenment.[6]

As a point of embarrassment, many saw the Black church as a counterfeit spirituality. They viewed it as counterfeit because they believed it was "forced" on Black people, and today we are still trying to make sense of our identity. Several of those who (wrongly) didn't view Christianity as an indigenous African spirituality began exploring other options, and this led to the rise of Black mystery religions, ideologies, and cults. You will learn that all of these movements share two major—and seemingly attractive—views. They believe that Christianity is the religion of the oppressors, and they teach and promote the idea that Blacks need dignity formation—without the interference of white people.

During the time of the Great Migration of the twentieth century, there were many religious shifts spurred by immigration and migration, and these were not limited to the various movements of African American Christianity. During this time, and especially in urban contexts, notable numbers of people of African descent began to establish and participate in movements outside of Protestant Christianity. Many turned to theologies that provided new ways of thinking about history, racial identity, ritual, community life, and the collective future of Black people.[7] As you will see throughout this book, race and spirituality are inseparable to most of these groups.

A BIBLICAL UNDERSTANDING OF DIGNITY

What is the appeal of these groups on the issue of Black dignity? Let's begin with an understanding of what we mean by "dignity." Dignity is something we see in the Bible from the beginning. It is core to the creation narrative in Genesis 1, and it is God's top priority to restore creation's dignity after Genesis 3. When we refer to "dignity," we are talking about God-invested value. Dignity has many layers, and Christians believe that our dignity and value is rooted in

God's creation of mankind and his purpose for his creation. Genesis 1 explains that God created all the animals according to their own kind (Gen. 1:21–25), but he created humans according to his own image and likeness (Gen. 1:26–27). All human dignity is derived from God by virtue of him saying that we are "very good" (Gen. 1:31) and by the care he took in his creation of us: fashioning man from the dust, blowing life into him, fashioning woman from man and blowing life into her, and giving us purpose in connection with God. Both body and breath are valuable to God, and they should be valuable to us as well. The fall of human beings into sinful disobedience only disrupted and removed our connection to God; it did not take away our inherent value and worth.

The book of Genesis uses two terms, "likeness" and "image," to describe human beings who in some way reflect the form and the function of the creator. We likely reflect God's form in a spiritual sense rather than a physical sense. The phrase "image of God" refers to "the God-given mental and spiritual capacities that enable people to relate to God and to serve him by ruling over the created order as his earthly vice-regents."[8] We also reflect this image through our created bodies. Psalm 139 affirms this: "For it was you who created my inward parts; you knit me together in my mother's womb. I will praise you because I have been remarkably and wondrously made. Your works are wondrous, and I know this very well" (Ps. 139:13–14 CSB). The psalmist finds his self-value in God's value of him.

In the psalmist's mind, humanity finds value not just in our being redeemed through Jesus, but in our being created by God. This is particularly important because while we affirm that our identity is in Christ, our value didn't start at justification but at *creation*. Our identity in Christ is a culmination of our value—it is not the beginning of our value. God valued us even while we were sinners (Rom. 5:8). Our ethnic value doesn't change in salvation, but it is given redemptive clarity as it is brought under the cross.

RESTORING BLACK DIGNITY

The importance of dignity is frequently lost among all of the historical, exegetical, and rhetorical arguments that go into apologetic engagement. This is one of the concerns we seek to address in this book. We urgently need a restoration of the human dignity that was broken by the historical narrative of racial injustice in America and the West. If we fail to address the recovery of the *imago dei* (image of God) in the *imago Christi* (image of Christ), the enemy will continue to molest people caught in his cultic web. Here are some ideas for how we can engage in this critical work of restoration.

Get Rid of All the Images of White Jesus

Umar Johnson, a psychologist and the self-proclaimed "Prince of Pan Africanism," frequently challenges the color of Jesus portrayed in Christian visuals and art. He refers to the money given in Black churches as "white Jesus money" and accuses those who make such gifts of being consciously irresponsible, of wasting that money by not using it to impact Black communities instead.[9]

We need to rid the church of the images of white Jesus. We do this not merely because the white image has been wrongly used for centuries, but because we are aware of the way this image has been used by mystery cults in Black communities. Suffice it to say, *many* Blacks feel that images of a white Jesus are a stumbling block to the gospel. Paul states in 2 Corinthians 6:3, "We put no obstacle in anyone's way, so that no fault may be found with our ministry" (ESV). Yet images of a white Jesus have done exactly that—they have become an obstacle to belief:

> By wrapping itself with the alleged form of Jesus, whiteness gave itself a holy face. But he was a shape-shifting totem of white supremacy. The differing and evolving physical renderings of white Jesus figures not only bore witness to the flexibility of racial constructions but also helped create the perception that whiteness was sacred and everlasting. With Jesus as white, Americans could feel that sacred whiteness stretched back in time thousands of years and forward in sacred space to heaven and the second coming.[10]

Ridding the church of images of white Jesus is a very practical step to take. And this effort would be noticed, sending shock waves throughout Black communities. African Americans might see this as evidence that the American church is finally bearing fruit in keeping with repentance. It can begin by making a change in how the white church visually communicates Jesus. This may be costly, as stained-glass windows, books, and paintings would need to be removed.

Even now, as I'm writing this chapter in a café, a fifty-year-old African American man was looking at the books piled around me. Remarking on the topic of Jesus, he casually said, "You know he wasn't a white man, right?" As happy as I was to hear him say this, I am aware that there is a huge need to correct the relationship that Black Americans had with the whitewashed Jesus. We all recognize that Jesus wasn't a white European, yet we still need to take radical steps to correct this portrayal, which for many Black people is a sign of ongoing white cultural supremacy.

Correct Efforts to Minimize Black Dignity in Scholarship

The year 2019 marked the 400-year anniversary of the first twenty inden-tured servants' arrival in Jamestown, Virginia. These individuals would even-tually become some of America's first slaves. Slavery was legalized in 1641, transitioning the seven-year indentured servitude system into a permanent sentence. Blacks went from being people to a form of "black gold."

We need more than affirmative action to correct the centuries of broken dignity experienced by Black people. The evangelical church, under the lead-ership of American Blacks, needs to work on a dignity restoration program that addresses everything from publishing to art and education. We need to educate the church about the influence of scholars like Adolf von Harnack and others who have whitewashed history in the academy. Dr. J. Daniel Hays wrote several articles fleshing out this historical bias in the academy throughout the modern era:

> One of the interesting (and troubling) things that I have encountered during this study is a lingering racial bias within the academy, which is still dom-inated by White scholars . . . What do I mean by racial bias in academic works today? I am not referring to the blatant racial prejudice that was relatively common in the historical/religious scholarship of the nineteenth and early twentieth centuries, although, as I mention below, many of these works are still in print and being used. Most everyone in the academy today knows that racial bias or prejudice is morally bad, as well as unscholarly.[11]

Hays goes on to talk about how many white scholars view addressing racial bias as a less important endeavor in scholarship. Neglect of this kind, whether intentional or unintentional, is damaging and creates the perception of image sabotage. We see revisionist colorization in suggestions that Egypt's prowess came from a small group of elite whites, and in efforts to hide the historic and ethnic background of countries like Cush and Ethiopia. Keener brings some refreshing accuracy, countering these efforts in his recent four-part commen-tary on the book of Acts. He points out that the Greek title "Ethiopia" techni-cally included all of Africa south of Egypt and that the title used for Candace (the Queen) indicates that the Nubian kingdom of Meroë is specifically in view here.[12] Meroë's Nubia was then a Black African kingdom between Aswan and Khartoum.[13] My point in referencing this is to argue that this type of detailed clarity—a willingness to admit that Black people held positions of authority in biblical times rather than an effort to whitewash history—is needed even more today. These efforts to change will need to be made repeatedly and will require repentance and copious grace. Brotherhood in this endeavor involves working together to fulfill the law of Christ by carrying one another's burdens (Gal. 6:2)—including the burden of correcting faulty scholarship from the past.

Create Images Intentionally for Black and Brown Children

In the 1940s, Doctors Kenneth and Mamie Clark conducted an experiment on children known as "the doll test." Via "the doll test," the doctors tested children's responses to Black and white dolls that looked the same (other than skin tone) and recorded which doll they chose. They conducted this test to show the impact of segregation on the self-worth of Black children. Most children chose the white doll. In 1950, Kenneth Clark wrote a paper from the study that was used by the Supreme Court and influenced their comprehension of the impact of segregated education on Black dignity. This is their statement:

> To separate [African American children] from others of similar age and qualifications solely because of their race generates a feeling of inferiority as to their status in the community that may affect their hearts and minds in a way unlikely ever to be undone.[14]

Dr. Kenneth Clark was dismayed that the court failed to cite two other conclusions he had reached: that racism was an inherently American institution and that school segregation inhibited the development of white children, too.

> The issues highlighted by "the doll test" remain a major concern today, one that still needs to be redeemed. Countless black parents I know speak of this in child rearing. From superheroes to Bible shows to homeschooling curriculum, there is a pressing need for images that positively portray black and brown children, and many black parents have a difficult time finding images that affirm the dignity of their children. Even my white friends who have adopted black children are appalled at how blind they had been to this prior to their adoption of a black child. But this has always existed for blacks, often accompanied by outright racism through the constant promotion of white images.[15]

My oldest son is a great artist. He began sketching at a pretty young age, and he would always draw white folks, even when he was creating heroes. I once asked him, "Son, what color do you wish you were?" and he answered, "White!" As we worked through these beliefs, it became obvious to me that he had been deeply impacted by all of the images of whiteness that he had experienced over the years. From that point forward, my wife and I intentionally looked to give him positive Black images. We exposed him to global culture, and he has grown to love people of all different cultures—including the person God has created him to be.

Recover the Imago Dei as a Foundational Bible Doctrine

I believe we must reintroduce teaching on the image of God (*imago Dei*) as a part of the foundational biblical and gospel education we provide for all believers. In the book of Acts, the Jerusalem Council deemed that particular issues were foundational to the Christian education of gentiles. Similarly, the western church today needs to recover as a core part of our teaching that people are created in the image of God. We need to constantly remind ourselves that because of our history with racism and slavery in this country, we have differing values we attach to people—despite our "belief" that we are all created in the image and likeness of God.

As we teach creation, fall, redemption, and consummation, we must zoom in on the concept of human dignity, taking time to repent of the teachings that the church has overtly and covertly communicated about Blacks in the narrative of American history. Because Christians have participated in creating false doctrines about Black humanity, there needs to be open dialogue and repentance until this urban legend is fully eradicated from Christianity. Dr. Evans engages this in his landmark book *Oneness Embraced*. He writes, "On one side, I was being told that I was created in the image of God and therefore had value. On a pragmatic basis, however, it appeared to me that the benefits of possessing that divine image were reserved for white people because it seemed that they were the real benefactors of God's kingdom on earth."[16] Dr. Evans felt that the freedoms of the kingdom had been given to others but were kept from him. Economic, educational, political, theological, and life development opportunities (and the runways that lead to them) are readily afforded our white Christian brethren, and African Americans see the gaping holes that expose these inequities. Because of this, many fall prey to anemic ideologies and cults which scratch the uncomfortable itch they feel, an itch that suggests the Christian church has not fairly divided the blessings of the gospel.

In all of these efforts, we must begin by taking seriously the fact that Black dignity is a core need, one that must be engaged in honest and restorative ways to meet the current crisis. To love people is to value them and to uphold their inherent dignity. Who can do that better than the Lord Jesus Christ?

CHAPTER 2

ALL WHITE EVERYTHING

Jerome Gay

CHRISTIAN SCHOLARSHIP rarely acknowledges that people of color had significant roles in both Scripture and the early church. Over centuries, primarily white historians have whitewashed Christian history, making it seem like a religion founded and perpetuated by white Europeans. This has led many Black people to question whether they have any place in the Christian church—and has pushed many to seek belonging in religious identity groups outside of the church.

On February 15th, 1974, the show *Good Times* aired an episode called "Black Jesus." *Good Times* featured a strong Black family—with loving parents, creative children, and caring neighbors—living in a Chicago housing project. The star of the show was the flamboyant James "J. J." Evans Jr., with his rousing signature wail "Dy-no-miiiite!" On this episode, J. J.'s brother, Michael, hangs J. J.'s painting of a Black Jesus on the wall next to the family's framed print of a conventionally rendered white Christ. "A Black family should have a Black Jesus on the wall," Michael says, amazed by the picture. When their mother Florida Evans comes home and notices, a debate ensues. She argues of the white Jesus, "When I was a baby, I don't know what I saw first: my momma, my poppa, or this Jesus. Now he's the one I know and love, so let's close the subject." Then she adds the clincher, "If Jesus was Black, the Bible would've said so." To that, Michael grabs a Bible and objects, "But it does say so." Then he begins reading from Revelation: "The hairs of his head were white, like white wool, like snow. His eyes were like a flame of fire, his feet were like burnished bronze, refined in a furnace, and his voice was like the roar of many waters" (1:14–15 ESV). (This verse is more symbolic than literal, and while Jesus's race is a component of his ontological makeup and he certainly wasn't a white man, this verse isn't about his race—it's symbolic for his judgment and power.)

Florida grabs the Bible from Michael with a look of disbelief. "Oh Lord have mercy, it sure do say that, don't it?" she says. Michael concludes, "Momma, how do we know Jesus wasn't Black? He could've been from the lost tribe of Israel, they were supposed to be Black." In true *Good Times* fashion, the segment ends with levity as J. J. responds, "If ever a people were lost, we're it."

Florida's statements highlight how the American church has responded to the idea of a Black Jesus and how proponents of the white Jesus myth have fought vehemently to perpetuate the Christian faith as one almost exclusively influenced by white people. Florida told her son to "close the subject." Closing the subject and refusing to address whitewashing have effectively kept the white Jesus myth active for centuries. Statements like "His race doesn't matter" or "Talks like this get away from the core message" and "I'm colorblind" are often deployed to close the subject. But this only nurtures the delusion that Jesus was white and contributes to people making the eternal decision to reject Yeshua (Christ) based on this erroneous assertion.

When thousands of Black and brown people are turning away from the faith in part due to the perpetuation of a white Jesus, we must ask: Why? When an entire faith is misrepresented, we must ask: Why? When whitewashing eclipses the core message of the gospel, we must examine why white Jesus is the only Jesus most people know. The reason is whitewashing. Whitewashing has taken place for centuries, and it has tainted the Christian faith.

DEFINING THE TERM "WHITEWASHING"

So what exactly is whitewashing? The term "whitewashing," like the term "white privilege," can elicit a vast array of responses, including vehement ridicule. I've found that opponents of the term "whitewashing" and the concept it represents rarely ask how we're defining it. Instead, they assume and respond to their self-created narrative on the subject.

Like much of the 'Christianese' used in churches all over the world, definitions are essential to understanding and engagement. With this thought in mind, I want you to think of whitewashing beyond the political propaganda used by "the left" to divide us; instead, it is a historical reality that still affects the way we think about and present the Christian faith. This will help us to engage the concept with a more balanced perspective as we review historical realities that shape how we engage Scripture, humanity, and Christian history.

The Cambridge dictionary defines whitewashing as "an attempt to stop people from finding out the true facts about a situation."[1] This is an attempt to hide facts in order to control a narrative. An example of whitewashing is the use of white people to represent people of color in film and history. This second definition serves as a picture, a metaphor that sheds light on what has been done to the Christian faith over the centuries. The version of Christianity that has been presented to us in the West for centuries is largely void of any ethnic diversity. That's a significant problem.

Whitewashed Christianity refers to the affinity of white Christian scholars to dominate the Bible, Christian art, literature, and history with white people at the expense of authentic ethnicity and true scholarship in order to resonate most deeply with the experiences, presuppositions, and worldviews of white audiences. As Ernest Grant says, "whitewashing occurs institutionally and structurally when the contributions of the African Diaspora to theology, ethics, and culture are largely ignored, and the influence of people groups of European descent are accentuated."[2] Another term related to the concept of whitewashing is "eurocentrism." Eurocentrism is placing the experience, culture, and philosophy of people of European descent at the center of personal understanding and culture. Essentially, it's making what is "white" universal. Eurocentrism is a particular kind of ethnocentrism that elevates and, in most cases, deifies whiteness based on the false belief that whites are superior and other races are inferior.[3]

WHY WE MUST CONFRONT WHITEWASHING

The whitewashing of Christianity and its Eurocentric focus has led to growing sentiment among people of African descent, as well as people across the globe, that Christianity is a Western-created, European-influenced, white-owned religion of oppression. While this is historically inaccurate, there are legitimate reasons that many people have adopted this assertion. As Dr. Vince Bantu explains, "Christianity has been perverted into a mechanism of tyranny by many Western nations."[4] The main reason for this growing sentiment is historical and cultural whitewashing, as well as the under-emphasized reality that the gospel took firm root in Africa, the Middle East, and Asia long before it reached the West.

In order to accurately present the gospel and the Christian faith, we must understand that Christianity is not the cultural property of any single racial or ethnic group; rather, it has always existed as a family of chosen people composed of every nation, tribe, and tongue. Because many non-Western people groups have been made to feel culturally alienated from the gospel, it is imperative that we explore the neglected history of non-Western Christianity.[5] We must confront whitewashing. As we explore whitewashing in this chapter, we'll see that it must not only be confronted but diagnosed within Western evangelicalism and opposed by all who claim Christianity as their theological home.

This doesn't mean that every white scholar is racist, nor does it mean that every white Christian scholar was complicit in the historic whitewashing that plagues Christianity in the West today. However, we must not ignore how the history of white supremacy has affected the presentation and propagation of the Christian faith, especially in the West. When we look at whitewashing historically, we'll find that it was dishonest, deliberate, and—when intentionally or passively ignored—destructive.

Whitewashing Is Dishonest

A tactic of white supremacy has been to intentionally remove any African influence from the presentation of Christianity and its history. Just peruse Saint Vladimir's Press, do a Google search, or look up church fathers on Amazon, and you'll see almost every African church father and African martyr presented as a white man or woman. We see this in art that inaccurately portrays Middle Eastern Jewish biblical figures and North African church fathers as white. "White Jesus," says Dr. Eric Mason, theologian and pastor of Epiphany Fellowship, "has done more harm historically than the Confederate flag."[6] Sadly, Dr. Mason's statement is true.

Education about church history oftentimes starts with the Reformation in Europe instead of with Israel and Africa and thus bypasses North African influence. For instance, the library of Alexandria of the third century provided the standard of the European university used in practically all of medieval Europe, but Africa and Africans are rarely given credit or acknowledged for their contributions. People like Basil the Great, Gregory of Nazianzus, and Gregory of Nyssa (all fourth century) are generally credited with developing and clarifying the theological doctrines of God the Father, God the Son, and God the Holy Spirit. The reality is that these Cappadocian fathers were shaped by the exegesis of African Christians like Origen, considered to be one of Africa's greatest scientific investigators of sacred text, as well as African scholars like Didymus the Blind and Tyconius. Additionally, almost every piece of literature in seminaries and institutions of higher education that mention African fathers like Augustine present them as white men. This dishonesty isn't accidental, it is deliberate, as we'll see in the next section.

Whitewashing Is Deliberate

The historic version of Christianity presented in America often doesn't acknowledge the diversity found within Scripture and history. This isn't an accident, nor are those doing the printing, proclaiming, and proselytizing aloof to the reality of color in the Bible and the African influence on the Christian faith that preceded the European reformers and Puritans. Numidia, Mauretania, Byzacena, and Libya are home to tons of martyrial oratories, cemeteries, and churches that date back to the fourth and fifth centuries and some that date to well before the Constantinian conquest. Yet many of our seminaries, lectures, and publications leave out this rich history.[7]

Why? Because whitewashing is deliberate. To present an accurate narrative of Christian history that includes Africa rather than starting with the Protestant Reformation of the sixteenth century causes those who are happy with a whitewashed narrative to lose their power. What power? Power to control and propagate a narrative that favors the idea that Christianity is primarily shaped by, influenced by, and the property of white people. While this notion is false, it's functionally true when we look at Christianity in America, both histori-cally and presently. J. Daniel Hays points this out by addressing the fact that several of the twentieth-century giants of Old Testament studies, for example, were located in pre-WWII Germany, where racism was not only frequent but widely accepted and extremely influential on the thinking of intellectuals. Additionally, the colonial outlook of many pre-WWII British intellectuals had a strong influence on biblical scholars and archaeologists in Britain as well. Because of the veneration of these white scholars by other white scholars, their racial prejudice was overlooked, and many white scholars continue to be influenced by their views.[8]

Whitewashing Is Destructive

The destructive nature of whitewashing is seen in high definition when we consider that slave owners painted the Bible white in order to justify chat-tel slavery. Developing and spreading fallacies like the Curse of Ham and Aristotle's Climate Theory while ignoring the Black presence in the Bible was essential to slave owners' attempts to convince Black people of their tainted identity. Sadly, this hasn't changed much. When books ignore the African heritage of many within Scripture, they support the myth that Jesus was a white man with twelve white disciples.

What makes whitewashing destructive is that it presents God as only using one group of people. Also troubling is the fact that institutions who hold themselves to high standards of orthodoxy and historical accuracy actually and functionally support the false notion that God uses just one people group. When we fail to acknowledge the Black presence in redemptive history, we leave people of color with questions about the role they play in God's plan. Whitewashing is a barrier to the message of hope—and an unnecessary one at that.

The realities of whitewashing seem pretty obvious, but many people deny that it's an issue that needs addressing. For instance, they argue that the gospel isn't for one group of people. I agree with that, but I argue that the gospel wasn't shared by only one group, either. They argue that race doesn't matter. This argument not only reveals their assumption that their version of history and their anthropological experience is universal and therefore applies to everyone, but it also fails to acknowledge that they've used race in their favor to paint the Bible and Christian history largely white. Perhaps most concerning is that those who refuse to address the reality of whitewashing reveal a lack of Christian love in their failure to consider how whitewashing affects people of color and the Christian faith in general. Whitewashing wrongly validates and champions the implicit cultural and historical bias within conservative evangelical communities, bolstering the notion that people of color will remain unequal to our white counterparts, regardless of our credentialing or accomplishments.[9]

You can't support or ignore whitewashing while championing truth, love, and orthodoxy. Whitewashing is destructive because it's a lie—a blatant, diabolical lie. It's a hermeneutical lie to read white people on every page of Scripture and wonder why Black people question if the Christian faith is a white man's religion. It's destructive because it hands primarily people of color to Black Religious Identity Cults (hereafter BRIC). It's destructive because it presents a truncated gospel that holds one group of people as more valuable than others. It's destructive because it contributes to lostness while opposing the Christian mission to depopulate hell through the spread of the authentic gospel.

Whitewashing, when not confronted, exacts the same vitriol on society as white supremacy. In many ways, whitewashing is an extension of white supremacy. White supremacy is the fanaticism and obsession over "whiteness" that leads to the dehumanization, degradation, and disenfranchisement of those not considered "white", thus making whiteness the standard for all other people groups. When we allow Christianity to remain whitewashed, we allow a false narrative to infect our faith; and we lead many people into embracing an inaccurate biblical framework that presents false depictions of Eurocentric Bible figures as fact without remorse or repentance. This is why whitewashing is not something we can ignore. We must confront it with truth.

ASPECTS OF WHITEWASHED CHRISTIANITY

There are two primary aspects of whitewashed Christianity: historical whitewashing and class whitewashing. Historical whitewashing occurs when literature, whether children's books or academic textbooks, presents practically all biblical characters as white men and women. Historical whitewashing occurs when nearly every church father is presented as a white man, despite his true heritage. People of European heritage don't receive this treatment. When someone is European, historians have assumed they're white and presented them as such in literature and art. Yet when someone is African, historians for centuries have comfortably assumed they are white—or worse, rewritten history to present them as white. This is especially true for those who have done something significant as it relates to hermeneutics, homiletics, theology, education, and/or scholarship. That's why Athanasius, historically nicknamed "The Black Dwarf" based on his dark skin and short stature,[10] is portrayed as a white man resembling Saint Nicholas. This is not only dishonest, it's also diabolical. When we present a God who is homogenous in whom he uses, we undermine the faith we claim. It also undermines our claim to be committed to truth. Yes, we're committed to the truth—yet Christians have been willing to rewrite history when the truth is that most of Christian history involves people of color.

Class whitewashing occurs when we present people of color in Scripture and history almost exclusively as slaves. This is most clearly seen in how scholars present the Cushites in Scripture. Scholars present this people, known for their archery skill and leadership, almost exclusively as slaves, even though they're mentioned almost more than any other group in the Old Testament (though not nearly so often by most scholars).[11] Why would we present an African tribe living hundreds of years before the antebellum South as slaves who had nothing to contribute but their manual labor? Why would we do this without sources to confirm it? This characterization is indicative of a subconscious—and in many cases conscious—racial bias. Presentations of people of color in this way demonstrate poor scholarship and expose how these scholars view African and other ethnic contributions to faith, scholarship, and history as insignificant and not worthy of scholarly effort.

Historic and class whitewashing have contributed to the false narrative that Christianity is a white man's religion—that God only used white people in Scripture and that only white scholars can determine what is accurate and historical for the world to consume. This narrative is dangerous and contributes to the lostness of people because it presents God as one who is guilty of the sin of partiality. The false belief that Black people didn't contribute anything significant to theological and cultural change—with the exception of Harriet Tubman, the civil rights movements, and a few athletes—is presented as gospel truth. And this is what the world sees: a white God committed to an agenda of salvation that includes all people but who places white people at the helm of leadership, influence, innovation, and revival.

WHITEWASHING CHRISTIAN HISTORY IN SCHOLARSHIP AND ART

In 2016 the hashtag #OscarsSoWhite brought to the forefront the decades-long concern that the Oscars nomination list tends to feature exclusively white actors. The fact that 94 percent of voting members are white might account for this disparity. That's not a strong indicator of a desire for diverse perspectives at the decision-making table, is it? But what does Hollywood have to do with Christian history? Much like the Oscars' voting membership, white people—and more specifically, white men—have been the only ones at the table determining how we view and interpret history. White men have sometimes rewritten history to make it fit a white narrative, and this is even true as it relates to the Christian faith.

The Christian faith is filled with people from diverse backgrounds who have contributed to its expansion and growth. Yet this aspect of Christian history has been hidden for generations, leading us to embrace an incomplete narrative of the faith and a view that Christianity is a mono-ethnic religion. The presentation of Christianity in literature and art only propagates this incomplete narrative.

To understand where the white superiority myth arises, we need look no further than the Roman historian Publius Cornelius Tacitus and his work *Germania*. This work is the origin of what Kelly Brown Douglas calls the Anglo-Saxon Myth.[12] In *Germania*, Tacitus describes Germanic tribes as aboriginal people "free from the taint of intermarriage." Said another way, Tacitus purports that these white tribes were somehow pure and superior, and the source of their superiority was in their blood.[13] Tacitus's perspective on race and purity spread rapidly after his writing was published, and his views weren't restricted to Rome. In fact, Thomas Jefferson referenced him in a letter to his granddaughter, heralding him as "the first writer of the world without exception." Jefferson not only embraced Tacitus's writings but some of his ideology as well, which informed his own view of white people as superior and other ethnicities as inferior. Jefferson saw himself and other Anglo-Saxons as people chosen by God to implement systems of government, and he also considered white Americans to be the New Israelites, God's chosen people.

In a letter to his wife, John Adams says, "Mr. Jefferson proposed the children of Israel in the wilderness, led by a cloud by day and a pillar of fire by night; and on the other side, Hengist and Horsa, the Saxon chiefs from whom we claim the honor of being descended, and whose political principles and form of government we have assumed."[14] Notice how Jefferson, influenced by Tacitus's ideology, made the original Hebrew people Anglos? This is the historic pattern of white supremacy and whitewashing. If God's chosen people are exclusively white, then all others must be inferior and even cursed (as many would assert). This should come as no surprise from a man who revised the Gospels to fit his commitment to Enlightenment ideologies in what was called *The Jefferson Bible: The Life and Morals of Jesus of Nazareth*.[15]

What Tacitus, Jefferson, and many Puritans, missionaries, and scholars have intentionally ignored is the overwhelming presence of melanin in the Bible—but this is the point of whitewashing. In order for whitewashing to continue and for these false narratives to perpetuate, the Black and brown presence in Scripture must be ignored. Whitewashing opened the door for making Adam and Eve, Abraham, Moses, David, Ruth, Mary, and Jesus white artistically. There are countless examples of people of color in Scripture who were connected to Jesus's earthly lineage. For instance, four of the five women mentioned in Matthew's account of the genealogy of Christ (Matt. 1:1–16) were of Hamitic descent—Tamar, Rahab, Bathsheba, and Ruth. John Mark, who wrote the gospel of Mark, was the son of Aristopolus and Mary. His Gospel was likely the first written, based on a theory known as Markan Priority, which suggests that the Gospel of Mark was used as a source by two of the other Gospel writers, Matthew and Luke.[16] John Mark was a Cyrenian Jew. Many Jews had fled to Africa for safety, and the two primary places to which they fled were Cyrene and Alexandria. They blended in well in Africa because, like the African people, many of the original Jews had melanin—they were people of color.[17]

A BROAD WHITE STROKE

Whitewashing has affected our understanding of history and the Bible, and sadly, the arts have also been complicit in supporting this movement. From children's book illustrations to Michelangelo's frescoes on the ceiling of the Sistine chapel, just about every artistic image we see presents the biblical figures as white. No example stands out to me more vividly than the 1956 movie *The Ten Commandments*. Charlton Heston plays the biblical figure Moses, and an array of white people were cast as Egyptians and the Hebrew people. I remember watching this movie and wondering: where did all the Africans go? Pharaoh was white, his African queen was white, and Moses, Joshua, and Aaron were all white.

This illustrates what people of color are referring to when we talk about an unfair—and in this case, unbiblical—underrepresentation of people of color in presenting the biblical story and the history of the Christian faith. It's impossible to read the Bible and think that everyone we read about is of European descent, yet this truth has been largely ignored in art, literature, and movies for years. Thankfully, the Bible presents an authentic reality of God including and using people of color in his divine plan.

Jesus Was Ethnically Jewish

Jesus was ethnically and religiously Jewish, and he considered them his people—his tribe. For instance, John states: "He came to His own [Judah], and those who were His own [Judah] did not receive Him. But as many [Jews] as received Him, to them He gave the right to become children of God, even to those who believe in His name" (John 1:11–12 NASB). In John 4:22, Jesus clearly distinguishes himself from gentiles: "You [gentiles] worship what you do not know; we [Jews] worship what we know, for salvation is from the Jews" (John 4:22 NASB). It is clear that Jesus did not deny his Jewish ethnicity. In fact, the very first verse of the New Testament clearly proclaims Jesus's Jewish ethnicity: "The book of the genealogy of Jesus Christ, the son of David, the son of Abraham" (Matt. 1:1 ESV). The author of Hebrews declares that Christ descended from Judah (Heb. 7:14).[18] Scripture also records Jesus's mother Mary's Jewish heritage, letting us know that she too was ethnically Jewish (Luke 3:23–38).

When you examine Jesus's genealogy, you'll find a vast array of ethnicities (as well as his Jewish roots) that suggest a white Jesus is historically inconsistent with his earthly lineage. Yet portrayals of Jesus in Bibles, children's books, art, and film consistently portray Jesus as white. This whitewashing of Jesus isn't accidental. Rather, it has been utilized as a tool for white supremacy, Black inferiority, and institutional control.

Tabatha L. Jones Jolivet, a professor of higher education and one of the authors of *White Jesus: The Architecture of Racism in Religion and Education*, says that there has been a whitewashing process over time and that white Jesus is a function of white supremacy. "White Jesus is so much more than an icon. It's not neutral because it has been proliferated and it's expanded in terms of its presence over centuries and it has been largely tied to what we call an imperial project. The agenda of a nation state." Unfortunately, attempts to confront the reality of the role white supremacy played in the formation and propagation of white Jesus tend to be dismissed as a liberal agenda meant to divide. The historical evidence proving that Jesus was not a white man is largely ignored, and the status quo of whitewashing is preserved.

Where Did White Jesus Come From?

The image of Jesus as white did not originate in the Bible, so why is it such a widely accepted fallacy, even today? Many white evangelicals are guilty of thinking anachronistically—meaning they assume that the past was largely like the present. We find a great example of this anachronistic thinking in medieval art and paintings, where the artists present Jesus as a European male wearing medieval European garb as opposed to first-century Jewish attire.

The fallacy of white Jesus is something we are introduced to at an early age. When you pick up a children's Bible, most of the artwork depicts the men and women of the Bible as white. Consequently, many Westerners adopt the faulty notion that the central figures of the Christian faith were white Europeans when in reality they were African and Middle Eastern. One factor that may contribute to the survival of the white Jesus fallacy is that Scripture does not provide a precise physical description of Jesus. None of the Gospels offers a physical description of Jesus or says much about his appearance. The book of Acts describes Jesus as the "light from heaven" that temporarily blinded the Apostle Paul (Acts 9:3), but it doesn't describe his appearance any further. Revelation 1:14–16 is the closest we have to a physical description of Jesus, but even that description is primarily symbolic: "The hair of his head was white as wool—white as snow—and his eyes like a fiery flame. His feet were like fine bronze as it is fired in a furnace, and his voice like the sound of cascading waters. He had seven stars in his right hand; a sharp double-edged sword came from his mouth, and his face was shining like the sun at full strength" (Rev. 1:14–16 CSB). The Revelation text isn't portraying Jesus as Black—but it's certainly not portraying him as white, either. If we were to take this description literally, Jesus would look like something resembling a piece of candy corn: white hair at the top, followed by the yellow and orange of bronze being heated in a furnace.

Artistic images of Jesus didn't appear until around the fourth century. The early church fathers disagreed about the attractiveness of Jesus, but not necessarily his ethnicity. The African church father Tertullian (220) didn't think that Jesus would have been that appealing based on Isaiah 53:2, which says, "He grew up before him like a young plant and like a root out of dry ground. He didn't have an impressive form or majesty that we should look at him, no appearance that we should desire him" (CSB). The African theologians Origen (AD 248) and Augustine of Hippo (AD 430) disagree, arguing that he must have been beautiful based on Psalm 45:3, which says, "Gird your sword on your thigh, O mighty one, in your splendor and majesty" (ESV).

While images of Christ preceded the adoption of Christianity as the religion of the Roman Empire, an influx of artistic images of Christ occurred during the reign of Constantine. Emperor Constantine legalized Christianity[19] and ended Christian persecution with the Edict of Milan in 312 AD. The depictions of Jesus from this period reflect Jesus as a Roman and not like the darker-skinned Jews. From this point forward, most art portrays Jesus as a white man rather than a dark-skinned, Middle Eastern Jew. For instance, the Walls of Santa Sabina in Rome (AD 430–32) portray Jesus as a white man turning water into wine and multiplying two fish and five loaves to feed thousands.[20]

In the third and fourth centuries, portrayals of Jesus varied, some portraying him with a beard and others portraying him as beardless. Around the sixth century, a long-haired, bearded Jesus became the predominant image. By the late Middle Ages, the beard had become almost universal. Michelangelo later portrayed Christ as a clean-shaven, Apollo-like figure in the Sistine Chapel (1534–41).[21] His frescoes also portray God as a white man reaching for a white Adam, which helped to normalize portrayals of a Judeo-Christian God as European.

By the 1500s, slavery was an institution of European civilization, and ethnic images of Christ were almost erased because those in power controlled the printing and the narrative. Edward J. Blum and Paul Harvey, who explore the history of white Jesus in their book *The Color of Christ: The Son of God and the Saga of Race in America*, argue that at this time "whiteness was not made sacred in the form of Jesus, in part, because whiteness itself as a marker of racial identity and power did not yet exist."[22] But this began to change in the years following the American Revolution. By the early 1800s, new printing technologies and advances in transportation combined with the rise of multiple missionary societies to change everything. Soon the "white Christ" was everywhere, and the remains of the gospel-centered Puritans, who actively opposed oppression, failed to temper the spread of his portrait. Some of them even contributed to the spread of white Jesus.

White Jesus at this point in history became the accepted image of Christianity in the West. Unfortunately, this picture of Jesus was not a symbol of hope, redemption, and renewal, but one of hierarchy, degradation, and domination. Why was Jesus white? Because any Savior who resembled the enslaved would undermine the mission of unregenerate slave owners and their attempts to misuse Scripture to oppress people of color.

White Jesus on the Big Screen

White Jesus has been popularized in virtually every form of media, from print to the big screen. In the 2004 film *The Passion of the Christ*, Mel Gibson chose to have Jim Caviezel, a man with European features, play the role of Jesus. And almost every other character in the movie was also played by a white person. *The Bible* miniseries, which debuted on the History Channel, deployed the same playbook, as Mark Burnett and *Touched by an Angel*'s Roma Downey presented a whitewashed narrative of Christian history to more than seventy million people. Russell Crowe played Noah in *Noah*, Christian Bale played Moses in *Exodus: Gods and Kings*, and the previously mentioned *The Ten Commandments* featured a whole cast of white people portraying African and Middle Eastern figures including Charlton Heston as Moses, Anne Baxter as the African Nefretiri, Yvonne De Carlo as Zipporah, and John Derek as Joshua. These portrayals make it acceptable and normative for Jesus, who is God in the flesh (John 1:14), to be viewed as white—subtly implying that white is now sacred.

ACKNOWLEDGE AND CORRECT

As we began this chapter, I noted how the term "whitewashing" had risen in prominence yet again recently when actress Jada Pinkett Smith accused the Oscars of being "so white." Pinkett Smith was outraged by the lack of diversity among the Oscar nominees in 2016, and she decided to boycott the Oscars. But not only did she not attend the show, she also promised she would not even watch it on television. The hashtag #OscarsSoWhite took off, and soon thousands of people had joined Jada in her quest to ensure that more people of color are recognized for their talent.

What can we do to change centuries of whitewashing the Christian faith? The first steps include loving confrontation, honest conversation, and concili-ation. Next steps might include starting new organizations and institutions or new artistic endeavors that reject the whitewashed Christianity of the past. Jada Pinkett Smith and her husband, Will Smith, didn't want the #OscarsSoWhite movement to die once the Oscars had ended, so they started the organization Careers in Entertainment to raise awareness that talent among people of color often goes unnoticed and highlight the steps needed to change things. Their goal was not simply to address and express apathy toward whitewashing in Hollywood, but rather to acknowledge and correct the issue.

I share the same hope. My goal isn't to simply call out the whitewashing we see in Christianity. I hope we can acknowledge its effects on our own percep-tion of the Christian faith, to see beyond the limited narrative of white evan-gelicalism and to embrace the larger narrative of Christian history—one that highlights how God has used and still uses all people in his redemptive plan.

CHAPTER 3

WHAT IS URBAN APOLOGETICS?

Eric Mason

EVANGELIZING IN Black communities is harder than ever. People are walking away from the church, seeking to find their identity outside of Christianity, and believing the lies Black Religious Identity groups are telling them. Urban apologists are working tirelessly to win them back.

When I began my college career at Bowie State University in 1991, I—like many African Americans in the '80s and '90s—stepped into a new hotbed of identity ideologies. Many Blacks entering college at this time (particularly a historically Black college), would be wearing some type of cultural accessory that pointed to their connection to Africa, from African medallions made of leather to t-shirts depicting the continent of Africa using some African artistic pattern. This was a significant time for Blacks wrestling with our ethnic and cultural identity. You would see brothers in the student union selling books and oils like Blue Nile, sandalwood, frankincense, myrrh, or an oil version of a popular brand like Cool Water, Joop, Obsession, or Faccanoble. It was a fun time. These vending stands were filled with resources promising to fill the void of our Black minds with the truth white men had deprived us of to prevent us from knowing who we were.

Books by authors like John Henrik Clarke, Dr. Ben-Yosef Jochannan, Cheikh Anta Diop, Walter Williams, Chancellor Williams, and George G. M. Jackson shook up an entire generation of Blacks. These individuals had either been brought up in the church or claimed they were Christians, but now they were enlightened by so-called master teachers who offered them something new—knowledge of self. Most of these "master teachers" had received their direction from nineteenth-century white mystics like Alvin Boyd Kuhn, Helena Blavatsky, Gerald Massey, and Kersey Graves. Even Clarke speaks of the influence of these white individuals on today's Afrocentric thought in his "Great Debate"[1] with Mary Lefkowitz.

THE NECESSITY OF URBAN APOLOGETICS

Every twenty or thirty years, Blacks become newly aware that America is a strange land. Racism and injustice reawaken us to the reality that the tears in the fabric of the American story are still ripping, as they have been since 1619 when slaves first arrived at Jamestown. From Emmett Till to Rodney King to Hurricane Katrina to Michael Brown to George Floyd, each scenario reawakens in African Americans a profound awareness that things haven't changed a bit. When this happens, Christianity is recognized to be a tool that has often been utilized to perpetuate injustice toward Blacks. As a Christian who is Black, I am sometimes led to feel as if I am following the religion of my oppressors. It's like the Stockholm syndrome, a realization that everything you thought you knew to be right is wrong. There is a constant tension inherent in being Black and Christian in America, and this has now been etched into the psyche of many African Americans.

Consider the following quotes from proponents of what are commonly called "Black Conscious" communities:

> The so-called Negro must awaken before it is too late. They think the white man's Christianity will save them regardless of what happens, and they are gravely mistaken. They must know that the white man's religion is not from God nor from Jesus or any other of the prophets. It is controlled by the white race and not by Almighty Allah (God).[2]

> It shows how man can manipulate a religious text to support and justify their evil actions, in this case against black people. Whitenization by the Europeans and Roman Empire proved this to be true. The brainwashing began in Europe and spread easily to America. 500 years after white slavery, 1,000+ years after Arab slavery it is still evident today as people of African descent are still subjected to more social, economic, and political oppression than any other race in the world. Arabs and Whites today have been known to call black people "monkeys" and "slaves."[3]

> I remember going to Sunday school class, and the teacher would pull these cardboard cutouts of Moses and Noah out of the box . . . and they were invariably old, white men in robes. They looked like my next-door neighbor, but in robes. Imagine as a child to have that inculcated in me that all of the heroes of Christianity are white. I do think that's kind of wrong.[4]

These quotes are from several representatives of "Black Conscious" communities, and they all agree that Christianity is *not* good for Black people. Commentary like this creates a type of cognitive dissonance for Black people that is difficult to overcome. As Christian apologists, we should not turn away from this challenge. It simply means we have a lot of work to do, and this is one of the many reasons why an approach I call urban apologetics is needed today. The miseducation and falsehoods being promoted by these groups is understandable, but it is not excusable. I say it is understandable because it is true that Western, white European Christianity has worked hard to destroy Black identity. However, these conscious communities have gone beyond a response to this dignity destruction and have thrown the baby out with the bathwater by jettisoning the entire Christian faith. They have not done the necessary homework to look closely at the truth. An urban apologetic defuses the false origin stories these groups promote.

Black Christians are always being interrogated by representatives of the Black Conscious community. We invariably get a mouthful that critiques our acceptance of Christianity because whites who called themselves Christians played a central role in the kidnapping and enslaving of Blacks. Many Blacks have been taught that Africans' first contact with Christianity was through the slave trade. Many see Christianity's historical role in slavery as a key factor in the destruction of the Black mind. They view Christianity as a European creation used by white oppressors as a tool to keep Blacks in bondage. And there is merit to this argument. During the era of slavery in the West, there was a false form of Christianity that justified the kidnapping of humans. Did proponents of this form of Christianity create an abridged Bible called "the slave's Bible" to prevent slaves from having a clear and comprehensive understanding of the gospel? Yes. Did certain so-called Christians make Blacks out to be less than human, thereby defiling the *imago dei* that is within every human being? Yes.

For the past one hundred years, since the founding of the Moorish Science Temple in the early 1900s, the Black community has struggled to offer robust theological answers to the challenges our community faces. The intellect, theology, and enablement has always been there, but until recently, we have not seen a concerted effort to address the objections and questions raised by proponents of the Black consciousness movements. In more recent years, we've been blessed by pioneers like Dr. Carl Ellis, Thom Skinner, Dr. Tony Evans, Haman Cross, Walter A. McCray, John Perkins, Dwight McKissic, Chuck Singleton, and many others. Even the Impact Movement led by Charles Gilmer in the '80s and '90s has been a great help to us. These leaders and movements have addressed some aspects of Black suspicion toward Christianity and the gospel. However, in the present internet age and with the predominance of social media, YouTube, and meme education today, the game has changed. Objections spread more quickly. Falsehoods about Christianity have a longer lifespan. This is why a uniquely urban apologetic that addresses these movements and other Black objections to Christianity is even more necessary in this information age.

URBAN APOLOGETICS DEFINED

What is urban apologetics? "Urban" is a popular word today and has been steadily growing in usage for the past four and a half decades. It points to the city. Before it became a slang term, "urban" had the connotation of concentrated complexity. It is a geographical landscape with a high concentration of cultures, politics, intellectual ideologies, houses, wealth and poverty, ethnic people groups, traffic, economy, art, and spiritualties.

Somewhere along the line, however, "urban" became the code word for Black, brown, and poor. This is the underlying foundation behind how "urban" is used in the corporate world today. Urban divisions of companies are devoted to marketing their products to Black and brown people. Black, brown, and poor have now become *the* popular culture because of the surging popularity of hip-hop and its viral spread via the internet. Urban culture is now popular culture, and today, urban isn't merely a geographical locale. It is a mobile culture we encounter in a myriad of contexts, even in rural and suburban geographic locales.

"Apologetics" is a term coined from 1 Peter 3:15: "But in your hearts regard Christ the Lord as holy, ready at any time to give a defense to anyone who asks you for a reason for the hope that is in you" (CSB). The word translated here as "defense" comes from the Greek word *apologia*. In context, apologetics is a response that abides in Christ and engages that presence in one's mind, emotions, and will by showing others that transforming work through a defense of the faith. Apologetics is a reasonable defense of the gospel based on the eschatological and imminent hope one has in Jesus, or as one lexicon puts it: "As a legal technical term, apologetics is a speech in defense of oneself, *reply, verbal defense* (2T 4:16); as a religious technical term, it is a *defense* of the gospel message from false teaching (Ph 1:7)."[5]

Jesus tells the disciples in Luke 12 not to worry when doing apologetics, but the Holy Spirit will aid them with their knowledge: "Whenever they bring you before synagogues and rulers and authorities, don't worry about how you should defend yourselves or what you should say. For the Holy Spirit will teach you at that very hour what must be said" (12:11–12 CSB). Jesus shows us that giving a defense (or apologetics) isn't merely an exercising of the intellect, but it is a commitment and trust of the soul for more than a debating exchange.

Jude 3 is another key text when it comes to explaining the biblical place of all forms of apologetics: "Dear friends, although I was eager to write you about the salvation we share, I found it necessary to write, appealing to you to contend for the faith that was delivered to the saints once for all" (Jude 3 CSB). The words "contend" and "faith" are both key terms we need to understand. "The faith" is the body of knowledge that is trustworthy for us to believe, the core of what makes Christianity *Christianity*. In the Pastoral Epistles, "the faith" is used frequently in this way as a summation for the theological DNA of believers, their biblical-theological catalog of faithful doctrines and beliefs (1 Tim. 1:2, 4; 3:9, 13; 4:1, 6; 5:8; 6:10, 12, 21; 2 Tim. 1:13; 2:18; 3:8; 4:7; Titus 1:1, 9, 13; 3:15). The faith is something to be protected. Here is a short list of some of the core tenets of the Christian faith:

- Justification by faith (Rom. 5:1)
- The person and work of Jesus Christ (Isa. 40–66 and Gospels)
- The oneness and distinct persons of the one God (Eph. 1)
- Salvation by grace through faith in Jesus (Eph. 2:8–9)
- The sufficiency of Scripture (Matt. 5:17–18; 2 Tim. 3:16–17)
- The reality of eternal punishment (Rev. 19–20)
- The eternal presence and kingdom of God on heaven and earth (Rev. 21)

Contending for these core tenets is a key role of apologetics. "Contending" means "to fight for, to make a strenuous or labored effort in someone or something's behalf."[6] The word "contend" translates a Greek word (*epagōnizomai*) that refers to athletic contests, such as a wrestling match. Paul hints at this association in his use of a cognate verb in 1 Corinthians 9:25: "Everyone who *competes* in the games goes into strict training. They do it to get a crown that will not last, but we do it to get a crown that will last forever" (emphasis added).[7] The ancient world was as crazy about sports as our world today, and the imagery of an athletic competition would have been easily understood.[8]

The church fathers living in the era after the apostles' death gained the nickname "the apologists" because many heresies arose during this time (e.g., the Judaizers in the NT, Marcion, the cult of Serapis, Docetists, Arians, etc.). During these years, the church needed to lay the foundation of what it meant to continue the commandments of Jesus and the doctrine of the apostles. Among those on the front lines contending for the faith were church fathers like Justin

Martyr, Origen, Tertullian, Clement of Alexandria, Cyprian of Carthage, and Lactantius the Berber. These fathers were the pioneers of apologetics, and their influence is felt to this day.

There are several ways we can categorize the various approaches to apologetics today, including:

- Classical apologetics: This form of apologetics stresses arguments for the existence of God as well as the historical evidence supporting the truth of Christianity.[9]
- Evidential apologetics: This form of apologetics stresses the need for evidence in support of the Christian truth claims. The evidence can be rational, historical, archaeological, and even experiential.[10]
- Experiential apologetics: Some Christians appeal primarily, if not exclusively, to experience as evidence for the Christian faith. Some appeal to religious experience in general, and others to special religious experiences. Within this second category are some who focus on mystical experiences and others who identify what they believe are particularly supernatural conversion experiences.[11]
- Historical apologetics: This form of apologetics stresses historical evidence as the basis for demonstrating the truth of Christianity.[12]
- Presuppositional apologetics: Usually, a presuppositionalist presupposes the basic truth of Christianity and then proceeds to show (in any of several ways) that Christianity alone is true.[13]

In this book, I'm introducing something I call "urban apologetics." When I use "urban" in "urban apologetics," I am referring specifically to our defense of the Christian faith against Black objections and how Christianity meets the unique needs and answers the unique questions of Black people. Urban apologetics utilizes several of the above approaches in a symphonic manner. We employ classical apologetic approaches when we are talking to a Black atheist or agnostic, many of whom value scientific explanations over faith-based assertions. The evidential model is particularly helpful when faced with challenges like "Prove to me that Jesus existed" or "Where are all the tombs of the characters in the Bible?" or "Christianity was created in Europe." Underlying most of the statements or questions we encounter in urban apologetics is a revisionist narrative. Such narratives appeal to and affirm many people's experiences with racism and injustice. To refute these unstudied revisionist narratives, we can draw on elements of both historical and experiential apologetics. Our job in urban apologetics is to prayerfully engage these issues with humility and care.

WHY WE NEED URBAN APOLOGETICS

Urban apologetics is doing the work of sharing the gospel by giving an answer and a defense of Christianity to Black people in light of the intellectual, emotional, and ethnic identity concerns of minority communities. It is giving Black people a reason for the hope of the gospel amidst the cultural, historical, spiritual, and theological barriers Blacks have to the Christian faith. And at the core of urban apologetics is a restoration of the *imago dei*. Racial injustice and inequity have created a complex need to affirm humanity while challenging human sinful pride. Scripture demands that we treat all people as bearers of God's image (Gen. 1:26–27; James 3:9).

Urban apologetics also seeks to speak truth into a world that has become characterized by lies. We live in a world of bootleg truth where Black Religious Identity Cults (BRICs) peddle pieces of the truth or promote material they try to pass off as truth. Because many people haven't learned to recognize truth from error, the real from the fake, they believe the lies. They have nothing to compare it to. Most of the ideologies or cults out there have a foundation in the Judeo-Christian worldview. They approach their rejections of Christianity and their framing of so-called truth in light of the Christian story; urban apologetics seeks to demonstrate that only Christianity proves to be reasonable and true as a worldview.

Urban apologetics also dispels and addresses the multitude of urban legends, historical myths, theological fallacies, exegetical improprieties, scientific misnomers, sociological revisionism, spiritual synchronism, and reductionist views of Christianity that exist in the Black community. Much of what we combat in urban apologetics are arguments that were once popular in previous generations and are now reemerging with an ethnic slant. For example, we're seeing a reemergence of the theory that Christianity is a copy of an Egyptian religion—an issue that was addressed and dispelled decades ago.[14]

Because the Black community deeply distrusts white people and European ideas, many Blacks tend to be easily swayed by any suggestion of white corruption, and Christianity is an easy target. When BRICs suggest that Christianity is a white religion instituted by white Europeans, many Blacks believe them. Yet in reality, Christianity spread from Jerusalem to Africa and *then* to Europe. Christianity's headquarters were in Alexandria, Egypt well before Christendom formed in Rome.

The willingness of people to believe that Europeans spread Christianity to Africa highlights an even bigger issue. As Thomas C. Oden explains in his book *How Africa Shaped the Christian Mind*,

Modern intellectual historians have become too accustome[d]
premise that whatever Africa learned, it learned from Europe[
of seminal Neoplatonism, however, its trajectory from Afri[c
(a south-to-north movement) is textually clear. But why is it so e[
or dismiss this trajectory?[15]

Erroneous beliefs about the origins of Christianity in Africa can be traced
to the undercurrent of racism we see in both secular and Christian scholarship.
As more Blacks were educated in the Western world, it wasn't long before that
prejudice began to be exposed. As I mentioned earlier, in my own historical
studies of Cush (the Black African kingdom along the Nile to the immediate
south of Egypt) and the role that the Cushites played in the biblical world, I've
encountered a lingering racial bias within the academy, which is still dominated
by white scholars. What do I mean by a racial bias? I am not referring to the
blatant racial prejudice that was relatively common in the historical/religious
scholarship of the nineteenth and early twentieth centuries, although many of
these works are still in print and being used. Instead, what we encounter today
is a subconscious or subtle racial bias—often unintentional, but real nonetheless. This racial bias is something that permeates all facets of society, including
Christian historical scholarship, and it has created great challenges for African
Americans' efforts to share the gospel with other Blacks. Subconscious and
complicit racism has blighted the fields of harvests in the Black community.
Today we fight racism in the world and in the church, contend with Blacks who
play into whiteness by denying racism, and resist the mystery cults and Black
ideologies that are destroying our communities. Urban apologetics is not an
easy task. We have our work cut out for us!

DOES COLOR MATTER?

In the epistemological landscape of truth, does color matter? Not particularly.
Yet white people's efforts throughout history to paint all of Christian history
with a white and European brush has made skin color a problem. Instead of
leading the way in confronting racism, Christian Western scholarship has
followed in the footsteps of the secular revisionists. This whitewashing of
history is repugnant to God. It is divisive to paint history with one's preferred
color rather than researching the real ethnicities of people mentioned in the
Bible and in the past history of the church. It is an affront to the good news
itself to suggest that God only saved and worked through white Europeans.

I can't blame my Black brethren according to the flesh for their constant suspicion of Christianity. Apologetics exists because of the sinfulness of all men and women, and urban apologetics explores how that sin affects ethnic minorities in particular. It is necessary, sadly, because of the sinfulness of racism and injustice in our world. Can you imagine people rejecting the gospel because they believe it is only for white people, thinking, "Since it is so white, maybe it is only for whites"? May it never be!

Our task is to give answers that respond to the psychological trauma that Blacks have experienced as Western Christendom has merged with the historic (non-Western) Christian faith. Since the time of the early church, Christianity has had to deal with the problem of one group of people wanting to exclude another. The question of whether Christianity is only for a particular ethnicity is not a new question—it goes all the way back to Peter's vision about the salvation of the nations (Acts 10) and to the Jerusalem Council (Acts 15). Galatians 2 further demonstrates that exclusion of people based on ethnic dividing lines is a core gospel issue.

Yet in the end, we are called to preach the gospel to all people, regardless of race or background, and we do this in the power God provides. Paul Says in 1 Corinthians 2:1–4,

> When I came to you, brothers and sisters, announcing the mystery of God to
> you, I did not come with brilliance of speech or wisdom. I decided to know
> nothing among you except Jesus Christ and him crucified. I came to you
> in weakness, in fear, and in much trembling. My speech and my preaching
> were not with persuasive words of wisdom but with a demonstration of the
> Spirit's power. (CSB)

Paul here appeals to the Corinthians' own conversion. It was the powerful preaching of the weakness of the cross, not humanly powerful rhetoric, that had saved them (1:18).

Apologetics isn't about winning the argument; it is contending for the soul of the hearer. At times, we are fighting for the bystanders, even if the specific person being engaged isn't responsive. Make no mistake: although we are dealing with the barriers of ethnic identity, racism, and injustice, ultimately, we are trying to help people recognize their own sinfulness (John 16:8). Our desire is that the Holy Spirit will convict them of their need for the gospel; we do not wish to merely speak about the atrocities that were committed to Black people. We will not ignore these atrocities, but we must not let them deter us from highlighting *every* person's need for the saving power of the gospel of Jesus Christ in our lives.

CHAPTER 4

BLACK CHURCH HISTORY AND URBAN APOLOGETICS

Tiffany Gill

NOWHERE IS the link between history and apologetics more urgent than in the urban context. Failure to recognize the role and significance of African American church history hinders the expansion of the gospel and the witness of Christ in these communities. This chapter addresses some of the theological implications of failing to give a full accounting of Black church history. It reflects on the ways in which the Bible articulates the importance of learning and recounting history, especially the history of the oppressed. It briefly recounts key moments in Black church history, concluding with some practical ideas for applying Black church history as an apologetic.

After the hopeful promise of freedom from 250 years of brutal enslavement gave way to the nightmarish reality of segregation and racial terror, African Americans in the early twentieth century fought for the survival of their people. It was the era known as the "nadir," a low point in the long quest for freedom and equality.[1] They watched as Black men's bodies swung from trees—lynched for the audacity of demanding to be treated with respect. They lamented the economic and sexual exploitation of Black women, relegated to back-breaking domestic labor in white homes. As African Americans struggled to envision a meaningful future, they formed organizations, they marched, they wrote, and they prayed. They also turned to their rich past for inspiration to endure the uncertainty of what was to come.

In 1926, during this season of despair, Dr. Carter G. Woodson, the second African American to earn a PhD in history from Harvard University, established what was then called "Negro History Week," later renamed Black History Month. He wanted to remind African Americans that the crises of their current day should not define them and that they should draw wisdom and strength from the deep well of their past experiences. Fueled by his unwavering belief that understanding the past in all of its fullness and complexity was not only necessary for African Americans but had the potential to transform the nation as a whole, Woodson dedicated his life to collecting, interpreting, teaching, and chronicling Black history.

In an article published in the *Journal of Negro History*, Woodson summarized the motivation of his life's work and declared, "if a race has no history it has no worthwhile tradition, it becomes a negligible factor in the thought of the world, and it stands in danger of being exterminated."[2] Of the many words he penned throughout his long and fruitful career, these are among his best remembered and most often quoted. This statement resonates deeply in part because it reflects a God-ordained truth. Reclaiming history is not a political act—although it has political implications. Neither is it a part of a radical agenda designed to exalt some while bringing shame to others. Historical literacy is an essential component of our faith and must be a fundamental pillar of apologetics. Nowhere is this link between history and apologetics more urgent than in the urban context. Failure to recognize the role and significance of African American church history hinders the expansion of the gospel and the witness of Christ in these communities.

Admittedly, significant challenges arise when we try to give a full account of Black church history. This history forces many white evangelicals to reckon with the truth that many of their denominational structures, seminaries, most revered leaders, wealth, and doctrine were forged in the cauldron of white supremacy and Black subjugation. Many African Americans outside the faith find it difficult to reconcile the God of the Bible with the God of those who have been most complicit with racial inequality, and as a result they dismiss Christianity as "the white man's religion." Still others—namely, African Americans of the millennial generation within the Christian faith—dismiss the traditions and theology of the Black church as out of touch with modern realities and instead see themselves as the manifestation of "their ancestors' wildest dreams," as if our foremothers and fathers didn't have dreams of their own.

In this essay, I'll address what is lost when we fail to give the full accounting of Black church history. This essay reflects on the ways the Bible articulates the importance of learning and recounting history, especially the history of the oppressed, and then provides a brief exploration into key moments in Black church history. Finally, this essay concludes with practical ideas about how to apply Black church history as an apologetic.

This essay does not offer a comprehensive overview. Rather, it is merely a piece of a larger, longer conversation that the American church needs to have about its neglect of Black church history. This history should be taught from pulpits, community centers, Sunday school classrooms, living rooms, prisons, university classrooms, and seminaries.

THE THEOLOGY OF REMEMBRANCE

Carter G. Woodson's personal dedication to the study and dissemination of history pales in comparison to the many biblical imperatives for God's people to remember the past. For example, more than a dozen Old Testament books, along with the New Testament Gospels and the book of Acts, chronicle key moments in the history of the people of Israel. Scripture describes remembering history as a spiritual discipline designed to increase one's faith, as well as a method of discipleship to instruct future generations.

One of the most powerful examples of the use of history as a means of discipline and discipleship is Psalm 78. Considered the longest of the historical psalms penned by Asaph, a prophet and musician who was a part of King David's royal court, the first eight verses provide a detailed account of the role of historical knowledge in a community of faith:

> My people, hear my instruction;
> listen to the words from my mouth.
> I will declare wise sayings;
> I will speak mysteries from the past—
> things we have heard and known
> and that our ancestors have passed down to us.
> We will not hide them from their children,
> but will tell a future generation
> the praiseworthy acts of the LORD,
> his might, and the wondrous works
> he has performed.
> He established a testimony in Jacob
> and set up a law in Israel,
> which he commanded our ancestors
> to teach to their children
> so that a future generation
> —children yet to be born—might know.
> They were to rise and tell their children
> so that they might put their confidence in God
> and not forget God's works,

> but keep his commands.
> Then they would not be like their ancestors,
> a stubborn and rebellious generation,
> a generation whose heart was not loyal
> and whose spirit was not faithful to God. (CSB)

In the opening verses, the psalmist explains that his goal is to instruct God's people and that he would be reflecting on the past to provide this instruction. The fourth verse proclaims that God's people must not hide the past from their children, but instead they must boldly declare the wondrous and praiseworthy things God has done on their behalf. In other words, God's people must not only *know* history but are commanded to *share* it with the next generation as a record of God's faithfulness.

Godly legacy
↑
Obedience
↑
Confidence in God
↑
Remembering God's faithfulness

Overall, the psalm underscores a key point about history that believers must understand in light of defending and furthering the gospel. Remembering God's faithfulness leads to confidence in God, which leads to obedience and the perpetuation of a godly legacy. The reminder of God's faithfulness and the motivation to persevere have been essential to the Black church's survival.

REFORMING SLAVERY

Essays in this volume by Dr. Eric Mason and Jerome Gay provide credible evidence that Christianity's presence on the African continent predated the transatlantic slave trade, the violent plunder of Africa that forced over twelve million Black men and women into a life of servitude.[3] To be sure, the most robust Christian communities were in the northern and eastern regions of the continent and not in western or central Africa, where the majority of those who were taken as captives to the Americas originated. However, trade routes throughout the continent make it very likely that even West Africans would have encountered the faith before being forced onto slave ships.[4]

While the sixteenth and seventeenth centuries were not the first time Europeans encountered Africans, they proved to be pivotal eras in that long history. The encounter between these two continents coincided with one of the most important moments in Christian history—the Reformation. As Europeans struggled over the direction of the Christian faith and warred against one another for dominance, they made incursions into Africa in search of precious metals and other forms of wealth. Unfortunately, they soon determined that Africa's greatest resource was not the gold in its mines, but the people on its land.

Explorers from Catholic-ruled Spain and Portugal were the first to establish dominance in Africa and to make settlements in what is now North and South America in the so-called New World. The British soon followed, and many Protestants who were fleeing religious persecution viewed settling in the New World colonies as an opportunity to recreate society. Unfortunately, that new society was dependent on the extermination of indigenous people and forced labor of enslaved Africans.

Initially, both Catholics and Protestants shared the belief that those converted to Christianity should not be held in bondage. The British also feared that the teachings of Christ would encourage rebellion and cause Africans to believe that their common faith made them equal with their enslavers. For example, in 1724, a white minister in St. Ann's Parish, Virginia, explained that slaveholders were proud that few slaves had been baptized over the course of fifteen years since Africans became "worse slaves when Christians."[5] As such, there were few African conversions to Christianity in colonial British North America.

This failure angered the church and government authorities back home in England who, coming off the heels of the Reformation, feared that the unwillingness of the colonists to convert enslaved Africans only proved to the Catholics their lack of zeal to spread the gospel. They began instructing the colonists to evangelize enslaved Africans and began manipulating Scripture to support their efforts. In the 1720s, British missionaries from groups like the Society for the Propagation of the Gospel in Foreign Parts were sent to evangelize Africans in America—not because they cared about the destiny of their souls, but so that they could prove themselves superior to Catholics.[6] They used Ephesians 6:5, as if all the Law and the Prophets culminated in the message of slaves being obedient to their masters. However, enslaved Africans refused to accept a truncated, self-serving gospel, and the missionaries returned home to England unsuccessful. It wasn't until bondspeople encountered the religious revival known as the Second Great Awakening that African Americans began coming to faith in significant numbers.

AWAKENINGS

Starting in the 1790s, less than a generation after the Revolutionary War transformed the British colonies into the independent United States of America, religious camp meetings began spreading across the new nation. Marked by emotionally charged preaching and teaching, these revivals emphasized repentance and faith as the singular path to salvation and declared that no one was out of the realm of God's deliverance. For the enslaved, especially those who were born in the US and not Africa, this was their first encounter with the comprehensive gospel, and many embraced it with abandon.

The willingness of Baptists and Methodists to not only preach the gospel to Blacks but, in some cases, to ordain them as preachers led to the first generation of free and enslaved church leaders. For example, Andrew Bryan, born enslaved in 1737 on a plantation outside of Charleston, South Carolina, was led to the Christian faith and baptized by George Liele, the first Black man licensed to preach the gospel in Georgia. While a slave, and with the blessing of his master, Bryan assembled a small group of African American believers outside of Savannah, Georgia, and met with them regularly. As Bryan's nascent congregation grew, so too did fears from slaveholders, some of whom forbade enslaved people from listening to his sermons for fear that they would inspire desertions and uprisings. As a result, enslaved people, even those with permission to attend Bryan's services, were stopped, harassed, whipped, and jailed. Bryan was also assaulted and imprisoned. According to historical sources, Bryan "told his persecutors that he rejoiced not only to be whipped, but would freely suffer death for the cause of Jesus Christ." Upon his release, he continued to preach. And despite the opposition, his church expanded with new converts.[7]

Upon the death of his master, Bryan purchased his freedom and continued teaching and preaching the gospel. By 1790, over 500 free and enslaved Blacks attended his services. Four years later, Bryan organized his congregants and established a church that eventually became African Baptist Church. Free and enslaved Blacks hired out their services and pooled their scarce resources and raised enough money to erect a church in Savannah—the first Black Baptist church in the United States. By 1810, the church planted an additional two churches, all led by Black men.[8]

While Andrew Bryan was fortunate enough to plant a church in a traditional sense, more frequently enslaved people created and participated in what Albert Raboteau called the "invisible institution." Unlike Bryan, who was formally ordained, the leaders of these churches were "licensed only by the spirit."[9] After attending plantation services sanctioned by masters, enslaved believers would often steal away into the woods to participate in secret gatherings, despite slave codes that deemed gatherings of large numbers of Black people illegal. In spite of these restrictions and the threat of persecution, Black Christians created church services that incorporated African cultural practices like drumming and dance to teach Scripture and doctrine. With African Americans prohibited from learning to read or write, church leaders were often one of the few people in the community who managed to defy the law and become literate. In other words, enslaved people's most significant spiritual formation came from others *within* their community and not their enslavers. Leaders within the invisible institution equipped their flock to discern the difference between the truth of the Christian faith and the manipulation they were taught by slaveholders.[10] And while the promise of heaven gave them eternal hope, their faith also helped sustain them in the everyday.

Free Blacks in the North also faced persecution. In 1786, an elder at St. George's Methodist Church invited a man named Richard Allen to preach to the Black congregants. Richard Allen, who was born a slave in Delaware, had purchased his own freedom just three years earlier. He was preaching the gospel throughout the region to African Americans and was committed to living out his faith by working to end slavery in the rest of the country. When Allen was asked to preach at St. George's, he agreed. However, the predominantly white church practiced segregation and held an all-Black, pre-sunrise service at 5:00 a.m. so as not to upset the white congregants.

Despite these conditions, the number of Black worshipers increased at St. George's. Unfortunately, so too did the hostile attitudes of the white members. Tensions reached a fever pitch when Blacks were physically thrown out of a service while kneeling to pray. Richard Allen later recounted what happened that day:

The Meeting had begun, and they were nearly done singing, and just as we got to the seats, the elder said, "Let us pray." We had not been long upon our knees before I heard considerable scuffling and low talking. I raised my head up and saw one of the trustees, having hold of the Rev. Absalom Jones, pulling him off of his knees, and saying, "You must get up—you must not kneel here." Mr. Jones replied, "Wait till prayer is over." The man said, "No, you must get up now, or I will call for aid and force you away." Mr. Jones said, "Wait until prayer is over and I will get up and trouble you no more." With that he beckoned to one of the other trustees to come to his assistance. He came, and went to William White to pull him up. By this time prayer was over, and we all went out of the church in a body, and they were no more plagued with us in the church.[11]

That incident led to a historic moment in African American urban church planting. After the walkout, Reverend Richard Allen and fellow minister Absalom Jones proposed that it was time for African Americans in Philadelphia to organize a church of their own. Located at Sixth and Lombard Streets on land that Richard Allen had purchased in 1791, Bethel Church was dedicated in July 1794. Mother Bethel African Methodist Episcopal Church remains at this location today, and it is the oldest continuously Black-owned plot of land in the country.

African Americans did not blindly embrace the religion of their oppressors. In fact, the teachings of the Black church inspired some of the most powerful critiques of racism and the American slave regime. Slave insurrectionists Nat Turner and Denmark Vesey, preachers within their respective communities, saw in their faith an inspiration to overthrow slavery—with violence, if necessary. Frederick Douglass offered scathing criticism of the church's failure to acknowledge the slave's plight. In his famous 1852 speech, "What to the Slave is the Fourth of July," the abolitionist declared "the church of this country is not only indifferent to the wrongs of the slave, it actually takes sides with the oppressors. It has made itself the bulwark of American slavery, and the shield of American slave-hunters."[12]

While historical accounts of the Black church often acknowledge the importance of these men, I'd like to turn our attention to the ways that Black women were also part of the theological foundation of the Black church. More than 150 years before author and activist Jonathan Wilson-Hartgrove identified the hypocrisy of "slaveholder religion," a form of Christianity more concerned with upholding the tenets of white supremacy than the teachings of Christ, a free Black woman named Maria Stewart penned powerful missives refuting narratives about Black inferiority. Born free in Connecticut in 1803, Stewart became a follower of Christ after the death of her husband in 1829. A year later, she declared that she had been called to be a "strong advocate for the cause of God and the cause of freedom." Stewart was the first woman of any race to address public audiences containing both men and women, and she provided piercing insight into the specific ways that racism and sexism intersected to impact the lives of Black women. However, her critiques were always rooted in her unshakable faith in Christ and his redemptive power. In a speech that was delivered to an audience of free Blacks in Boston and later published as a pamphlet, Stewart offered this reflection, demonstrating a powerful understanding not only of Scripture but the US Constitution:

> Many think, because your skins are tinged with a sable hue, that you are an inferior race of beings; but God does not consider you as such. He hath

formed and fashioned you in His own glorious image, and hath bestowed upon you reason and strong powers of intellect. He hath made you to have dominion over the beasts of the field, the fowls of the air, and the fishes of the sea. He has crowned you with glory and honor; has made you but a little lower than the angels; and, according to the Constitution of these United States, he has made all men free and equal.[13]

In this and other speeches, Stewart grounded her argument for freedom and equality in Scripture. She stood before audiences, defying the cultural mores of nineteenth-century America about what was appropriate for women and African Americans. She questioned the biblical basis of holding African-descendant people as human chattel based on her interpretation of the Constitution and her rich theological understanding of *imago dei*.

In the years before the Civil War, women like Stewart worked alongside Black men and white antislavery activists to end slavery, and in the process created an unprecedented transatlantic movement based on biblical principles of equality. To dismiss the holistic Christianity of African Americans before the Civil War as merely the "white man's religion" ignores enslaved and free Blacks' robust and theological critique of the religion of white slaveholders and their allies. Their pursuit of Christ would only continue after emancipation. Unfortunately, so would the legacy of the slaveholder's religion.

RECONSTRUCTING A PEOPLE

In the immediate aftermath of the Civil War, millions of newly freed African Americans sought to rebuild their lives. Among the first things they did was to establish churches in their communities. They pooled their meager resources, and with their own sweat and labor, they chopped wood and laid bricks to build their churches with their own hands. In addition to meeting the spiritual needs of their communities, these churches housed what were called Sabbath Schools. Legally prohibited from learning how to read and write while in bondage, freed people, ranging in age from toddlers to the elderly, gained literacy in the pews of the churches they built.

These church-based schools laid the foundation for many of the Historically Black Colleges and Universities (HBCUs) that exist today. Building upon the legacy of the white philanthropists who created Cheyney University in 1837 and Lincoln University in 1856, the American Baptist Home Mission founded Shaw University in North Carolina in 1865 to provide a theological education to freed Blacks. Just two years later, Moses Adams, a Black pastor in Holly

Springs, Mississippi, began a school in his church's basement that became Rust College. That same year, a group of ministers met in Augusta, Georgia, at Springfield Baptist Church, one of the nation's oldest independent Black churches. These men would go on to establish Augusta Institute with the goal of helping to prepare Black men for the ministry. Augusta Institute would later move to Atlanta and become Morehouse College. Of the 101 HBCUs that exist today, about 40 are Christian founded or based. The impact of these HBCUs cannot be overstated. During the many decades of Jim Crow segregation, these institutions faithfully educated the Black doctors, lawyers, teachers, nurses, social workers, activists, educators, ministers, and artists who sustained Black communities. They opened their doors to Black scholars and professors who were unable to secure employment at predominantly white schools.[14]

Although African Americans in the post-civil rights era now have more options in higher education, these colleges and universities remain vibrant and important institutions in Black life. HBCUs only account for three percent of all colleges and universities in this country, however, over twenty percent of African Americans continue to earn their degrees at these schools. In a society and culture where Black life remains under assault, these institutions provide a venue where African Americans can celebrate their deep intellectual and spiritual legacy. Ironically, many of those within the African American community who most loudly criticize the Black church as a do-nothing, regressive, and irrelevant institution have benefitted from HBCUs that would not exist without the Black church. As we celebrate HBCUs and reflect upon their continued importance, we must never forget to celebrate their Christian roots.

The years after the demise of Reconstruction also saw the resurgence of white supremacist organizations like the Ku Klux Klan, who terrorized Black communities with rampant racial violence. Despite (or because of) this, it was also a period of rapid growth in church planting. The expansion of the church caught the attention of historian Carter G. Woodson, who chronicled the phenomenon in his 1921 book, *The History of the Negro Church*. For Woodson, the continued subjugation of Black people after slavery's legal end only underscored that emancipation did not translate into equality or true freedom. As such, African Americans had to build their own independent institutions to help them navigate the era of segregation. "The church then," Woodson opined, "is no longer the voice of one man crying in the wilderness, but a spiritual organization at last becoming alive to the needs of a people handicapped by social distinctions of which the race must gradually free itself to do here in this life that which will ensure the larger life to come."[15] Upon further investigation, Woodson found that while the Black population increased only twenty-six percent from 1890–1920, the number of church organizations, church buildings, and seating capacity all increased by over fifty percent. The value of church property, Woodson found, more than doubled.[16] However, the impact of this expansion would pale in comparison to the demographic shift on the horizon that would forever transform the Black church—the Great Migration.

A MODERN EXODUS

Life in the Jim Crow South became so unbearable that African Americans, like the Hebrew children before them, longed for deliverance and a promised land free of oppression. Lured by the hope of better economic opportunities, a chance to vote, and an escape from racial violence, between 1910 and 1970 over six million African Americans left all that was familiar to embark on a new life in cities like New York, Chicago, Milwaukee, Los Angeles, Detroit, and Philadelphia. At the end of the nineteenth century, ninety percent of the Black population lived in the South. By the time WWII started, almost half of all Black Americans lived in urban areas in the North and Midwest.[17]

City life was hard, and any visions of the North or Midwest as a promised land soon faded as African Americans struggled to find work, safe and affordable housing, and relief from law enforcement officials who harassed them at every turn. Black church leaders saw this dissonance between what migrants hoped for and what they found as a fertile ground upon which to sow the seeds of the gospel by meeting pressing needs. For example, under the leadership of Reverend Lacy K. Williams, Chicago's Olivet Baptist Church called upon religious leaders in his expanding city to "make better preparations for those new recruits" by providing venues for recreation and Christian education.[18] At Olivet, as in most Black urban churches, women assumed responsibility for meeting those needs. S. Mattie Fisher, one of the first Black social workers in the US, used her professional training not only to develop a comprehensive survey to assess the needs of Black migrants in her neighborhood but also to help Olivet establish the systems and programs to meet their physical and spiritual needs. Fisher saw no divide between her vocation and her spiritual calling. After helping to establish a school at the church, she explained, "There have been many conversions and connections with church as a result of our work. Three girls . . . have accepted Christ and are [now] active in the church." Despite charges from twenty-first-century evangelicals that it was during the Great Migration era that African Americans abandoned the true gospel for a "social gospel," Fisher was clear about the motivation for the works she did: "The greatest joy in the service comes when I can point to someone and say 'God used me to help that one find Himself.'"[19] Making disciples was always her highest goal.

Religious leaders feared that the bright lights and anonymity of modern cities would draw African Americans away from the church. However, data demonstrates an expansion that surpassed the Reconstruction era. African Methodist Episcopal churches doubled, while predominantly Black Baptist churches quadrupled. Urban areas also gave rise to small, nondenominational holiness churches. Often housed in storefronts, these churches provided a space for mostly poor and working-class African Americans to be more exuberant in worship than the mainline Black denominations.

However, for all of the ways that the church was growing, it also had to contend with challenges to some of the basic tenets of the faith. Migration gave rise to what Alain Locke called a "new Negro" identity, which manifested in increased political agitation for equality as well as a flourishing of artistic production that celebrated the beauty and resilience of Black identity.[20] It also gave rise to religious communities that, according to historian Judith Weisenfeld, "provided new ways of thinking about history, racial identity, ritual and community life and collective future."[21] "Religio-racial identity" groups like the Moorish Science Temple of America founded in Newark, the Nation of Islam established in Detroit, or Father Divine's International Peace Mission Movement based in Philadelphia sought to help migrants combat race-based discrimination. In many ways, these groups capitalized on what they saw as insufficiencies in American Christianity's challenge to white supremacy. As we're exploring in this book, Black churches in the urban context still face the onslaught of these groups in the twenty-first century and will only be able to address them if they understand what gave rise to them in the first place.

THE CHURCH AND CIVIL RIGHTS THEOLOGY

Although popular history remembers the civil rights movement of the 1950s and 1960s as an unprecedented phenomenon that seemed to emerge out of thin air, African American churches, as this essay demonstrates, have always fought for racial equality. What is different about this moment of intensified activism is that it forced the Black church to grapple openly with a fundamental question about the role of the church in social justice movements—a conundrum that twenty-first-century urban churches are still confronting. For example, as the civil rights movement began gaining momentum, it drew criticism from *within* the Black church. At the heart of the debate was the perceived dichotomy between the mission of the church to spread the gospel and win souls and the goals of the civil rights movement to promote racial justice. This dilemma led to one of the largest schisms in Black church history when half a million members of the National Baptist Convention (the largest Black denomination) left to create the Progressive National Baptist Convention. Among the mutineers was none other than Reverend Dr. Martin Luther King Jr. In many ways, the Black church still hasn't healed from that rupture, and the question of how to engage issues of racial justice in a way that honors God remains.[22]

Historian Jeanne Theoharis describes the "national mythologizing" that surrounds the civil rights movement as a story that is often told as a fable centered on heroic characters who solved the race problem once and for all.[23] African Americans have also not escaped the tendency to mythologize the civil rights movement. The lack of a robust understanding of the civil rights struggle and the theology of the movement has led many of the millennial generation to dismiss the accomplishments of those who preceded them. Much of this sentiment was captured by Tef Poe, founder of Hands Up United, a Black Lives Matter affiliated activist organization founded in the wake of the 2015 murder of Mike Brown in Ferguson, Missouri. In response to what he perceived as inaction by Black clergy, Poe declared that "this is not your mama's civil rights movement."[24] The phrase was later printed on t-shirts. In an article entitled "Why the Modern Civil Rights Movement Keeps Religious Leaders at Arm's Length," Rahiel Tesfamariam explained why the shirt resonated with her and her generation of activists. "The front lines of the fight for civil rights," she wrote "are no longer 'manned' by the traditional leaders of the Black community: well-dressed, respectable clergymen."[25] While there were issues of misogyny within the civil rights movement, Tesfamariam's oversimplification dismisses the ways that poor, rural, and devoutly Christian women like Fannie Lou Hamer were not only on the front lines of the violence and unwarranted incarceration of the movement but were also central to its theological approach.

Born in 1917, the twentieth child of sharecroppers in Mississippi, Hamer lived most of her life in poverty. Mrs. Hamer experienced the worst of white supremacy firsthand. For example, she was sterilized without her consent in 1961 after seeking treatment for a uterine fibroid tumor. She suffered greatly for her commitment to Christ and her belief that those created in the image of God were bestowed with dignity. Hamer lost her job, was thrown off the plantation she called home, was arrested, shot at, and beaten so bad in a Mississippi jail that she suffered permanent kidney damage—all for asserting that simple truth. Known for her booming voice and the singing of spirituals, she did not look or sound like the caricature of civil rights leaders that many

Black millennials project onto the past. Many Black millennials thus miss out on the ways that the movement continues to be instructive in the post-civil rights era.

RECOGNIZE, READ, RECORD

Many of the challenges facing urban Black churches in the twenty-first century are not new. Whether we are battling against a racist judicial system, white evangelicals who refuse to acknowledge our full humanity, or the resurgence of attacks from Hebrew Israelite religions, we should look to the past to gain wisdom and to remind us of God's faithfulness. However, as the demographics of cities change and the descendants of those who participated in the white flight of the 1970s and 1980s return, many historic Black churches are struggling to survive. For example, New Light Beulah Baptist Church in Philadelphia weathered so much during its ninety-nine years of existence, but it could not survive gentrification. As property values in the Graduate Hospital neighborhood, its home for sixty-one of those years, increased exponentially (more than 400 percent since 2000), the Black and working-class community surrounding the church became home to young, white professionals. Membership plummeted as a result, and the church was no longer able to sustain the costs of maintaining the building. In 2017, the few remaining congregants watched as the building was razed and a nineteen-unit condominium rose in its wake. Stories like this are all too common across the nation as urban areas undergo significant changes.[26]

In light of the rich and complex history of the Black church and the current threats to erase it, how should contemporary Christians embody a robust apologetic within an urban context? I have identified three things leaders and congregants in urban churches can do.

Recognize
- Recognize that the Lord has been at work in your community long before your church arrived.
- Churches, especially newer church plants, should work with respected elders within urban communities to ensure that the histories of these communities are not forgotten as cities undergo significant changes.
- Honor the legacies left by the urban churches and community organizations that came before you. This is especially important for church planters. Connect with local pastors and community organizers to see how your church can come alongside the work they are already doing.

Read

- Read well-researched books about the history of your city.[27]
- Read local and community news. Know your local elected officials and the legislation making its way through city council. In an era where folks are mesmerized by the divisiveness of national politics, Christians must keep their ear on the ground.
- Develop relationships with local colleges and universities and take advantage of their resources. Reach out to faculty members doing research pertinent to your community and invite them to give a lecture at your church. This may be the only time many of them get to interact with a faith community.
- Create a culture of literacy that is infectious beyond the walls of the church. Support your local public libraries. Create book clubs and reading groups as means of outreach.

Record

- Churches should be at the forefront of preserving the history and legacies of the communities where we serve.
- Bring back the office of church historian! Establish a system to chronicle meaningful moments in your church's history. Your church record keeping should not be reduced to numbers and financial spreadsheets but should tell stories of God's faithfulness.
- Collect oral histories of people in your community that do not attend your church as of yet. Create opportunities for intergenerational dialogues. Showing a genuine interest in people's lives goes a long way to building relationships that lead to conversion.
- Help people in your communities find their Christian roots. Invite local genealogists to conduct workshops at your church.
- Enlist the help of local historical societies. Visit local museums.

The Black church has survived against all odds. Its survival is quite possibly God's strongest apologetic for the power of the gospel within American Christianity. The Black church is a miracle. Her history should cause believers to fall to our knees in worship and gratitude for the ways the Lord has maintained a faithful and enduring witness among a people who, by every estimate, should have been only a memory. This remnant of Christ's bride has survived onslaughts from slaveholders who tried to wield the Bible as a mechanism of subjugation. She has stood defiantly against those who chastised her for trusting in the God of her oppressors and possessed the supernatural ability to discern the difference between God himself and those who claim to represent him. She continues to weather unrelenting displacement as the demographics of urban areas shift. Sharing the history of the Black church should not be a source of shame or guilt for God's people. Rather, we should all proclaim with loud and grateful hearts that she is still here and commit to do all we can to ensure that she remains a shining example of God's grace and faithfulness to his people.

CHAPTER 5

WHY THE BLACK CHURCH MUST BE RELEVANT

Zion McGregor

> *There arose another generation after them who did not know the LORD, nor yet the work which He had done for Israel.*
> —Judges 2:10 (NASB)

> *In those days there was no king in Israel; everyone did what was right in his own eyes.*
> —Judges 21:25 (NASB)

A CENTRAL preoccupation of African American culture has been to confront the wounds and scars of African American people, and historically the Black church has labored greatly in this effort. However, a new generation does not know the bridge that has brought us over troubled waters in the past. They see the church as dated and impotent and are exploring cults, sects, and new ideologies. They turn to the internet for the answers the church once provided. Today's African American church must engage the work of urban apologetics and learn to answer the popular barbershop questions people are asking while introducing the illuminating and transcendent truth of the gospel.

To be is to question. From the moment we are self-aware, our identity, origin, and purpose form the tri-entity that drives the car of our curiosity. It is a journey of wandering, of tasting and testing the religious produce available to us. For every question of life there is an answer. And yet, when those answers are colored by the pens of pluralism and subjective truth, they lose exactitude, specificity, and weight. Like the other travelers on this journey of life, African Americans need clarity and guidance as they wade through the waters of incalculable content and opinions on religion in general but Christianity specifically.

Apologists run the point in this effort. They sort out the absolute from the erroneous, the plausible from the irrational, and the facts from the unsubstantiated. They provide a proper understanding of Christian views in context and the implications of these views. Apologists expend this effort in order to defend the faith. It is a most urgent defense—the kind that, in the end, finds the fate of the soul hanging in the balance. This is why answers that are true matter. The Black church must be relevant in urban apologetics because our reality is construed and impacted by what we believe, and what we believe has eternal consequence.

THE RISING NEED FOR APOLOGETICS

During the first two decades of the twenty-first century, the need for apologetics has become apparent within the African American expression of Christianity. Millennial African Americans, largely from historically Christian families, have begun to feel dissatisfied with and pessimistic about the state of the African American community. Much like their ancestors, these grandchildren and great-grandchildren of the civil rights movement are hopelessly frustrated by the factors impacting their reality. The crime, gentrification, substandard healthcare, low-income housing, poor education, unemployment, predatory policing, and intentional disenfranchising legislation have all fueled the hopelessness being felt across the country in predominantly African American urban centers. Publicized scandals from both within and without the Black church community—including scandals within Catholicism and predominantly white Protestant communities—further added to the suspicion and mistrust. Critics of Christianity took to social media to draw widespread and unwanted attention to the church. Political loyalties were also seen as an accomplice that played a role in damaging the perception of what it meant to be Christian, further pushing many away.

But perhaps nothing played a greater role in stirring the suspicion of the African American community in recent years than the seemingly epidemic and violent unarmed killings of African American men, women, and children by police and the systemic injustice that followed. The killings of Trayvon Martin, Sandra Bland, Michael Brown, Philando Castile, Eric Garner, Tamir Rice, Botham Jean, Atatiana Jefferson, George Floyd, Breonna Taylor, and Ahmaud Arbery, which make up a mere fraction of incidents, left the community anxiously asking questions. Recognizing the damage done to African American personhood and failing to receive due justice, witnesses walked away angry, with many questions unanswered. While their anger was decidedly aimed at the police and justice system, there was collateral damage. The preceding events, wedded to the unanswered existential questions that followed, caused some pockets of the community to turn against its most enduring institution, the African American church.

A central preoccupation of Black culture is to confront candidly the onto-logical wounds, psychological scars, and existential bruises of Black people while precluding a move to Black insanity and Black self-annihilation.[1] Historically the Black church[2] labored greatly in this effort. And in many cases, it still does. However, a generation has arisen who does not know the bridge that has brought us over many troubled waters. They see the church as dated, impotent, and as little more than a show; thus, many have ventured out into a world riddled with cults and "isms," ideologies and sects. They have morphed into a tech-savvy society that turns to the internet for the answers the church once provided.

NOW WHAT?

How did the church lose her voice? Where did her influence go? Some urban apologists attribute the unique crisis facing the African American Church (and by extension, the community) to the collapse of proper Christian virtue. A collapse in the church's commitment to biblical principles and essential Christian doctrine, the absence of intentional community evangelism, and the dogged unwillingness to accommodate contradicting societal shifts bears much responsibility. To some, these virtues may have an elitist ring. But once the church gives sanctuary to lazy pseudo-scholarship, materialism and sec-ularism, syncretism and subjectivity, it loses its relevance and everything else falls apart.

The church cannot pretend that it does not bear some measure of culpa-bility. Over the past two decades, few pastors seemed to be aware of or took seriously the attitude shifts toward the church within the African American community. This lack of awareness is perhaps due to an age gap between the pulpit and pew. It could also be the historically individual aspect of pastor-ing, which can often be quite arbitrary within the African American church. As a result, those who readily dismissed the shifting tide of attitudes toward the church seem to have done so from the perspective of a preferred real-ity. Their eyesight, fixed on the rearview mirror of an increasingly distant church tradition, is constantly obstructed by *"remember when the church used to . . ."* nostalgia. This romanticized view of big mama's church teases their longing in the present while leaving them nearsighted to the future. Others would seem to suffer from a type of astigmatism. They are able to see but not rightly discern the scope of the threat. This has been corroborated over the past several years as well by countless conversations amongst numerous multi-generational believers across denominational lines. Their testimonies were reflections of their inquisitive experiences with church leaders and teachers.

With each story I began to hear an echo. When the opportunity presented itself to ask a question surrounding both essential and secondary doctrinal issues, as well as struggles with certain moral demands of the Christian life that stand at odds with the movement of secular culture, their bewilderment, concerns, and questions were never clearly addressed—or worse still, dismissed. They were often given a rhetorical placebo and told not to worry about that. Others were simply encouraged to attend a particular Christian education ministry for better understanding. The problem, however, was that these were church-going, mid-week-attending members. And yet, many of them who lacked a working knowledge of the teachings of the Christian faith were left to fend for themselves, vulnerable to competing philosophical and religious voices. This should not be. Samuel DeWitt Proctor wrote,

> Persons who are pursuing answers to life's most imponderable questions, who are sorting out alternate lifestyles and competing paths to fulfillment, who are yearning for fellowship and conciliation with God, who are seeking strength sufficient to follow Jesus, deserve to find something better than an imposter masquerading as God's servant.[3]

Proctor highlights how the pulpit must always be able to attend to the questions of a curious culture. He defends laypersons' expectations to seek out the counsel of clergymen who have sanctified Christ as Lord in their hearts, ever ready to make a defense to everyone who asks of them to give an account for the hope that is within them (1 Peter 3:15). At the time of the COVID-19 pandemic, heretical clergy, rogue religions, and pagan philosophies are becoming increasingly prevalent and aggressive in their campaign for the followship and devotion of humanity. In the face of such threats, the pulpit must be careful and intentional to share and demonstrate—in attitude and aptitude, deeds and defense, leadership and love—the absolute and all-encompassing message and truth of the gospel of Jesus Christ. Good answers to challenging questions followed by clear acceptance or rejection of the gospel provides the clarity needed for what the Apostle Paul refers to as "the building up of the body of Christ" (Eph. 4:12 NASB).

Urban apologetics, which focuses on the implications of the truthfulness of the gospel among people of color, labors in this arena of faith as a clarion voice and an agent of truth. It is the companion of evangelism and the champion of discipleship. It is the ministry arm that helps the church be what the apostle Paul called "the pillar and foundation of the truth" (1 Tim. 3:15 CSB). It is my ultimate intent to sound the alarm and to stir committed followers of Christ to become a community skilled in making a defense of the Christian faith and in applying that message to the various questions posed from within the church and from without.

An Apologetic within Apologetics

Urban apologetics is a relatively new concentration. Born out of a need to respond to specific and unique challenges to the Christian faith within the African American community—such as the rising tide of Black Religious Identity Cults (BRICs) and the so-called conscious community[4]—a diverse cluster of Spirit-led urban apologists began to organically emerge. In the simplest of terms, urban apologetics is a cultural apologetic. It is a derivative division of Christian apologetics that engages the unique challenges of faith plaguing the African American community with informative answers palatable to the African American experience.

As a ministry, urban apologetics has the power to give clarity to puzzled believers and critical detractors, aiming to influence right believing with right thinking to best help defend the Christian faith. Christopher W. Brooks, a recent contributor to the study of urban apologetics, offers an expansive perspective when he writes, "The task of urban apologetics should be to show that Christ and the gospel have much to say about issues such as economics, health care, hunger, energy, homelessness, and immigration."[5] In addition to Brook's commentary on the subject, we must add identity to the list, as identity is recognized as a major root issue driving BRIC movements and the sweeping dominance of the conscious community.

Urban apologetics is useful for the edification of the Black church. It shapes and maintains a Christian consciousness that can be articulated intellectually, demonstrating rationale value. African church fathers such as Augustine came to confess Jesus Christ in part due to well-reasoned apologetic arguments. With all of this in mind, if there is to be the reclamation of a generation lost and an attempt to apply a preventive inoculation to future denials and doubts, we must inject urban apologetics into the life of every local congregation.

INQUIRING MINDS AND THE SKEPTICS WHO LOVE THEM

Much like our ancient congregational ancestors of the first three centuries, the church today shares the challenge of living in a society that seems to be growing either indifferent or hostile to its presence. Having yielded the public square over the course of the twentieth century, Christianity now more than ever finds itself in contest with alternative understandings of God and religion—all campaigning for the minds and, consequentially, the souls of men. So serious is the matter of defending the faith within our present era that we find this urgency even when we venture outside of evangelical and mainline Protestant traditions. In 2008, while on a visit to the United States, Pope Benedict XVI addressed a question on the challenges of rising secularism and intellectual relativism in the public square. He responded,

> In a society that rightly values personal liberty, the church needs to pro-mote at every level of her teaching—in catechesis, preaching, seminary and university instruction—an apologetics aimed at affirming the truth of Christian revelation, the harmony of faith and reason, and a sound under-standing of freedom, seen in positive terms as a liberation both from the limitations of sin and for an authentic and fulfilling life.[6]

The Black church finds no exemption. African American religion under-went a rapid process of diversification in the early decades of the twentieth century, particularly with the appearance of a wide array of Holiness, Pentecostal, Spiritual, Islamic, and Judaic sects.[7] Most of this diversification remained largely affiliated with Christianity. The Islamic and Judaic sects were the exceptions.

Today, post-modernity has left an increasingly secular and uncivil civilization marked by pluralism and estranged to absolute truth. The social and theological errors that do moderate damage in our society are doing harm in excess within the African American community. The inevitable and unavoidable pendulum of false ideas has been swinging in our direction for some time. Every African American congregation—even those some might expect to be impervious to the threat of the present wave of offensively minded BRIC movements—is a target. No one is safe. The vast majority of churches, however, carry on aloof or unaware, still tethered to the familiar comforts of denominational customs and historic practices.

This is what undermines the witness of the church within the African American community. When the church ceases to be the witness of the life and ministry of Jesus Christ, when our message and methods are hard to determine and seldom yield transformation, when our moral claims are incompatible with the witness of our lives, and (worst of all) when churches stop making converts, the church loses its relevance. And when our relevance is lost, inquiring minds become a vacuum. Skeptics, like the serpent in the garden, strike from the shadows to introduce or heighten the poison of doubt. Considering what is at stake, the Black church must be relevant. Urban apologetics can help.

URBAN APOLOGETICS CLARIFIES MISCONCEPTIONS ABOUT THE CHRISTIAN FAITH

It is impossible for any knowledgeable, Bible-reading believer to listen to the dissenting arguments from the various factions at odds with Christianity without realizing how terribly these factions misunderstand the faith. We often find that critics have never read the Scripture that is foundational to the very religion they are rejecting. Framing the faith inaccurately as a result of their misunderstanding, they imagine their own version of Christianity and stand at odds with it. In some cases, the Christianity that they take issue with looks nothing like the biblical faith. Thus, they offer oversimplified objections like these:

- Christianity has no connection to Africa.
- Christianity is a Greco-Roman creation.
- Christianity is a forgery of Kemet.
- Jesus Christ was a prophet but not God.
- Shakespeare wrote the Bible.
- Christianity is the white man's religion.

These are just the tip of the iceberg. Christopher W. Brooks shares additional insight when he writes, "What I discovered, however, is that just as natural as it was for me to possess a high confidence in the applicability of the gospel to the contours and nuances of life, there were also those who were equally convinced of the utter irrelevance of the eternal teachings of Scripture as it pertained to the critical concerns of our day."[8] These challenges illuminate the urgent need for the African American church to aggressively engage in urban apologetics.

Urban apologetics, when rightly incorporated, tackles these and other such fallacies. Systematically, the discipline enables any Christian who has been discipled and has command of the essential Christian teachings to debunk and clarify false claims, using everything from archeology, to history, to primary source literature of the ancient Near East, to the holy Scriptures themselves. Clearly explaining the misconceptions of the faith allows apologists to properly center the narrative on the gospel, potentially opening the door for the redeeming message to go forth and be received. This is illustrated by Jesus in John 4:7–26 and by Philip in Acts 8:26–40.

Jesus as Apologist

The narrative account of Jesus and the Samaritan woman at the well is an extraordinary example of apologetics working in tandem with evangelism. Here we find a Samaritan woman going to a well to draw water. She is of a mixed nationality. Upon arriving, she meets a Jewish Rabbi—an encounter ripe for conflict, considering that Jews and Samaritans were hostile toward one another (John 4:9). The Jews despised the Samaritans as the worst of humanity and demonically possessed. The Samaritans mocked and scoffed Israel for only accepting the Torah in most quarters. This is the backdrop of the meeting. Jesus engages her with a question. She responds from the perspective of their cultural norms, reminding Jesus that he is a Jew and she is a Samaritan, missing the fact that Jesus is dignifying her humanity. Jesus presses on. He doesn't allow the Jim Crow-like culture of prejudice and misogyny to prevent him from the ultimate goal of witnessing to this woman. He takes her comment and pivots to his real intent. The conversation moves to talk of her five husbands. This, perhaps, is Jesus's way of drawing attention to her life and sin. She then brings up the divisive debate between the two nations concerning their different takes on where God is to be worshiped. And finally, she gets to the central essence: the expected advent of the Messiah. Jesus's engagement, dignity, gentleness, and clarification of her misunderstandings eventually led to a conversation about Christ. This is Jesus, the master apologist. He is so patient and persuasive in his conversation that the woman leaves her water pots and returns to the city testifying to her experience with Jesus and inviting others to come and see for themselves.

Philip as Apologist

Not all encounters are contentious or hostile. The Ethiopian eunuch, an officer in the court of Queen Candace, Queen of Ethiopia, and his encounter with Philip is one such example. The Ethiopian is not a believer in Jesus the Messiah when we first meet him. And yet, he is reading the scroll of Isaiah. His reading of Isaiah, and his pilgrimage to Jerusalem suggests that he was familiar with, and adherent to First Temple Judaism. The proselytism of one from so distant a land is perhaps tied to the reported relationship between two ancestral monarchs: Solomon, king of Israel, and Makeda, the Ethiopian queen of Sheba (1 Kings 10).

The Ethiopian eunuch is reading Isaiah 53, but he can't make any sense of it. After being directed by the Holy Spirit to the caravan, Philip runs over and asks him, "Do you understand what you are reading?" (Acts 8:30). From there, Philip seizes upon the opportunity to give clarity to the high-ranking Ethiopian and shares "the good news about Jesus" (Acts 8:35). A predetermined rendezvous between God's witness and the Ethiopian resulted in more than one mere covert; once the Word of God was clarified and explained, it led to the gospel being introduced to Ethiopia and the African continent in the first century.

In these examples, we can see the significance of apologetics. Urban apologetics functions in this same manner as it relates to the urban context and those who identify as atheists, as BRIC members, or simply as decidedly non-Christians. Urban apologetics has the same unique task and the same hope as the apologists of the Bible—to clarify and explain the truth of Scripture in context in order to share the good news of Jesus Christ, save souls, and change lives.

URBAN APOLOGETICS GUARDS AGAINST THE PROLIFERATION OF FALSE TEACHINGS WITHIN THE AFRICAN AMERICAN EXPERIENCE

My parents taught me that the world is filled with easily transmittable bacteria, diseases, germs, and viruses. They instructed me to wash up every evening before eating because of all the things and people that I had come into contact with at school. As you can imagine, there were occasions when the rebellious boy in me would skip washing my hands and proceed to eat. Inevitably those aforementioned undesirable microbes would make their way into my system. Luckily for me, the human body comes equipped with an immune system, which protects the body from disease by producing antibodies. These antibodies are a type of protein stimulated within the blood to counteract the presence of foreign substances that the body recognizes as alien.

Apologetics is the immune system within the body of Christ. Within a healthy Christian community, the apologist identifies, engages, and dispels false and dangerous teachings—be they from within or without the church—that attenuate, distract, or pervert the redemptive end of the gospel (Rom. 3:21–26; 5:1, 8) and the edifying aim of maturity (Eph. 4:12–13). Apologetics works against the greatest obstacles to the reception of the gospel—namely, false teachings, misinformation, and the proliferation of pseudo-intellectual BRICs.

Likewise, urban apologetics is the immune system of the Black church.

It drives away false teaching and restores truth to the throne of the mind. False teaching is displaced not by the accommodating subjectivism that masquerades as truth but by biblically dependent, theologically sound, historically corroborated, and practically experienced truth. Prior to Dr. Martin Luther King's leadership of the civil rights movement, W. E. B. Du Bois, for half a century, promoted the notion that the pursuit of truth must be the primary goal of Black people. If this indeed must be the primary goal of Black people, the Black church must be ground zero for all that is true.

The Superbug

Some attacks on the faith are not directly false as much as they are misleading, with the goal of stirring rebellion or proliferating bad doctrine. Some are subtle but nonetheless dangerous. Arguably, the greatest of these was used in the garden. The adversary of God, in the guise of a serpent, planted the seed of rebellion with one question, and man has paid for it ever since. His question was laced with a lie: "And he said to the woman, 'Indeed, has God said, "You shall not eat from any tree of the garden"?'" (Gen. 3:1 NASB). The lie is easy for us to spot and correct: God forbade Adam and Eve from eating from the tree of the knowledge of good and evil (Gen. 2:17). The real evil in this statement is the toxic demon of doubt: "Did God say?" With this framing, the adversary was able to sow doubt into Eve's mind, and that same doubt continues to be sown within the minds of people throughout the world.

Urban apologetics is the countermeasure to the disease of doubt. This doubt comes in many forms. And yet, one must remember that doubt is not a Christian virtue. It is not an attribute to be celebrated or encouraged as it is among the apostates, Gnostics, and heretics. Instead, it is seen throughout Scripture as an instrument wielded to sabotage the salvation of the soul. Thomas the apostle teaches us this well. Thomas, also called Didymus (meaning "twin"), finds himself bitten by the superbug of doubt and poisoned with a stubborn strain of disbelief (John 20:24–29). Despite having witnessed countless miracles firsthand—Jesus turning water into wine at the wedding in Cana (John 2:1–11), restoring life to the dead son of the widow of Nain (Luke 7:11–18), calling back to life the deceased daughter of Jairus (Mark 5:21–43), or raising Lazarus from the dead (John 11:1–46)—none of these experiences seemed to have persuaded Thomas enough to believe the eyewitness testimony of his fellow apostles.

The doubt of Thomas has a happy ending to it. Though he is reluctant to accept the account of his friends, Jesus shows up in dramatic fashion and invites him to touch his wounds. And with this invitation, Jesus issues an imperative rebuke to Thomas and to all who would disbelieve the gospel after him: "Stop doubting and believe" (John 20:27 NIV). Thomas is quickly convicted and repentant. Shocked and awed, with fear and trembling in his voice, Thomas makes a full about-face when he utters, "My Lord and my God!" (John 20:28). This is why urban apologetics matters. When rightly applied in word and demonstrated in life, as with Thomas, the gospel of Jesus can exterminate the superbug of doubt.

It should be no surprise that doubt has many abusers. One of the more popular drivers of doubt and modern skepticism within the African American community is the perceived need for identity-derived faith. In certain quarters of the community, individuals and factions insist that the practice of religion must have some sort of connection to their own ethnicity or native land. To some in the Black community, this identity crisis requires the belief in and worship of a God that looks like or is in some way directly tied to them and their African ancestry. Apologetics corrects this narrative by drawing attention to the universal attributes of humanity, especially our common sin.

In the twentieth century, the Black church became the primary arena for the pursuit of African American identity, independence, equality, and complete freedom.[9] The true genius of the Black church, however, resides in the fact that it has given status, dignity, and respect to common people who were often invisible in American society.[10]

During a lecture at Southwestern Baptist Theological Seminary, Dr. Carl Ellis Jr. put it this way: "Ethnicity has beauty only as it derives understanding that we are in God's image."[11] Much like a flu shot, when a congregation is properly inoculated with urban apologetics, the biblical awareness helps to build up an ethnic, emotional, intellectual, and—most importantly—theological resistance to the tempting and attractive false doctrines, heresies, and religious identity dogma.

The revelation of our helpless and universal condition is meant to draw all of us to the conclusion that we cannot save ourselves. We need a savior, and God the Father has provided one for us by giving his only begotten Son, Jesus the Messiah, as the sacrifice in our stead. Urban apologetics rides shotgun to evangelism in the worthy effort to affirm the truth of Jesus Christ over against the pluralistic nonsense that cannot save.

Apologetics and Scripture

In Matthew 4, Jesus has an encounter with the devil, who entices Jesus three times. Employing and spinning Scripture, the tempter aims to coerce Jesus to his own wicked ends in an effort to derail his ministry and purpose. Jesus, however, counters each address with God's Word. Interestingly, it is with

Scripture that Jesus is ultimately able to force the devil to flee. In this account, Jesus relies exclusively on the authority, power, and primacy of the Word of God. When believed, understood, and rightly used, the Word of God counters the false teachings of any adversary. To this end, the church must be more intentional in adopting methods that help believers internalize the Scriptures to the point that they are ready and resilient when responding to arguments against the viability of the Christian faith.

URBAN APOLOGETICS IS A PERSUASIVE TOOL FOR CHRISTIAN WITNESS

When Benjamin Franklin wished to convince the people of Philadelphia of the need to incorporate street lighting to the city, he didn't try to persuade them with mere lectures or pamphlets. Instead, Franklin began by hanging a beautiful lantern in front of his home. He routinely polished the glass so that not even the most minor speck or smudge would dampen the light. Every evening as the sun and moon traded places, Franklin would carefully light the wick. People could see the light from a distance. And as they walked by and came closer into the light, they found that it helped them notice and avoid sharp stones along the illuminated pavement. Over time, other citizens began placing lanterns outside of their homes as well. And as Franklin had hoped, soon the citizens of Philadelphia recognized the need for standardized street lighting.

In like manner, urban apologetics is an illuminating instrument that is about one thing if nothing else: theologically correct answers that affirm the plausibility and rationale of the Christian faith by shining a light on and debunking the unique and challenging errors presented by various BRIC movements, with the goal of persuading all who hear to believe the gospel.

Apologetics Is Indispensable to Our Message

Incorporating apologetics into our preaching strikes a preemptive blow to the looming arguments, concepts, ideas, and philosophies that pursue the attention and affections of the soul at the soul's expense. The pulpit today must utilize apologetics with an unrivaled zeal. With every occasion, the sermon should be constructed and delivered in a manner that labors to convince the non-believer of the truths we proclaim while edifying the believer in the faith that they hold. Where there is confusion about the omniscience of God, apologetics should be intentionally woven into the sermon to prove the all-knowing nature of God. To this end, the church must explore every possible way to persuade and convince whosoever we encounter of the redemptive love of Jesus Christ. Further, when we consider the rich tradition of African American preaching—be it expository, narrative, or a mixture of the two—the tailored homiletic of the African American preacher and the culturally specific agency of urban apologetics make for a tool that is both offensive and defensive at the same time. This is the beautiful marriage of two disciplines. Apologetics, the great sentry of Christianity, tethered to proclamation of the gospel makes for a presentation that is objectively true, intellectually firm, and relevant to the full scope of our existence.

Apologetics Is Integral to Our Mission

Being ready is not just a matter of having the right information available. It is also about having a clear sense of purpose regarding the task of the church and the role apologetics plays there.

The *missio Dei* is reconciliation: God reconciling humanity back to himself through the person and work of his only begotten Son, Jesus Christ (2 Cor. 5:18; John 3:16). Outside of the church, urban apologists stand in defense of this faith. The public square is the space where they refute accusations and erroneous claims made against Christianity. It is also a place where they provide clear answers to the questions of seekers concerning essential doctrinal distinctives and misunderstandings. And since Jesus has entrusted his Word of truth to the church, the church is to be the guardian and disseminator of the truth.[12]

Apologetics Is Instrumental to Our Method

Urban apologetics is not merely academic. It is demonstrative. In a world where Christianity is increasingly challenged, a number of individuals and ministries have adopted apologetics as a method of defense and proclamation of the gospel. Certain tools help us to communicate the core truth of Scripture.[13] A critical method of urban apologetics is the incorporation of appropriate events and facts from African, African American, and Judeo-Christian history. These sources aid in exposing the fallacies, inconsistencies, and often incoherent arguments posited by various BRIC movements.

Within the African American church, the urban apologist serves to inform the local congregation on the unique threats to the community, identifying and responding strategically to them. Be it the lead pastor, elder, ministerial or staff member, the role of the urban apologist is vital to the relevance and revival of the church.

Social media has enabled a new generation of discipled believers to step into the arena as apologist and, guided by love and gentleness, to engage in debate with opposing camps. With prayer and intent to show the rationale of the gospel, confessional claims may result. Our methods serve the message.

To this end, if the Black church is to stay relevant and survive, it must acquire the intellectual agility to pivot and modify its methods of ministry to meet the needs of the day.

CONCLUSION

Urban apologetics does not ensure that the African American church will recover the generation it lost to confusion, deception, and indifference. And yet the African American church must make every effort to recover them nonetheless. When thoughtfully considered, urban apologetics answers popular barbershop questions while introducing the illuminating and transcendent truth of the gospel. Apologetics offers the truth that endows one with the capacity to see beyond what's there, comprehending the deeper revelation and why it matters.

The apologist and those versed in the vocation of the pastorate and public theology must remember that people in a postmodern and pluralistic society see creation through the lens of their own wants and prejudices. God has worked through the weakness of every sin-marked servant he's ever called. You and I are no different, and neither are our times. We will always face questions. Some will be general, but others will be unique to the African American experience. When those critical questions are raised, the Black church must be relevant—armed for action with the tools of urban apologetics—because our reality is impacted and understood by what we believe, and what we believe has eternal consequence.

PART 2

RELIGIOUS AND

ETHNIC IDENTITY

GROUPS

CHAPTER 6

THE NATION OF ISLAM

Damon Richardson

THE NATION of Islam gained popularity in the 1950s–1970s. Famous members like Malcolm X and Muhammad Ali brought notoriety to the group. But it's not a thing of the past. Understanding the historical development and beliefs of this group will equip apologists to interact with its members and lead them to the truth of Christ.

I remember playing hide-and-seek with my sisters as a child. One day I'd hidden so well that my sisters could not find me, and they had to resort to yelling, "Come out, come out, wherever you are!" Hearing their voices, I can recall being gripped by a profound thought, far beyond anything I could fully grasp at that time: "My sisters don't know where I am, but Allah does because he knows everything and he is on the inside and the outside of this closet."

How was it possible that at such an early age—still just a child—I could intuitively understand the reality of God's omniscience and omnipresence? It's remarkable considering I had been raised to believe the opposite. You see, I was raised in the Nation of Islam (NOI), and we had been taught that God is a man and only a man. We chanted each day, "God is a man—not a spirit or a spook, never has God been a spirit or a spook, God is a man, God is a man!" So how could a Nation of Islam youth, indoctrinated with the teaching that God (Allah) came in the person of Master "Fard" Muhammad, the Savior of the Lost-Found Nation of Islam in North America, come to know the truth of God's omniscience and omnipresence?

The Nation of Islam defined and shaped my childhood. The East Elmhurst section of Queens, where my family called home, was formerly home to many prominent members of the NOI, including Malcolm X and his Captain, Yusef Shah, both of whom lived on 97th Street, just up the block from one of my uncles. Malcolm was good friends with Queens realtor Mr. Butts of Butts Realty, who attempted to help Malcolm find a home after his house was firebombed. My Aunt Vera owned a funeral home in the building adjoining Butts Realty, and my grandmother lived just five houses down from it.

Many African American families like mine were attracted to the Nation of Islam because of its emphasis on identity, self-sufficiency, community, and dignity. Like many other incarcerated African Americans, my father committed himself to the teachings of the Nation of Islam because of its message of racial identification, reform, and Black uplift. Black prisoners easily identified with the metaphorical narrative that the Nation of Islam presented, which viewed all of America as a prison in which all Black people were incarcerated and whose only hope of true liberation was the teachings of "the Messenger."

The Nation of Islam gained popularity from the 1950s through the 1970s and gained notoriety through famous members like Malcolm X and Muhammad Ali. And it's still around today. Far from being a thing of the past, many African Americans are still drawn to the NOI today for the same reasons they were fifty years ago. Understanding the beliefs of the Nation of Islam and the historical development of this group will equip apologists to interact with its members and lead them to the truth of Christ.

THE HISTORY OF THE NATION OF ISLAM

By the time my family and I had become members of the NOI, it had become deeply rooted in many Black communities for almost half a century. Over the years the NOI has undergone a number of significant changes in leadership and structure, and each NOI leader modified or developed NOI's theology and doctrine based on his motive and objectives.

Noble Drew Ali

The Nation of Islam has its roots in an early Black nationalistic Islamic sect called the Moorish Science Temple of America, founded by Noble Drew Ali. Noble Drew Ali was born in North Carolina as Timothy Drew Ali. During his young adulthood, Ali traveled as a merchant seaman, and in 1913, he established the first Canaanite Temple in Newark, New Jersey in order to encourage racial uplift. The movement underwent several name changes in the 1920s: the Moorish Holy Temple of Science, the Moorish Science Temple of America, and the Moorish Divine and National Movement of North America, Inc. It was influenced by the first Great Migration (1916–1940), wherein many African Americans left the rural South in search of jobs in industrialized northern cities, and the preaching of Marcus Garvey (whom Ali credited in his *Holy Koran* as being his forerunner[1]), who was advocating a return of

African Americans to their motherland in Africa. Ali believed that it was more important for African Americans to discover their historical and cultural roots while remaining in their new home. He taught that Americans of African descent were originally Asiatic people who later immigrated to Africa. Such people are known in history as the Moors, a Muslim people of mixed Berber (Amazigh), Arab, and Spanish ancestry who settled in North Africa, most notably Morocco. Ali taught his followers that they had dual homelands and dual loyalties to both the US and Morocco.[2]

Noble Drew Ali taught that the true identity of Black Americans was ethnically Moorish and spiritually Islamic. Noble Drew Ali believed himself to be the final Prophet sent by Allah to the so-called Black people in America. His purpose was to declare that they were not negroes, Blacks, or colored, but Asiatics.[3] And their true religion was Islam, not Christianity—which was the white man's religion.[4] Noble Drew Ali's message was that the so-called Black people of America had lost their Moorish identity because of sin and disobedience to Allah. They had not honored their forefathers and had gone whoring after the gods of the Europeans. As a result they had incurred the wrath of God and been subjected to the horrors and indignities of slavery until such time that a Prophet should come and reveal their true identity, warn them of the wrath of Allah to come upon the earth, and redeem men of their sinful ways. Recognized by their fezzes, turbans, and names such as "Bey" and "El" (which had replaced their slave given names), the "Asiatics" were part of an early tradition within the African American religious experience that taught an alternative identity replacement ideology. Identity replacement ideologies reject the negro identity of Black people in favor of a nationalism that attempts to locate the true identity of Black Americans as the descendants of a particular ethnic, cultural, and religious group (such as Hebrew Israelites/Judaism and, in the case of Ali's movement, Asiatic and Islamic Moors from Morocco).

Ali produced his own divine text, scriptures called the *Holy Koran*, often referred to by his early followers as *The Circle Seven Koran*. This text had nothing in common with the Qur'an of orthodox Muslims. Instead, Ali's Holy Koran was a mix of freemasonry, eastern mysticism, esoteric teachings, and moral principles taught throughout history via wisdom teachers such as Buddha, Confucius, Abraham, Jesus, and Muhammad, emphasizing the fatherhood of God and the prophethood of Noble Drew Ali. According to historian C. Eric Lincoln, the Moorish Science Temple was nothing more than a "mélange of black nationalism and Christian revivalism with an awkward, confused patina of the teachings of Prophet Muhammad . . . it was not Islam, but it signified a dim awareness of Islam."[5] Moorish Science doctrine also emphasized love, truth, peace, freedom, and justice as divine law,[6] along with economic empowerment and the social, ethical, spiritual, and moral uplift of the so-called Negro.

The first Temple of Moors was established in 1913 in Newark, New Jersey, and by 1925, other temples had been organized in Chicago, Detroit, Hartford, Pittsburgh, and other midwestern and northeastern cities. Internal strife over Ali's leadership in Chicago led to the downfall of the movement across the nation. After one of the rival leaders was killed, Noble Drew Ali was arrested. Although he was quickly bonded out of jail, he died under suspicious circumstances in 1929 shortly after being released from prison. Following Ali's death, various leaders claimed to be the reincarnation of Ali in an effort to gain control of the Moorish Science Temple. Soon after, splinter groups emerged. One such faction was led by W. D. Fard, believed to have been a minister under Ali, who founded the Lost-Found Nation of Islam in 1930.

W. D. Fard

Most scholars agree that W. D. Fard founded the Nation of Islam in 1930. What is debated, however, is Fard's identity, as he had no less than fifty different aliases. The Nation of Islam teaches that W. D. Fard, or Master Farrad Muhammad, was a light-skinned Black Arab with wavy hair from Mecca and was Allah in person. According to NOI teaching, Fard appeared like a white man so that he could maneuver among whites unsuspectingly and teach the Black man his true identity. Early followers attest that Fard claimed to be from Mecca and later began to identify himself as a prophet. The later leader Elijah Muhammad stated that when he asked Fard about his identity, Fard responded, "My name is Mahdi, I am God."[7] Some scholars have suggested that Fard was of Pakistani origin, while his FBI file contends that he was from New Zealand, born to a British father and a Polynesian mother.

Fard was known on the streets of Detroit as a seller of merchandise such as clothing and silk, and he used his peddling skills to teach Black residents of Detroit's Black Bottom and Paradise Valley neighborhoods that their true identity was Asiatic (most likely borrowing this idea from Noble Drew Ali). He taught that they were descendants of the god-tribe Shabazz, the original man, lost in the wilderness of North America. In Detroit, Fard established the first Temple of Islam, and soon after, he established a second in Chicago. Other temples were opened in Milwaukee, Washington, DC, and several other cities.

Under the leadership of W. D. Fard, the Lost-Found Nation of Islam became a proto-Islamic, separatist movement in the tradition of Noble Drew Ali. This means that it holds to the notion that Islam is the *natural* religion of the so-called Negro, even before Muhammad the prophet of Mecca ever taught it. The NOI is also quasi-Islamic like Ali's Moorish Science Temple, meaning that it mixes aspects of Christianity, Islamic symbols, rituals, principles, and various forms of mysticism with Black nationalism. Like its Moorish Science predecessor, the NOI is essentially "an unexplainable hodgepodge of beliefs, a cult built on religious hokum and the gullible desperation of simple rural blacks lost in the big city."[8]

Fard established a sophisticated organizational structure for Temple leadership and instruction, which included a temple minister and assistant ministers for the proclamation and propagation of NOI doctrine. The Fruit of Islam (FOI) is a paramilitary unit of men that served as guards for Temple ministers. The FOI is led by a captain who is responsible for training and drilling soldiers and assisting the minister in various duties that serve the mission of the NOI. Using a curriculum comprised of his own teachings along with elements of liberal arts instruction, Fard established the University of Islam, a primary and secondary parochial school for the education of Muslim children. Fard also created the Muslim Girl's Training (MGT) class to teach young women in the Nation of Islam the role of women in the home and in the Nation, as well as principles of home economics.[9] Fard also pioneered the core values of self-knowledge and self-determination, upon which the NOI established bakeries, fish markets, and other businesses as a means of economic liberation and social dignity. Additionally, Fard is responsible for the creation of most of the NOI's more notorious doctrines, such as its cosmology or creation narrative and the story of Yakub (explained in more detail later).

Elijah Muhammad

In 1931, Fard recruited Elijah Poole, a Southerner from Georgia. Like Noble Drew Ali, Poole had migrated with his family to the North in search of jobs. Elijah Poole heard Fard's teaching at the Temple of Islam, enthusiastically accepted it, and quickly rose through the ranks. He claimed that he was personally discipled by Fard for three and a half years and was chosen to be his messenger. He was soon appointed by Fard himself to be the "Supreme Minister" of the Lost-Found Nation of Islam, and his name was changed by Fard to Elijah Karriem and then finally to Elijah Muhammad.

After a number of incarcerations, Fard disappeared in 1934, creating a leadership vacuum that Elijah Muhammad quickly filled. Elijah Muhammad began to claim that he was the messenger or prophet of Allah and that Fard was Allah in person. He led the group through the 1930s all the way up until his death in 1975, and under his leadership the movement expanded into cities across the

US and more than quadrupled in membership. Some estimates track its growth from approximately 500 to over 100,000 at its height (during the Malcolm X era). The "Lost-Found" designation was dropped from the name, and the group began to simply be called "the Nation of Islam." Elijah Muhammad's death in February 1975 led to a number of serious factional disputes and internal conflicts including mosque attacks, assassination attempts on NOI leaders, and an ideological paradigm shift brought on by his successor, his seventh son, Wallace Delaney Muhammad. Wallace Delaney Muhammad led the NOI away from most, if not all, of his father's earlier teachings and toward the embrace of Islamic orthodoxy.

Malcolm X

The recruitment of Malcolm X was a notable highlight of Elijah's tenure as leader. Just as Elijah was the star disciple under Fard's leadership, Elijah found his new star disciple in a highly articulate, charismatic, and intelligent ex-convict named Malcolm Little. Malcolm Little was born in Omaha, Nebraska, in 1925. Like Elijah Muhammad's father, Malcolm's father, James Earl Little, was also a Baptist minister. His family relocated to Lansing, Michigan, due to the constant threats they received from the Klan as a result of his father's Garvey-inspired, Black nationalist, back-to-Africa preaching. Six years later, Malcolm's father was murdered by a KKK white supremacist subset known as the Black Legion. Malcolm was converted to the teachings of the Nation of Islam through the influence of his brother Reginald, who was already a member of the NOI. Reginald shared the teachings with Malcolm when he visited him in Charlestown State Prison in Boston, Massachusetts, where Malcolm was serving a ten-year sentence for armed robbery.

For a time, Malcolm and Elijah Muhammad shared a close relationship. Malcolm even lived with Elijah Muhammad and his family and drove his car. Elijah Muhammad highly favored Malcolm, and he appointed him as minister of the Boston Temple and later, in 1954, as minister of Temple 7 in Harlem. Elijah Muhammad also appointed Malcolm as his national spokesperson for the Nation of Islam and charged him with establishing new Temples (later called Mosques), resulting in the exponential growth and popularity of the fringe movement.

Yet Elijah's love for Malcolm brought about great disdain and jealousy among some of the other ministers. Their relationship fell apart after Malcolm responded to John F. Kennedy's assassination by saying, "Being an old farm boy myself, chickens coming home to roost never did make me sad; they always made me glad." As a result of this statement, Malcolm received a ninety-day suspension from the Nation of Islam, which was never lifted. This ultimately forced Malcolm out of the Nation he dearly loved. Malcolm's decision to leave the NOI was made public at a press conference in New York on March 12, 1964, where he also announced the formation of two new organizations, the Muslim Mosque Inc. (an orthodox Islam mosque) and the Organization of Afro-American Unity (OAAU), a pan-African and Black nationalist organization.[10]

After Malcolm's split with the NOI, tension grew between him and Elijah Muhammad. Malcolm, now renamed El Hajj Malik El Shabazz, began to expose the hypocrisy of Elijah Muhammad through radio, television, press interviews, and public speaking around the country, to the embarrassment and infuriation of Muhammad and top NOI officials. In a speech given on February 15, 1965, he accused the Nation of Islam of conspiring with the KKK and the Nazi Party.[11] This alleged conspiracy involved some negotiations for land in Georgia. He also alleged that secret meetings had been held in Atlanta where he (Malcolm) and the minister for the Atlanta mosque had been present with KKK leaders. Malcolm also investigated and made public a paternity scandal involving Elijah Muhammad. He personally interviewed many of the women involved in the scandal, some of whom said that they'd had multiple children from Elijah Muhammad and some of whom were silenced with excommunication from the Nation. Malcolm X was assassinated nine days after making these revelations, and this speech was likely the impetus for his murder.

The Nation of Islam was suspected to be behind Malcom's death, a suspicion which resulted in a retaliatory firebombing of Temple 7 on February 21, 1965, the same day as Malcolm's assassination. After Malcolm's death, the Nation of Islam went through a short period of decline and unpopularity, attributed to what many people believed to be the Nation's role in Malcolm's murder.

Louis Farrakhan

Shortly after Malcolm's death, Elijah Muhammad appointed Louis X as minister of Temple 7 and as the national representative of the Nation of Islam, both positions previously held by Malcolm, and gave him the name Farrakhan. Louis Farrakhan was born Louis Eugene Walcott on May 11, 1933 in Bronx, New York, and was raised in the Roxbury section of Boston, Massachusetts, by his mother in a deeply religious Episcopalian home. Farrakhan's rise to prominence began in 1955 when he converted to the Nation of Islam at a Saviours' Day Convention in Chicago after an invitation from a friend. Farrakhan was noted for his oratory skills, which developed through his imitation of his teacher and mentor, Malcolm,[12] and which led to his appointment as assistant minister to Malcolm and soon after as minister of Temple 11 in Boston.

Farrakhan was noted to have sided with Elijah Muhammad against his mentor, Malcolm, and to have made numerous incendiary remarks believed to have instigated the climate within the NOI that led to Malcolm's assassination.[13]

Farrakhan's popularity in Harlem as the minister of Temple 7 helped to revitalize NOI membership, and his name began to be whispered as a possible successor to Elijah Muhammad. These rumors were disappointed by the decision of the NOI's leadership to unanimously appoint Wallace Delaney Muhammad, Elijah Muhammad's son, as successor to his father and as the third leader in the NOI's history at the 1975 Saviours' Day Convention, just two days after Elijah Muhammad's death. Wallace was suspicious of Farrakhan's opportunism, a perspective reportedly long held by Elijah Muhammad and members of his family.[14] He relocated Farrakhan to Chicago, changed his named to Abdul-Haleem Farrakhan, and appointed him to serve in a small mosque. Farrakhan initially cooperated with the new leader's direction to move the Nation away from its fringe origins toward orthodox Islam; he taught orthodox Islam for three years as Imam Farrakhan under Imam Wallace Delaney Muhammad's leadership. Yet he eventually grew disenchanted, discontent with the direction of what was now known as the World Community of Islam. He resigned in 1978 after announcing his plans to rebuild the former Nation of Islam in line with the doctrine of the late Elijah Muhammad and Master Fard Muhammad.[15] Farrakhan held his first Saviours' Day in 1981, and his newly formed group restored most of the original teachings of the earlier NOI. They also reestablished *The Final Call* periodical, the original name of the paper started by Elijah Muhammad in 1934 and rebirthed by Malcolm X as *Muhammad Speaks* in 1960. He also restored the FOI and the NOI's separatist policies.

Wallace Delaney Muhammad

Born October 30, 1933 in Detroit, Michigan, as the seventh child of Elijah and Clara Muhammad, Wallace Delaney Muhammad was named by his father in honor of the NOI founder W. D. Fard Muhammad. Following his family's relocation to Chicago shortly after his father took the helm of leadership, Wallace was reared and educated in the NOI's parochial school, named Muhammad University of Islam (MUI), now named Clara Muhammad University of Islam, after his mother.[16]

Wallace grew up under the teachings of his father and the Nation of Islam, but as a teenager he began to wrestle with incongruencies and discrepancies between orthodox Islam and the brand of Islam propagated by his father. In a 2003 interview on a PBS program called *This Far by Faith*, Wallace spoke candidly about his appointment as the minister of the Nation of Islam Temple in Philadelphia and how he used his education and knowledge of Arabic and the Qur'an to teach the members orthodox Islamic practices such as Islamic prayers and Qur'anic readings, none of which had ever been done in an NOI temple.[17] As his rejection of his father's divinity became public, as well as what many considered as his siding with Malcolm over the paternity scandal involving his father, Wallace was excommunicated by his father from the NOI five times. He was finally reinstated in 1974. This was a tumultuous period very similar to Malcolm's post-NOI experience; he and his family were constantly harassed and threatened by members of the NOI who considered him a traitor.

After the death of Elijah Muhammad in 1975, Wallace was swiftly appointed Supreme Minister of the Nation of Islam as the obvious successor of his father. As he settled into his new role, Wallace quickly began to dismantle many of the long-held NOI views. Within a year, he had changed the name of the Nation of Islam to the World Community of al-Islam in the West, which was later changed again to the American Muslim Mission in 1978, and to the Muslim American Society in 1985. Wallace also changed his own name to Warith Deen Mohammed, changed the title of "minister" to "imam," renamed temples as mosques, changed the dress code, and disbanded the FOI (the NOI's paramilitary unit). Among his theological reforms were several renouncements: the teaching that Fard was Allah in person, his father's status as a prophet, and NOI cosmology (including the history of Yakub, which taught that whites were "blue-eyed devils"). Concerning the absurdity of his father's doctrines, Warith Deen Mohammed stated, "I believe much of the Nation of Islam's theology was intentionally made ridiculous so that we would one day be too smart for it, and would look for something better, and would search for our own way to freedom. That's what I think my father wanted."[18]

Change did not come without dissent; some followers did not agree with the reforms toward Islamic orthodoxy. After the death of Elijah Muhammad, many NOI families were faced with the dilemma of remaining faithful to the teachings of Elijah Muhammad or abandoning them and following Warith Deen Mohammed into the practice of orthodox Islam. Many families transitioned into orthodox Islam and followed Warith Deen Mohammed and his newly named American Muslim Mission. Others joined the splinter NOI groups that formed under the leadership of individuals such as John Muhammad (Elijah Muhammad's oldest brother), Silis Muhammad, the Caliph Emanuel Abdullah Muhammad, and Louis Farrakhan. The splinter group led by Farrakhan was the largest of the NOI splinter groups.

The Nation of Islam Today

As of this writing in 2020, Louis Farrakhan is the eighty-seven-year-old leader of the Nation of Islam. He has led the reorganized group for forty-two years, ever since he grew disenchanted with the reforms toward Islamic orthodoxy brought in by Warith Deen Mohammed. Farrakhan recalls the period between 1975 and 1978 when he was relocated to Chicago and eventually left the reformed NOI as a time of having "gone to sleep."[19] Farrakhan had taken time to travel throughout some Arabic countries in Africa, Asia, and the Middle East. Upon returning to the States, he happened upon a former member of the Nation of Islam named Jabril Muhammad. After reading Jabril's manuscript on the life of Jesus, Farrakhan became inspired by the part where Jesus told Peter that he would deny him three times—which Farrakhan interpreted as his own leaving and being unfaithful to Elijah Muhammad's teachings. He then decided to rebuild the former NOI, restore its original tenets (including the separatist ideology abandoned by W. D. Muhammad), and reinstate the strict adherence to the policies of discipline that had previously been required of members.[20]

Today, the Nation of Islam led by Louis Farrakhan is rife with controversy. Some of this began with anti-Semitic statements made during Farrakhan's support of the Rev. Jesse Jackson's presidential candidacy in 1984. Farrakhan's strong critique of the US government, accusing it of funding the crack epidemic and developing AIDS as an effort to destroy Black communities, as well as his praise of Adolf Hitler as "a very great man"[21] has earned him the infamous reputation as a "Prophet of Rage"[22] and even a "Black Hitler."[23] In 1995, Farrakhan called for a political demonstration that drew almost one million African American men and boys to the National Mall in the US capital, a massive event that is remembered as the "Million Man March." The demonstrators heard from various speakers including Farrakhan himself, who called upon men to embrace their responsibilities as fathers, sons, and brothers and focused on "spiritual and moral uplift," economic independency, and "patriarchal family values."[24] After the success of the Million Man March, the Nation of Islam began to grow rapidly under Farrakhan's leadership, expanding into African countries, the United Kingdom, and the Caribbean. During the early 2000s, Farrakhan delivered speeches in large cities throughout the US, regularly drawing crowds of more than 30,000.[25] Under Farrakhan's leadership, the Nation of Islam has not just preached social reform and socio-economic solutions to the problems of Black crime and economic disparities; true to its core values of self-reliance and economic independence, it has practiced these values by establishing a presence in drug-infested housing projects in Washington, DC, and other major cities, forcing drug dealers and criminal elements out. It has also established a clinic for AIDS patients in Washington, DC, and brokered truces between the Bloods and Crips street gangs in Los Angeles.[26]

It is not surprising that despite Farrakhan's popular anti-Jewish rhetoric, the Nation of Islam, as well as Farrakhan, is still highly regarded in the Black community as a champion of the Black underclass. This is due to its commitment to uplifting African Americans, a support that is built on a mutual respect that is far more cultural and racial than religious and ideological. We find evidence of this among African American hip-hop culture, artists, actors, and intellectuals who reference NOI principles in song, credit NOI work in Black communities, and dialogue with Farrakhan in State of the Union–styled roundtable discussions. This is complemented by the reciprocal support that the NOI has given to Black artists and their works, including sponsored events in the Black community that promote Black culture, which generates a solidarity that is built on mutual concern for the plight of African Americans rather than religious agreement.[27]

African American millennials hear in Farrakhan and see in the NOI a fearless leadership, a voice unafraid of challenging the white establishment and unencumbered by the caution exhibited by other African Americans in "speaking truth to power." This is reinforced by what Kelleter calls "the litmus test for white acceptance," a reference to Jesse Jackson's distancing from Farrakhan during his 1984 presidential bid over Farrakhan's anti-Semitic remarks.[28] That event set a new precedent and standard, and to this day a Black politician's position in the political mainstream is determined largely by his or her stand on Farrakhan, which in turn strengthens Farrakhan's criticism of failed Black leadership and white control of politics. It reflects African American suspicion of the agendas of African American politicians as well as a determination of many Black people not to be told who they can and cannot have as a spokesman.[29] In other words, the more Farrakhan is vilified in the media, the stronger his reputation is among many African Americans who may not share his beliefs and ideology but believe he has the best interests of Black people at heart and can provide solutions to many of their greatest ills.

While the NOI under Farrakhan's leadership has appeared to tone down some of its racially inflammatory rhetoric, often sounding more conciliatory, its conservatism on issues such as abortion and homosexuality keep it at odds with African American mainstream politics. Yet paradoxically, this endears it to theologically liberal African American Christian congregations who are often conservative in family values and work ethics. Interfaith dialogue, politicized references, Black cultural metaphors, event-oriented emphases, use of the Bible and Qur'an during teaching and public speeches, and use of traditional Black rhetoric styles often help Farrakhan feel right at home in many Black churches, where he preaches and pushes NOI doctrines cloaked in Christian theological terminologies and Black church colloquialisms. One popular megachurch pastor, after having Farrakhan preach at his church, remarked to his congregation, "I've heard as much gospel out of you today, as I've ever heard from anybody. Can Farrakhan preach, does he preach the gospel? Does he preach Jesus? He's done it today, and he's done it with conviction. Now those other little ole idiosyncrasies or whatever they may be ain't worth talking about."[30]

Interestingly, the NOI under Farrakhan's leadership in 2010 publicly embraced the L. Ron Hubbard founded principles of Dianetics (a set of ideas and practices regarding the metaphysical relationship between the mind and the body), as practiced by Scientology. Farrakhan has made the Scientology practice of auditing a requirement for NOI ministers and expressed a desire that every member of the Nation of Islam become an auditor. Auditing is the one-on-one counseling process used by an individual called an "auditor" to facilitate an individual's ridding themselves of their "engrams," which, according to the practices of Scientology, are mental images of past experiences that produce negative emotional effects in one's life.[31] This seemingly unlikely relationship between Scientology and the Nation of Islam has influenced and exposed millions of African Americans to this dangerous cult. While NOI Black separatist ideals would seem to rule out partnership with a predominantly white church, there are some theological overlaps that help to explain the relationship. It is commonly reported that Scientologists believe that they live under an alien dictator called Xenu, though some scientologists deny that this aspect of the doctrine exists. The Nation of Islam holds that the white race was created by a mad scientist named Yakub. In Scientology, the best version of self is the "clear" status—being free from past negative influences; in the Nation of Islam, being mentally resurrected from the dead means to be lifted above the impact of white culture and influence upon Black people through application of the teachings of Elijah Muhammad.[32]

The Nation of Islam today, under the leadership of Louis Farrakhan, places less emphasis on "Master Fard Muhammad" as Allah in person and more emphasis on the newly developed concept of Elijah Muhammad's messiahship. References to Elijah Muhammad as Jesus are often made during the preaching of Farrakhan and other ministers of the NOI. The Nation has seemingly departed from its view that there is no life after death, holding instead to the idea that Elijah Muhammad, while "absent" now, is still alive. These aspects of NOI teaching will be explained in further detail in the theology section of this chapter.

THE LIFE OF A NATION OF ISLAM FAMILY

As I mentioned earlier in this chapter, my family became members of Temple 7B in Corona, Queens, an annexed mosque of the famed Temple 7, where Malcolm X had once been minister and which has since been led by Louis Farrakhan. The minister of 7B, known to us simply as Minister Larry, went on to become the international representative of the Nation of Islam under Farrakhan and is better known to members of today's NOI as Minister Abdul Akbar Muhammad.

Our Nation was a post-Malcolm Nation. It was barely seven years after his assassination, and none dared mention his name. There was an unspoken rule forbidding any discussion that involved him. My father became a member of the FOI, the Nation's paramilitary group, and my mother baked bean pies and carrot cakes for the Nation to raise money for our Temple (as well as to make some extra money on the side). She used her earnings one year to attend Saviours' Day in 1974, which was the last time Elijah Muhammad would address the Nation before his death in 1975.

Growing up Nation of Islam meant that we were big Muhammad Ali fans. Ali was not just the people's champ—he belonged to us, and we proudly watched every fight. I can remember as if it were yesterday falling asleep during the Ali vs. Spinks fight in 1978 and my mother waking me up to watch the final seconds of the fifteenth round as Ali unambiguously defeated Spinks to reclaim his title and become the first boxer to win the heavyweight championship three times. He was *our* Ali.

Growing up in the Nation of Islam meant education that featured drilling and recitation of the doctrine of God from the Supreme Wisdom Lessons written by Fard Muhammad. It meant looking up at the night sky, spotting the lights of planes, and thinking we had just spotted the "Mothership" (more on this later). My earliest and fondest memories are the smell of scented body oils and the fragrances of burning incense, the latter of which is a common feature of Nation of Islam households. Along with those aromas came a picture of Master Fard Muhammad and Elijah Muhammad, his messenger.

After the death of Elijah Muhammad, our family decided not to follow any leader but to instead hold as best as we could to the NOI's foundational teachings. This meant that we still honored Saviours' Day every February 26 to honor the birth of W. D. Fard. We continued to abstain from eating pork, refused to attend church, and refrained from celebrating "pagan holidays" such as Christmas and Easter. What I did not know at the time was that God was sovereignly orchestrating situations in my family and events around us that would lead us away from the teachings of the NOI and into faith in the glorious gospel of Jesus the Christ.

THE THEOLOGY OF THE NATION OF ISLAM

From the historical overview above, we can see that the character and practices of the Nation of Islam have been heavily dependent on the Nation's leadership. The theology and doctrine of the NOI also shifted depending on the leader, as each leader developed or modified it based on his motive and objectives. In the following sections, we'll explore the doctrines of the NOI in the hope that an urban apologist will gain an organized perspective of what NOI members believe and why they believe it. Since the goal here is apologetic, we will focus primarily on the NOI's contentions related to Christianity.

Deity

The Nation of Islam claims that they believe in one God, like monotheistic, orthodox Islam. But the NOI is actually polytheistic, teaching plainly that there have been many gods throughout history and that the first god created himself out of triple darkness from a single atom seventy-eight trillion years ago. After the death of the original god, the universe was ordered and ruled by a divine council of twenty-four Black gods. Twenty-three of these are called scientists, and the twenty-fourth is God (or Allah) over all the others.[33] These gods also determine history in advance and they produce other gods in 25,000-year time cycles; those gods in turn produce other gods. The NOI considers Fard Muhammad to be one of those gods who came to redeem Black people, who are also considered gods, albeit in need of restoration from a fallen mentality back to godhood. Whites are considered a race of devils or evil gods. Thus, in NOI theology there is one supreme God, Fard or Allah, as well as inferior gods—some good and some evil. Elijah Muhammad clearly stated this:

> There are two on the scene at the present time; An evil God and a good God. When we say "Allah" that Name means God and covers all Muslims. All Muslims are Allahs, but we call the Supreme Allah the Supreme Being. And He has a Name of His Own. This Name is "Fard Muhammad."
>
> "Fard" is a Name meaning an independent One and One Who is not on the level with the average Gods (Allahs). . . . The reason why we call Him the Supreme Being is because He is Supreme over all beings and or is wiser than all. The Holy Qur'an teaches: He is wiser than them, meaning all the Gods before and all who are now present.[34]

According to the Nation of Islam, gods are not immortal: "There are not gods who live forever." They are men and are therefore not eternal. Their lifespan may range though their influence endures: "Their wisdom and work may live six thousand or twenty-five thousand years, but the actual individual may have died within a hundred or two hundred years, or the longest that we have a record of, around a thousand years."[35] Thus, they believe the original god who created himself died at some point, as did all the other gods after him.

The Trinity and Jesus

The Nation of Islam denies and denounces the Christian doctrine of the Trinity as a damnable lie and teaches that it is an illogical heresy created by the white man. Again, in Elijah Muhammad's own words:

> Even the very basic principle of Christianity is wrong and false (three Gods in one). And that one of them had to die, He being the Son of the Father, to save the wicked world of the Caucasian race is the most damnable teaching against your peace and happiness. It takes you right out of life.[36]

Elsewhere he stated, "It is foolish to believe in three gods—foolish to make Jesus the Son and the equal of His Father (the one of 2,000 years ago)."[37] Therefore, according to NOI doctrine, Jesus was a mere man—a prophet but not God—and Jesus never claimed to be God or to be equal with God. In a text known as *The True History of Jesus,* written by Elijah Muhammad, he retells the New Testament Gospel narratives and reinvents the history of Jesus. His is among the most bizarre historical revisions of the life and times of Christ ever produced. Ironically, Elijah accuses Christian preachers, teachers, and theologians of revising history in order to mislead people.

Virgin Birth

The NOI claims that theologians invented the virgin birth story by claiming that Mary was impregnated by the Holy Ghost. According to the NOI, this fake account twists the actual account that they learned from the Jews, who accused Joseph of "acting like a ghost and visiting her under the cover of darkness and making Mary pregnant."[38] Elijah Muhammad claimed that he was taught this directly by Allah in the person of Master Fard Muhammad, who he claimed also taught him that Joseph impregnated Mary while he was married to another woman. From this other wife, Joseph had six children in as many years of marriage. Joseph only married Mary after she told him that he fathered her unborn child and that this child would be the last prophet to the white race.[39] The Nation of Islam claims that it was "deceitful theologians," "writers of Christianity," and "the Pope" who invented December 25 as Jesus's birthday in order to deceive people into worshiping Nimrod, who they teach was born on December 25.[40]

Deity of Jesus

The NOI rejects the deity of Jesus as Christian fiction. In their view, the Jesus of the Bible was killed after being on the run for twenty-two years, at which point he realized that he was 2,000 years too early to convert the Jews and to win others over with his teachings on freedom, justice, and equality.[41] According to NOI doctrine, all of the messianic prophecies of the Old Testament, as well as some New Testament verses that talk about the day of the Lord, refer not to Jesus of Nazareth—whose mission, in their view, was unsuccessful—but to a future Jesus. He will be the resurrector of the mentally dead and the shepherd of the symbolically lost sheep.

Like orthodox Islam, the NOI teaches that when Jesus refers to himself as the Son of Man (e.g. Matt. 25:31), he is referring to a *mahdi* or messiah, a Christ yet to come. Sunni Islam teaches that this messiah is the seventh-century Mohammed of Mecca, and the NOI teaches that this messiah is W. D. Fard.[42] Elijah Muhammad taught that the angelic prophecy of Matthew 1:21, "he will save his people from their sins" (which he incorrectly quoted as Matt. 1:23), referred to a modern Jesus, and the people to be saved were the lost and found members of the Black Nation.[43] He said elsewhere that Jesus "did not consider himself to be God or a son of God or equal of Him. . . . Jesus was only a man and prophet of Allah."[44] He further warned Black people, "God is in person, and stop looking for a dead Jesus for help, but pray to Him whom Jesus prophesied would come after Him. He who is alive and not a spook."[45]

Jesus's Death and Resurrection

According to Elijah Muhammad, Jesus of Nazareth didn't die on the cross. Elijah Muhammad offers this alternative narrative: Jesus was standing under an awning of a Jewish merchant's store in Jerusalem while it was raining, teaching passersby. The store merchant became upset and called the "sheriff deputies." Two officers arrived, seeking to arrest Jesus for the bounty on his head, which was $2,500 worth of gold if Jesus was dead or $1,500 in gold if he was alive (not thirty pieces of silver, as the Bible teaches). One of the officers asked Jesus, since the Jerusalem authorities were going to kill him anyway, if he would not instead allow him to take Jesus's life and get the full reward since he was a poor man with a wife and family to care for. Jesus obliged, essentially knowing that his mission to the Jews was a bust. He bravely faced death at the hands of the officer, who marched him down the block in front of a vacant, boarded-up store, where he had Jesus place his arms straight out from his sides with his back and arms flush against the wall. The officer proceeded to stab Jesus straight through the heart, and Jesus died instantly. According to Elijah Muhammad, God in the person of Master Fard Muhammad told him directly that "the blood stopped circulating in his veins that instant also . . . therefore, his body was chilled so quickly by death, that his hands and arms were left stretched in the same position that the soldier demanded him to make." In other words, Jesus was killed instantly by the officer, which "left him looking like a crucifix against the wall of a vacant store."[46]

Christological Developments

Nation of Islam doctrine seems to contradict itself and change over time. For instance, it was taught under Elijah Muhammad that Master Fard Muhammad is God (Allah) and the long-awaited Messiah—the future Jesus predicted by the historical Jesus of the Gospels and the Mahdi of the Muslims. Yet Elijah Muhammad later claims to be the Son of Man or Messiah with a messianic allusion from John 10:9. He states, "I am the Door. By no means can you get by except you come by me . . . your prayers will not be heard unless my name is mentioned in them . . . I have the key to your salvation, and I have the key to your hell . . . There is no escape for you today . . . the only way is through me to Allah (God) . . . me first, for you cannot get to Allah (God) without getting to me first."[47] The current leader of the NOI, Louis Farrakhan, suggested that Elijah Muhammad was the true Jesus when he stated that Jesus wasn't born in Bethlehem of Judea but rather in Sandersville, GA.[48] Ironically, this statement was made on Easter of 1989, the very same day that I came to faith in Christ.

Humanity

The Nation of Islam teaches that the Black man is the original man, descended from a race of gods called the Tribe of Shabazz, who came to Earth from the moon sixty-six trillion years ago. In this weird anthropology and cosmology, one of the Black gods (also called "scientists") who was responsible for creating the moon decided to blow up Earth with explosives. A remnant of the surviving Tribe of Shabazz relocated to Africa with their leader Shabazz, where they developed kinky hair over time. African Americans who have gone through enslavement and have lost the knowledge of their true identity originate from this tribe.[49]

Whites, according to NOI teaching, were created as a race of devils from a genetic experiment. One of the twenty-four scientists, Yakub (the Jacob from Genesis), discovered how to manipulate two germs within humanity to create a race of devils to make havoc, mislead Black people, and rule them for 6,000 years. This experiment, according to the NOI, took 600 years and was conducted on the Island of Patmos.[50]

Eschatology

According to the NOI, a UFO or spaceship referred to as the Mothership was built on the Island of Nippon (Japan) by some of the original scientists (Black gods). The Mothership would bring about the final judgment and destruction of the white race and Christianity in the battle of Armageddon, which is referred to in *Message to the Blackman in America* as "The Battle in the Sky."[51] This Mothership (or Mother Wheel) is said to carry 1,500 smaller spacecrafts (small wheels) that will carry out the attack. The Nation of Islam claims that the Mothership and its smaller spacecrafts are referred to in Scripture as Ezekiel's wheel in the middle of the wheel (Ezek. 1:16). In recent times, Farrakhan has stated that Elijah Muhammad is aboard the Mothership and communicates with him, protects him when he travels, and is often sighted in places where he speaks.[52]

In William A. Maesen's article "Watchtower Influences on Black Muslim Eschatology: An Exploratory Story," he points out a number of doctrinal similarities between the Nation of Islam and the Jehovah's Witness.[53] Maesen contends that Elijah Muhammad borrowed heavily from the Watchtower Society's second president, Joseph Rutherford. Listed below are the most significant similarities for our discussion:

- The Watchtower Society taught that the Time of the Gentiles ended in 1914 but later deferred so that more preaching would prepare the world for the final judgment. The NOI, twenty-eight years later, taught that the white man's time was originally up in 1914, but Allah delayed the final end so that Black people could hear Elijah Muhammad's message of Islam.
- The Watchtower Society taught that the millennium (or the last 1,000) years would begin in 1870 and then later changed that date to 1975. The NOI teaches that in 1914 the world entered its final 1,000 years since the creation of the white man 6,600 years ago.
- The Jehovah's Witnesses teach that the Battle of Armageddon will end Satan's rule; the NOI teaches that the same battle, also referred to as "the Battle in the Sky," will end the devil's rule (the white race) and Christianity, including Black adherents to Christianity.

- Both teach of a surviving remnant of 144,000. For Jehovah's Witnesses, that number was previously taught to be survivors of Armageddon, but they now teach that these are already in heaven, and they are the only elect who will live in heaven. The surviving remnant of Armageddon, whose number is unknown, will live in paradise on Earth. The NOI teaches that the surviving remnant of Armageddon (144,000) will be reconverted to Islam upon survival and will also live and rule on Earth.
- Both groups teach that souls are not immortal and there is no eternal hell. The Watchtower Society teaches that the dead are asleep and will be awakened at the judgment, at which point the righteous will live on Earth and the wicked will be annihilated. The NOI does not have a doctrine of the resurrection but teaches that heaven and hell are states of the here-and-now, conditions of this life. There is no hereafter other than life on Earth for righteous Black people, who will rule Earth after Armageddon. They will live mortal lives and reproduce.

Similar to the teachings of the Jehovah's Witnesses, salvation according to the NOI comes by works—strict adherence to NOI doctrine and moral living. Salvation for the NOI simply means deliverance from white rule and influence; it is not an otherworldly experience or transformation of bodily existence upon the earth.

One might find it baffling that the NOI could teach such far-fetched doctrines and still retain a sizeable membership. But keep in mind that the Bible contains accounts of miracles that come across as difficult to accept for many modern people; and remember that NOI offers an apologetic for doctrines like Yakub, pointing to technological developments in cloning, the popularity of UFO sightings, and breakthrough research in genetics, all of which supposedly bolster the scientific plausibility of these teachings.

HOW SHOULD CHRISTIANS RESPOND?

In our response to the teaching of the Nation of Islam, it is very important that we begin with prayer. Prayer should be made for those who follow the NOI, including requests for God to convict NOI members of sin and reveal their need for salvation.

Keep in mind that many NOI adherents have underlying identity issues and socio-economic concerns that have motivated their interest and involvement with the group; subscription to doctrine is often more of a byproduct or end result, not necessarily the impetus for their allegiance to the Nation of Islam.

Genuine relational conversation and a demonstration of interest in the person should precede conversations about theology.

Responding to NOI Concerns and Values

Because the NOI teaches self-reliance, moral discipline, Black nationalism, and economic self-sufficiency, those values may resonate most with the person that you are concerned about. In response to this, you can point to the Black church and its historical work in the African American community as well as their impact in the area of education with the founding of Historical Black Colleges and Universities (HBCUs). You could also point to the contribution the Black church has made in local communities.[54] Be sure to mention the civil rights movement, which was not singlehandedly led by Dr. Martin Luther King Jr. Thousands of Black churches across denominational traditions, both pastors and congregants, came together to effect the changes that still benefit African Americans today, such as the right to vote and the end of segregation. This is a rich history of involvement on behalf of the Black community, from the time of Reconstruction through the modern area. The Nation of Islam, in contrast, took a sidelined, apolitical approach to involvement.

Responding to NOI Doctrines

While personal interest must come first, the theological problems of the Nation of Islam cannot go unaddressed. Since the Nation of Islam is syncretistic (a union or fusion of beliefs from multiple belief systems), mostly a hodgepodge of Christian and Islamic doctrines that have been reinterpreted, a presuppositional approach to apologetics may be most effective. The NOI doesn't make a strong appeal to archaeological, philosophical, or historical evidences to support their theological claims, and that type of evidence may not be helpful in arguing.

Working from the presupposition that the Bible is God's Word (although they claim it's been tampered with), show carefully in Scripture that biblical monotheism (belief in God's oneness) is antithetical to belief in the existence of multiple gods. The NOI teaches henotheism, that many gods exist and different gods rule the universe at different times; there are twenty-four scientists, and Fard is the Supreme God or Allah (albeit not the original Allah of creation). Yet the Bible is very clear that there is only one God (Deut. 6:4), and God in his eternal being is *not* a created man (Num. 23:19) but is spirit in his being (John 4:24).

Do *not* attempt to explain the Trinity at this point, as it might do more to hurt the conversation than to help. Demonstrating Jesus's divinity may be more effective at countering the NOI teachings that Jesus was a mere prophet.

The NOI is fond of claiming that Jesus never claimed to be God, however several verses support Jesus's own claims by indicating that he possesses the attributes of God. The "I AM" statements of Jesus are his very own confession of deity that identify him as the God of Abraham and Moses in Exodus 3:13–15. In the Gospel of John there are at least seven "I AM" statements.

- "I am the bread of life" (John 6:35, 48, 51).
- "I am the light of the world" (John 8:12).
- "Before Abraham was, I am" (John 8:58)
- "I am the door of the sheep" (John 10:7 ESV; cf. v. 9).
- "I am the good shepherd" (John 10:11, 14).
- "I am the resurrection and the life" (John 11:25).
- "I am the way and the truth and the life" (John 14:6).
- "I am the true vine" (John 15:1; cf. v. 5).
- "I am he" (John 18:4–8) (Note that the original Greek omits "he," which makes his deity even clearer! When he asked them who they wanted and they replied "Jesus of Nazareth," his response three times was "I AM.")

In addition, we can point out that Jesus possessed all the biblical attributes of God, which undermines the NOI concept of mortal gods, finite gods, noneternal/preexisting gods, and spatially confined gods:

- Jesus is eternal (Col. 1:15–17; Heb. 1:2; Heb. 7:3; Rev. 1:8). Jesus has existed *before* all things; he is described with the Greek word *prototokon* (preeminent), meaning that he is not just before all things but is the cause or originator of them, the eternal one.
- Jesus is omnipresent (Matt. 18:20; 28:20). Jesus expresses a clear and unmistakable claim to omnipresence, stating that he will be present wherever believers gather in his name and that he would be with believers as they fulfill the commission to make disciples in his authority.
- Jesus is omniscient (Matt. 9:4; John 2:25; 16:30). Jesus demonstrated that he knew the unspoken thoughts of people as well as things no other person was capable of knowing, such as the unspoken and undetected motives in the heart.
- Jesus is omnipotent (Matt. 28:18; Col. 2:8–9; Heb. 1:1–4). Scriptures teach that God is Almighty, yet Jesus and others explicitly claim that Jesus, too, possesses all power.
- Jesus was preexistent (John 3:13, 31; 6:41–42, 62; 13:3; 16:28).

- Jesus is the creator of everything (Gen. 1:1; John 1:1–3; Col. 1:16; Heb. 1:2). This is one of the most powerful apologetic arguments for Jesus's divinity because it demonstrates that he is preexistent; greater than any man; not confined by time, space, and matter; possessing all knowledge and power, including the ability to create from nothing; and self-existent, having no beginning or end but being the cause of the heavens and the earth and all life therein.

Many other scriptural proofs exist, of course. However, it is important to remember that the person and work of Christ alone is what will unravel NOI doctrines. The dual nature (divine and human) of Christ, the crucifixion and resurrection, and faith in Christ alone are essential to salvation. You may want to consider these verses as you dialogue with someone who follows NOI teaching:

- *John 8:24*: In a context where Jesus's divinity by both action and claim is made as clear as in any other place in Scripture, Jesus states, "Therefore I told you that you will die in your sins. For if you do not believe that I am he, you will die in your sins" (CSB). This rules out any saviors coming after Jesus because belief in the deity of Jesus is stated by the Christ himself to be absolutely essential to salvation. Denial of his deity results in eternal damnation. Neither Fard nor Elijah Muhammad could rightly make this claim.
- *1 Timothy 2:5*: The Scripture identifies Jesus alone as the mediator between God and man. This places Jesus in a unique position as the only person who, as both God and man, could represent the demands of God to man and could present the needs of humanity to God. One mediator! Significantly, 1 Timothy 2:3 identifies God as Savior, a title that Titus 2:13 uses to refer to Jesus Christ. So just as there is only one mediator between God and man, there is only one Savior in Scripture. Both have been identified as Jesus, fulfilling Isaiah 43:11. Fard and Elijah Muhammad therefore cannot be God or Savior.
- *Matthew 24:23–26*: Jesus himself warned that both false prophets and false messiahs will arise after him, making claims to divinity and prophethood and even performing miracles. But Jesus's warning is threefold: (1) do not believe them (v. 23); (2) signs and wonders can lead people astray (v. 24); and (3) having been warned in advance, do not go out to follow them or follow up on the claims that the Messiah has arisen (vv. 25–26). This warning challenges any claim that the NOI makes concerning Fard and Elijah, as Jesus himself said not to believe

anyone who claims that another Messiah and Prophet (in the sense of Deut. 18:18) has come.

- *Acts 1:11*: The angels testified to the apostles who were watching Jesus ascend into heaven: "This same Jesus, who has been taken from you into heaven, will come in the same way that you have seen him going into heaven" (CSB). The NOI teaching that the coming Christ was Elijah Muhammad, not Jesus of Nazareth, is completely debunked here. The Word of God says that the same Jesus is the one who will return, not another!

In addition to those listed above, Deuteronomy 18:15–18 is a very important passage for this discussion because it promises that God will rise up a prophet like Moses:

The LORD your God will raise up for you a prophet like me from among your own brothers. You must listen to him. This is what you requested from the LORD your God at Horeb on the day of the assembly when you said, "Let us not continue to hear the voice of the LORD our God or see this great fire any longer, so that we will not die!" Then the LORD said to me, "They have spoken well. I will raise up for them a prophet like you from among their brothers. I will put my words in his mouth, and he will tell them everything I command him." (CSB)

The key question for the urban apologist is this: Was Elijah Muhammad that prophet, the one mentioned here in Deuteronomy? In your response, point out how the following characteristics rule out individuals like Muhammad of Mecca or Elijah Muhammad of Sandersville, GA.

- Moses and Jesus both brought salvation; the former brought physical deliverance to a physical promised land, and the latter brought spiritual deliverance and spiritual rest. Muhammad of Mecca did not claim to bring salvation, and Elijah Muhammad does not bring any salvific outcome.
- Moses and Jesus made covenants between God and man (Ex. 19–20; Jer. 31:31; Luke 22:19–20; John 1:17). Neither Muhammad made a covenant.
- Moses and Jesus both uniquely stood as mediators between God and man, averting the judgment of God through intercession. Jesus's intercession and mediation was greater than Moses's because he stood before God *as* God and man (Ex. 15:23–25; 19; Num. 16:42–50; 21:7–9; 1 Tim. 2:5; Heb. 7:25). Muhammad of Mecca never claimed to be a mediator,

and when did Elijah Muhammad mediate? What makes him the prophet that God himself prophesied would come?

- Moses and Jesus spoke with God directly, "face to face" (Ex. 33:11; Num. 12:6–8; Matt. 17:1–13; Mark 9:1–13; Luke 9:27–36). When both Moses and Jesus spoke directly to God on a mountain, both of their faces began to shine or radiate brightly immediately afterward (Ex. 34:29; Matt. 17:2)! Muhammad of Mecca claimed to hear from God in dreams, while Elijah Muhammad claimed that Fard was God (who, according to NOI doctrine, is human and not spirit), and therefore spoke with him physically. Neither of these men had unique, direct lines of communication with God, as did Moses and Jesus.
- Both Moses's and Jesus's ministries were attested to by miracles from God (both the Torah and the Gospels provide us the full account of the miracles of Moses and Jesus). Muhammad of Mecca and Elijah Muhammad performed no miracles!

The most important characteristic to highlight is that both Moses and Jesus had Scripture uniquely in common. Moses brought Scripture (Ex. 20), whereas Jesus was the Word incarnate (John 1:14). Jesus demonstrated in his unique life, complete obedience, and wise teaching that he had completely fulfilled everything in the Law (Moses's Torah), the Prophets, and the Psalms. This claim cannot be made by any human who ever lived other than Jesus—certainly not either Muhammad! And we can take it even further. If the Qur'an (recitation) is supposed to be new Scripture, why does it contradict the Old Testament in too many places to mention? Jesus did not say, do, or teach anything that contradicted the Old Testament.

MY PERSONAL TESTIMONY

Despite the incorrect teachings about God and the Christian faith that I'd been brought up on, God planted seeds of truth in my heart. Eventually, I came to distinguish the truth from the lies. Marital issues led my father and mother to separate, and my mother moved us from New York to Florida. It was there that we first encountered a Southern Baptist children's evangelist.

Mr. Brown, as he was affectionately called, would walk through the housing project where we lived every Saturday, passing out Sunday School flyers with Bible verses, Bible crossword puzzles, and pictures of biblical characters to color. Every time my older sisters and I answered the door to take a tract against our mother's wishes, Mr. Brown was sowing the seeds of the gospel in our hearts. It was Mr. Brown who gave us our first copy of the Bible, which we read in secret.

Mr. Brown had invited us to Sunday School a thousand times before our mother, seeking to find some Sunday morning activities for us, finally relented. Before we left, she gave us a litany of cautions against being proselytized. We were to simply go for the sake of being with friends and then come straight home. One year, however, Mr. Brown invited us to a Christmas party exclusively for those who could recite a selected memory verse from the New Testament. We had to beg, lie, and plead with our mother to allow us to go. When we were asked to recite the New Testament memory verse, my two older sisters and I proceeded to recite the entirety of Matthew 1, genealogy and all. Mr. Brown ultimately became a family friend; his planting of gospel seeds, along with God's hidden work in our lives at that time, would come to full fruition later.

After the passing of my father, we continued a lukewarm connection with Nation of Islam doctrine for some time, until my sister's boyfriend invited her to church with his family. Debates I had with her about salvation, Jesus, the Trinity, and the afterlife began to war in my mind. She seemed convinced and even knowledgeable about this faith in Jesus—something that was becoming more and more intriguing to me. Eventually I decided that I would start visiting her church to hear for myself what was being taught. The more I visited, the more interested I became. It was as if the Holy Spirit was pricking my mind, leading me to wonder if this was what I had been searching for all those years!

I now believe that the reason my earliest thoughts of God were not restricted to the doctrines the Nation of Islam taught us to believe is because of the draw of the Father to his son, Jesus, throughout my life (John 14:6). After a time of deliberation, I knew I could not sit through another sermon without giving in to my burning desire to tell God that I believed in his son Jesus. At sixteen years old, I came to the realization that I was indeed lost and that Jesus, not Master Fard Muhammad, had come to find me. The wilderness was in my heart, not North America. Our Savior had indeed arrived, and he had indeed come as a man; but he exists eternally as God, who is a Spirit and had come in the person of the Lord Jesus Christ to save sinners like me.

On March 26, 1989, I was born again, and a year later I was preaching the gospel and sharing my faith with an unspeakable joy. To date, my oldest sister has been brought to the saving knowledge of Jesus Christ through the instrumentality of my witness, and many years later, after the tragic passing of my second oldest sister, my mother is now a believer in the Lord Jesus Christ! God is faithful to deliver, even in the face of the deceptive teachings of the Nation of Islam, and I am living proof that he will seek and save those who are lost.

CHAPTER 7

ENGAGING HEBREW ISRAELITES

Eric Mason

BLACK PEOPLE in America are searching for their identity. The Black Hebrew Israelites claim they've found it and call people of color to awaken to their true identity as descendants of the ancient Israelites. Urban apologists everywhere must study their Scripture and equip themselves to interact with this often combative group.

I was attending an event at the historic Concord Missionary Baptist Church in the Oak Cliff section of the southern sector of Dallas, TX, and was leaving the parking lot when I saw a group of young men dressed in twenty-first-century fringes on the other side of the street holding "camp."[1] I immediately recognized them as Hebrew Israelites, and they were preaching against the Black church—and against me.

I didn't have a lot of time to spare before I had to catch my flight home to Philly, but I walked over to have a conversation with them. I tried to conduct myself in a loving manner, and a young man and I began to go back and forth. I asked him some questions, and he asked me several as well. It felt like a fun, enlightening exchange. Yet as I left, I heard them chanting Proverbs 28:1: "The wicked flee when no man pursueth" (KJV).

THE SEARCH FOR IDENTITY

The African diaspora of Blacks in the western hemisphere, particularly those of us in the United States, has led to an identity dilemma. Thus far, Christianity's most frequent answer to this problem has been misguided. Many Christians are content to say that Black Christians should find their identity in Jesus Christ alone. They may quote from Galatians to discount the value of ethnic identity: "There is no Jew or Greek, slave or free, male and female; since you are all one in Christ Jesus" (Gal. 3:28 CSB). Yet they are taking this verse out of context. What this verse is really saying is that ethnicity, social status, and gender don't give any of us a leg up in our relationship with God. We are all fallen and need to place our trust in Jesus for salvation.

Spiritually speaking, we all have the same identity—we are all descendants of Abraham through faith (Gal. 3:7). Yet becoming a Christian doesn't wipe out ethnicity. Consider Revelation 7:9: "After this I looked, and there was a vast multitude from every nation, tribe, people, and language, which no one could number, standing before the throne and before the Lamb. They were clothed in white robes with palm branches in their hands" (CSB). This verse tells us that in heaven, our ethnicity and language will not be wiped out or eliminated. Rather, our diversity with equality will show off the might and glory of the gospel of Jesus Christ. Ethnicity is part of the beauty of the *imago dei* and the creativity of the living God.

A GROWING MOVEMENT

Hebrew Israelite culture is another Black Religious Identity Culture (BRIC) that emerged from the vacuum in the American church as it preached and proclaimed a broken image of Blackness. For almost two and a half centuries, the language, culture, and humanity of Black Americans was beaten and bred out of us. Consequently, many Blacks have a deep longing to discover who they were prior to the trans-Atlantic slave trade. This has also led to the common belief that anything that has white origins is fundamentally flawed.

Hebrew Israelism today is a fast-growing Black identity movement that offers an easy on-ramp for Blacks who are familiar with Christianity or grew up in the church, have some familiarity with the Bible, and are interested in knowing more about Blackness and our history. Former Christians are one of the most targeted groups for the Hebrew Israelites because of the common ground between the two. For these churched people, it's an easy jump. The Hebrew Israelites use the ethnic identity gap these former Christians experienced as a baiting mechanism to draw unsuspecting Blacks into this false form of restored identity.

The Hebrew Israelites base their beliefs on a faulty understanding of the nation of Israel. Lifeway Research did a study on African American views on Israel, and some of the findings were surprising:

> Many African Americans said they think more positively about the nation of Israel because of the historic connections between the journey of their ethnicity and the journey of the Jews.

Around a quarter said their opinion of Israel has been positively influenced due to the historic parallels between the enslavement of Jews in
ancient Egypt and blacks in America (27%) and due to the similarities
between the two groups overcoming oppression: Jewish people in pursuing
the promised land and African Americans pursing civil rights (26%).

Interestingly, most respondents to the survey (62%) said they were
not familiar with the teachings of Black Hebrew Israelites, a group
that contends that black Americans are the physical descendants of the
ancient Israelites. Very few (4%) considered themselves to be a Black
Hebrew Israelite.[2]

Even though Lifeway Research states that "few" African Americans consider themselves to be a Black Hebrew Israelite, 4 percent is still a significant
number. If these numbers are projected against the Black population in the
United States, that is between 1.4–1.8 million professing members. That
would make Hebrew Israelites the largest Black identity group. Numbers
are difficult to come by, since the doctrinal formation in different camps of
Black Hebrew Israelites is very fragmented and unclear. What is clear is that
Hebrew Israelite members tend to be unified by their ethnic identity and a
deep disillusionment with Western forms of spirituality and the Western white
and Black church.

HISTORICAL DEVELOPMENT OF THE BLACK HEBREW ISRAELITE MOVEMENT

Most of this chapter will focus on the various camps within the Hebrew
Israelites and those who hold to similar beliefs. I'll begin with a brief history,
which is by no means comprehensive, but it gives a beginner's understanding
of where this movement began.

Influential Figures

The conscious community, which can include some Hebrew Israelite
groups, tends to elevate leaders of slave revolts and use these narratives for
their own purposes. One such narrative centers on an illiterate blacksmith
named Gabriel Prosser, who planned a slave rebellion in Virginia. According
to Israel United in Christ (IUIC) and other Hebrew Israelite groups, in around
1800, Gabriel Prosser began teaching that Blacks were the people of God.[3]
Historian Arnold Rampersad, however, has a different perception of Prosser's
self-perception:

Towering above all these characters as a man of action in the narrative is Gabriel Prosser himself. Gabriel is a man of action rather than of words and thoughts. Capable of enjoying sensual gratification but firmly resisting it as a substitute for freedom, he respects the Bible. Of the proslavery whites he says: "God's aiming to give them in the hands of they enemies and all like of that. He say he just need a man to make up the hedge and stand in the gap. He's going to cut them down his own self." But religion does not lead him to see himself as a prophet, to the gloomy fanaticism of which Nat Turner was accused. The real Gabriel identified with Samson, another figure of great strength who died for freedom, but Bontemps's Gabriel does not offer himself as a mystical instrument of God.[4]

Hebrew Israelite groups tend to expand history to fit their purposes, seeing Prosser as a prophetic and even messianic voice. They often add details to the narrative that aren't supported by scholars. In this case, the evidence suggests that Gabriel Prosser didn't promote a hyperspiritual narrative; he was motivated by the conditions of Blacks and found a vague inspiration in the biblical figure of Samson.

Another figure non-Christian Black groups love to co-opt into their narrative is Nat Turner. Nat Turner was another slave rebellion leader, and while most of these groups will never adopt his inspirational radicalism, they use him as an example of what a revolution looks like at its best. Hebrew Israelite groups frequently portray Nat Turner as a prophet or as the Black Moses of America. This is inspired by Turner's claims that he had visions inspired by God that seemed to reflect a race war between Black and white spirits.[5] However, historians tell us that Nat Turner was a Christian, not a Hebrew Israelite, nor did he see himself as a Hebrew Israelite. He was one of many slaves who valued the narrative of the Hebrews in Exodus and drew practical parallels from his situation to that of the ancient Israelites, but he did not claim any natural descent from them.

Yet another influential figure in the Hebrew Israelite movement is Rabbi Arnold Josiah Ford, an immigrant from Barbados who asserted that he was an Ethiopian Hebrew.[6] He taught hundreds of people in Harlem that they were Ethiopian Hebrews. He influenced and ordained Wentworth Arthur Matthew, who went on to found the Commandment Keepers Ethiopian Congregation in Harlem in the 1920s. Commandment Keepers was just one of the many groups influenced by Rabbinic Judaism prior to the rise of 1West in the 1960s.

Throughout history, many Black Christians have identified with the Israelites' experience of enslavement in Egypt. Many slaves longed to experience God's deliverance as the Israelites had. Even though they had never had a seminary class, most slaves naturally understood redemptive history, and in particular the narrative of the ancient Israelites, from their own life experience.

> In the Old Testament story of the enslavement of the Hebrews by the Egyptians, they found their own story. In the figure of Jesus Christ, they found someone who had suffered as they suffered, someone who understood, someone who offered them rest from their suffering. Moses had become Jesus, and Jesus, Moses; and with their union the two aspects of the slaves' religious quest—collective deliverance as a people and redemption from their terrible personal sufferings—had become one through the mediation of that imaginative power so beautifully manifested in the spirituals.[7]

Enslaved peoples' identification with Israel, Moses, and Jesus led to an ongoing expectation that God would release them from ungodly and unbiblical American slavery. Hebrew Israelites take this self-identification one step further. Not only do they identify and draw parallels with the Israelites of the Bible; they believe they *are* the Israelites of the Bible. This is the key difference.

Prophet William Saunders Crowdy

Although many people in the broader Hebrew Israelite community would disagree with this claim, William Crowdy is widely documented as the first to promote the idea that Blacks in America and the Caribbean are, in fact, related to the biblical Israelites. Jacob Dorman explains,

> The founder of the largest and one of the earliest African American churches to preach that Black people were descended from the ancient Israelites was Prophet William Saunders Crowdy, who had a revelation while clearing his fields outside an all-Black town in Oklahoma in 1892. The inspiration for one of the first Black Israelite churches is a metaphorically rich example of the search for roots among uprooted people.[8]

Crowdy's revelation from God about the identity of African slaves in America resonated with the comprehensive struggles Black people were experiencing and with their search for theological and spiritual answers. Crowdy was socialized in a racist environment where Blacks experienced some of the vilest forms of racism. His master was a harsh Confederate sympathizer, and Crowdy, like many Blacks, found great solace in the parallel narrative of the ancient Israelites.

At one point, Crowdy began hearing voices.[9] On September 13, 1892, he had what he called "a revelation" that involved starting a new church called the Church of God and Saints of Christ. Crowdy espoused several novel teachings, which were rooted in his so-called Seven Keys. Dorman explains,

> In the final part of the vision, Crowdy was given a book, which he ate, in reference to Revelation 10:10. The book contained the "Seven Keys," or revelations of the Holy Bible, which included a ban on wine, ritual foot washing, and a version of the Eucharist (or Lord's Supper), a "holy kiss" greeting, and strict adherence to the Ten Commandments. At its start, the Church of God and Saints of Christ adopted practices that had gained favor among Holiness churches of the Great Plains. Adopting Hebraic practices did not mean rejecting the language of Christianity, at least initially. The Seven Keys were the plan of salvation, "and if they searched the scriptures according to its direction they would not go astray and their blinding eyes would be opened to the marvelous light of the gospel of Jesus Christ," Crowdy taught.[10]

Even at this early point in the movement, we find an overall lack of theological clarity. Crowdy's Seven Keys were intended to be the foundational doctrines of salvation. Crowdy's teachings changed over time, yet one thing that we can say with certainty about Crowdy is that he had a desire to fight racism. Crowdy would go on to be known as a "World Evangelist" and would plant many new communities. Though he believed that African Americans were truly the ten lost tribes of Israel,[11] he allowed for his congregations to be mixed race, which differs from many modern-day Hebrew Israelite camps.

Today, if you visit the website of the Church of God and the Saints of Christ, you'll see core beliefs that deviate in significant ways from the Prophet Crowdy's revelations. Part of this lack of clarity can be traced to the prophet's syncretism between his own church and masonic teaching, a feature missing from some of today's Hebrew Israelite movements.[12]

1WEST CAMPS

Another stream of the Hebrew Israelite movement is the 1West camp. The name "1West" derives from the address where this particular form of the Hebrew Israelites first originated: 1 West 125th Street, Harlem. Over the years, this group has expanded and has had several breakoffs and offshoots, and all of these splinter groups are called "camps." The camps can be likened to congregations or different denominations. 1West is also known as The

Israeli School, Tanach School, or The Israelite School of Universal Practical Knowledge (UPK).

1West was started by Abba Bivens in 1969 after Bivens broke with a group known as the Commandment Keepers.

> Known as Abba Bivens—sometimes Eber ben Yamin, Yamyam, or simply "Pop Bivens"—he signed his name on official correspondence as Rabbi E. Bibbins in an ornate cursive hand. While some contemporaneous groups, like the Commandment Keepers and a Chicago group known as the African Hebrew Israelites of Jerusalem who migrated to Israel amid much controversy, receive a tremendous amount of popular and critical attention, Bibbins's life and legacy is a relative terra incognita. Materials I've found reveal that Abba Bivens was born Edward Meredith Bibbins in Philadelphia on July 31, 1896, the son of James C. Bibbins and Emilie Bibbins. He spent much of his life in Pennsylvania—marrying, raising a family and working as a public school janitor.[13]

Today, you will find that Bivens's name is revered in Hebrew Israelite camp circles. Others worked with him in the school to help create pieces of doctrine and solidify some missing elements that were lacking to create a level base for their followers. Figures like Ahrayah, Masha, Yaiqab, and Sharn all played a major role in this.[14]

The most widely known camps in the 1West movement of the Hebrew Israelites are the Israelite Church of God in Jesus Christ (ICGJC), Israelite School of Universal Practical Knowledge (ISUPK), Israel United In Christ (IUIC), Gathering of Christ Church (GOCC), Great Milestone (GMS), and Sicarii. The Southern Poverty Law Center has a more comprehensive list of the various Hebrew Israelite groups and camps and which states they are located in.[15] Many of them, though not all, have been labeled as hate groups. Yet it can be difficult to discern which groups of Hebrew Israelites are which. The reality is that there have been quite a few splits leading to a multiplicity of camps, as is common with many religious groups (even Christian churches). While they may broadly call themselves Hebrew Israelites and hold key beliefs in common, there is also sharp disagreement and diversity in the movement.

Encountering Hebrew Israelites

On the street you will often encounter a 1West group holding what they call "camp." 1West groups will typically establish a presence in high foot traffic areas and ask Black passersby, "What's your nationality?" Their goal in doing this is to wake up the "Negro" to the truth that Blacks, Hispanics, and Native Americans are really the original Israelites spoken of in the Bible. The question, "What's your nationality?" will typically produce a variety of answers. Most Black people in the western hemisphere don't know where their ancestors were taken from in Africa, and many African Americans struggle to call themselves American exclusively. So unwitting passersby often answer this question by identifying themselves as African American, Black, African, Caribbean, Trinidad, or another label. The 1West member will then respond, "That's not a nationality!"

Having left the passing person speechless, the 1West member then asks, "What if I can show you in the Bible that the so-called Blacks, Hispanics, and Native Americans are the Jews of this Bible?" They will ask the passerby if their father is Black, a question based on reading Numbers 1:2, which they see as a measuring rod for ethnicity: "Take a census of the entire Israelite community by their clans and their ancestral families, counting the names of every male one by one" (CSB). They cite this verse as proof that your nationality is determined by your father's nationality.[16] From there, they will walk the person through various verses about Black people in the Bible to convince them that their true nationality is as an Israelite.[17] One of their key assertions is that Jesus is Black, an argument they make from Revelation 1:14–15.

The 1West member will often move to seal the deal by turning to Deuteronomy 28. This begins an attempt to prove that God has replaced the biblical Israelites (the Jewish people) with the African Hamitic people.

The person listening to all of this is presented with a false picture of God. All of this is rooted in prideful ethnocentrism. In this exchange, the listener has their identity rooted in their ethnicity and then has a valued part of who they are affirmed—but with false information.

HEBREW ISRAELITE USE OF SCRIPTURE

This brief sketch of an encounter with a Hebrew Israelite illustrates how significant a role Scripture will play in a Christian's witness to this group. The urban apologist must be equipped with knowledge of Hebrew Israelites' use and misuse of Scripture so that true biblical teaching may prevail. Below, we will address the passages to which Hebrew Israelites most often appeal, interpreting them in context so that we may be prepared to give an answer.

This Is Us! Deuteronomy 28

Hebrew Israelites see Deuteronomy 28 as a key passage in support of their belief that African Americans, Afro-Caribbeans, Native Americans, and

Latinos comprise the true twelve tribes of Israel. They couple this identity claim with additional support from Genesis 49.

In Deuteronomy 28, Moses lists the blessings the Israelites will experience if they stay faithful to their covenant with the Lord, as well as the curses they will experience if they are unfaithful. The Hebrew Israelites claim that the curses in Deuteronomy are prophetic signs that can be used to identify the Israelites as a people. Ronald Dalton, a Hebrew Israelite author and documentarian (albeit not a camp member), comments on Deuteronomy 28:46 in his book *From Hebrews to Negroes*:

> "And they (the curses) shall be upon thee for a sign and for a wonder, AND UPON THY SEED FOREVER." Because of this they would also lose their heritage to be enslaved and scattered amongst nations that they didn't know neither the land nor the language. From what country has a majority of slaves been taken and scattered to the four corners of the earth? What race of people has been led into captivity to the many different nations of the world?[18]

Hebrew Israelites use Deuteronomy 28:46 to talk about the "awakening" they will have as a people, yet their interpretation of this verse is highly problematic. Biblical scholars agree that the curses spoken of in this verse were to be a sign of the Israelites' need for repentance, not a measure of whether or not you are an Israelite.[19] For instance, if my dad stated that he would give me a whippin' for something, he isn't prophesying; he is giving a condition based on an action.

Hebrew Israelites also place great emphasis on the King James Version of Deuteronomy 28:68, which describes what would happen to the Israelites who did not keep the law: "And the LORD shall bring thee into Egypt again with ships, by the way whereof I spake unto thee, Thou shalt see it no more again: and there ye shall be sold unto your enemies for bondmen and bondwomen, and no man shall buy you." Many Hebrew Israelites view this verse and the chapter as a prophetic warning about what will happen to Israel if they don't keep the law. They view this as a central sign to remind them of who they were in slavery.

A cursory reading of the text seems to have some parallels with Africans' experience of slavery. However, the King James version doesn't make clear to us what the original Hebrew is actually saying. Let's take a closer look.

"Into Egypt Again"

Hebrew Israelites will argue that the phrase "into Egypt again" in this verse is a figurative description for bondage meaning "house of bondage." Their point is that this isn't a literal reference to Egypt—anywhere can be a place of bondage. Egypt is used figuratively in Revelation 11:8, which makes sense given that apocalyptic texts like Revelation abound in figurative language. However, Deuteronomy 28 contains little to no figurative language and should be taken at face value as a reference to Egypt.

"With Ships"

Hebrew Israelites see the phrase "with ships" as a reference to the African slave trade, where Africans were kidnapped from Africa and taken to the "new world." They argue there isn't a time in history when Israelites were taken in ships back to the country of Egypt, as this passage suggests. A statement they will often make is, "We fit the curses!" Yet there are historical sources outside of Scripture that document a deportation of Israelites to Egypt. For instance, Flavius Josephus records the following in the first century:

> So this Fronto slew all those that had been seditious and robbers, who were impeached one by another; but of the young men he chose out the tallest and most beautiful, and reserved them for the triumph; (418) and as for the rest of the multitude that were above seventeen years old, he put them into bonds, and sent them to the Egyptian mines. Titus also sent a great number into the provinces, as a present to them, that they might be destroyed upon their theaters, by the sword and by the wild beasts; but those that were under seventeen years of age were sold for slaves.[20]

St. Jerome records a later event in which enslaved Israelites are transported to Egypt by ship. Recounting the failed Simon Bar Kokhba Revolt in AD 135, Saint Jerome states, "After the last overthrow of the Jews by Adrian, many thousands were sold, and what could not be sold were transported into Egypt, and perished by shipwreck, or famine, or were slaughtered by the people."[21] There may be other times this happened, of course, but these two accounts indicate that this did happen and need not be taken figuratively. They effectively dispel the myth that "Egypt" in Deuteronomy figuratively refers to America.

"There Ye Shall Be Sold Unto Your Enemies for Bondmen and Bondwomen"

Hebrew Israelites again argue that this part of Deuteronomy 28:68 has clear connections with the transatlantic slave trade. However, if we examine other translations of this verse, as well as the original Hebrew of this text, it immediately becomes clear that this is not what the verse is referring to. Compare three translations:

NASB: And there you will offer yourselves for sale to your enemies as male and female slaves . . .

ESV: And there you shall offer yourselves for sale to your enemies as male and female slaves . . .

CSB: There you will sell yourselves to your enemies as male and female slaves . . .

Notice that in each of these translations, the Israelites are selling *themselves*—they are not being sold. The Hebrew verb translated "sell" or "offer" (*makar*) is a reflexive verb form, meaning that the subject of the verb acts upon or with respect to itself.[22] So in this verse, the Israelites are not being sold, they are attempting to get enslaved, likely because they are indebted in some way. The point of this aspect of the curse is to warn the Israelites that if they break the covenant, they will be taken captive and will experience hard economic times, closed out from their captors' socioeconomic system. They will be so desperate and destitute that they'll voluntarily trade their freedom, selling themselves into slavery in order to obtain basic necessities.

"And No Man Shall Buy You"

Hebrew Israelites argue that "buy" here means "redeem"—as in redeem from slavery. The Hebrew word translated "buy" (*qanah*) refers to the acquisition of chattels or real estate and functions as the antonym of "sell" (*makar*) in the previous phrase.[23] Yet this passage does not use the Hebrew word typically translated as "redeem" or "buy back" (*gaal*; e.g., Lev. 25:48–53), nor can *qanah* and *gaal* be used interchangeably.[24] "Buy" here could be translated "buy back" in another context, but that wouldn't make sense here because the redemption clause only works if the subjects were actual slaves. As we discussed earlier, however, this text is not referring to the Israelites as slaves seeking redemption—they were *seeking slavery* in order to obtain food and shelter while in exile. This warning would strike the Israelites with tragic irony since they have just *escaped* slavery in Egypt; if they betray the LORD, their fate will be even worse than if they had never left Egypt in the first place. Close attention to the language and larger narrative of Deuteronomy simply confirms that this passage has nothing to do with the transatlantic slave trade.

Loss of Identity

The Hebrew Israelites also cite several passages of the Bible to suggest that following the exile, the Israelites were equated with the gentiles, who, according to the Hebrew Israelites, can't be saved. Yet the verses they cite more accurately communicate God's judgment on the Israelites for their failure to represent him *as* a nation and represent him *to* the nations, bringing them to worship the Most High God. The set apart, holy character of Israel has a missional purpose, made clear within Deuteronomy 28 itself: "The Lord will establish you as his holy people, as he swore to you, if you obey the commands of the Lord your God and walk in his ways. Then all the peoples of the earth will see that you bear the Lord's name, and they will stand in awe of you" (Deut. 28:9-10 CSB). To say that the gentiles can't be saved misunderstands the entire purpose of Israel's election!

Jeremiah 29 shows that even in exile, the Israelites were called to be faithful to the Lord. They weren't viewed as a heathen or gentile people but were expected to remain distinct and set apart. In exile, the Israelites are still Israelites—they do not become ethnically associated with the nations because they have been scattered. Jeremiah writes:

> This is what the LORD of Armies, the God of Israel, says to all the exiles I deported from Jerusalem to Babylon: "Build houses and live in them. Plant gardens and eat their produce. Find wives for yourselves, and have sons and daughters. Find wives for your sons and give your daughters to men in marriage so that they may bear sons and daughters. Multiply there; do not decrease. Pursue the well-being of the city I have deported you to. Pray to the LORD on its behalf, for when it thrives, you will thrive." (Jer. 29:4–7 CSB)

Hebrew Israelites frequently argue that this passage from Jeremiah refers to Judah rather than the northern tribes.

They further cite Hosea 1:8–2:1, which says that Israel is "not my people," arguing that Israelites in exile are no longer God's people. Israelites are functionally gentiles and heathens, no different from the other nations. They use this verse and apply it as a universal principle to all of Scripture.

Yet nowhere does the Bible refer to Israel—whether from the northern or southern tribes—as gentiles or as a part of the nations to which they are scattered. Hosea 1 is a formal divorce certificate that Yahweh issues to Israel; in fulfillment of the covenant curses of Deuteronomy, he takes his name and presence from them because they continually betray him. The Hosea passage simply means that Yahweh has covenantally divorced them—but their nationality isn't changed. Whether they are in covenant or out of covenant, they are always Israelites. The Hebrew name of Hosea's third child, Lo-ammi (meaning "Not My People"), was a symbolic proclamation that Israel had broken covenant with God (Ex. 6:7; Lev. 26:12). "I will not be your God" could be literally rendered, "and I will not be to you" or "and I am not 'I AM' to you" (compare Ex. 3:14–15). God's statement amounted to a decree of divorce,[25] but that decree was by no means permanent. God promises to remarry them through a new covenant made possible in Jesus Christ (Hos. 2:14–23). The picture Hosea paints is of a nation that is spiritually broken but ethnically unchanged.

"Jews" and "Gentiles"

The Hebrew Israelites' incorrect views regarding the salvation of gentiles are based largely on their incorrect understanding of terminology used for gentiles and the nations in Scripture. The term *nations* is a major theme of the Bible. In the Hebrew Israelites' theology and use of exegetical aids, they tend to use the semantic domain that best fits their arguments and bring their own presuppositions to a passage rather than letting the context or author's intentions speak.

Hebrew Israelites have an ethnocentric, Israelite-centered, law-oriented, and overly literal way of reading Scripture. One of the greatest challenges in engaging Hebrew Israelites is holding them to good methods of interpretation. Grammatical, historical, canonical, and Christological interpretation is a weakness in these camps, and because of this, they have a poor understanding of background context and the history of interpretation of a passage. They utilize the "precept" principle from the previously mentioned Isaiah passage, and this blinds their ability to have a clearer understanding of Scripture; in other words, they misuse Isaiah 28:10–13 as a general rule for biblical interpretation. This is particularly evident in their understanding of what the Bible says about Israel, gentiles, and the nations.

The New Testament makes it clear that God's purpose in salvation is to save Jews and gentiles. While a few camps of the Hebrew Israelites believe in gentile salvation,[26] fundamental to most of orthodox 1West doctrine is the argument that gentiles cannot be saved. Hebrew Israelite camps draw from the King James Version for support of this idea. They attempt to show that various people from Ruth to Cornelius were really "Hebrews in a gentile state of mind" or Northern Israelites. Passages such as Hosea 1:8–2:1 and Ephesians 2:11–22 are used to connect the break between the Northern and Southern Kingdoms spoken of in Hosea, showing that unity is now accomplished in Ephesians. But in the New Testament when someone is called a gentile or belongs to a non-Jewish nation, the biblical authors are not misreading the Hosea theme that Israelites are "not my [God's] people" like the Hebrew Israelites are. Most of the Jews in the New Testament are covenantally unfaithful like the Jews of Hosea's time, yet this does not make them gentiles. Neither Jesus nor the apostles ever refers to unfaithful Israelites as ethnically gentile.

Psalm 147

Psalm 147:19–20 are the key verses they use to build their argument of covenant exclusivity, that all salvation and biblical understanding belongs to Israel: "He declares his word to Jacob, his statutes and judgments to Israel. He has not done this for every nation; they do not know his judgments. Hallelujah!" (CSB). Every camp uses this verse to defend their particular understanding of the Bible and emphasize their role as the true Israelites. However, they misidentify themselves as ethnic Israelites and leave out the role of Israel as a light to the nations.

Here is a short list of passages you can study that speak of gentiles God saved and preserved in the Scriptures. These are people mentioned in the Bible who are clearly not Hebrews, yet God saved them with the ethnic Israelites.

1. From Adam to Noah to Abraham and Isaac, as this predates the formation of the nation of Israel (book of Genesis)
2. Job (Job 1:1 and possibly the last verse of the Septuagint)
3. Ruth (book of Ruth)
4. The Assyrians of Nineveh (book of Jonah)
5. Rahab and her family (Joshua 2; Hebrews 11:31)
6. Canaanite woman (Matthew 15:21–28)
7. The proselytes at Pentecost (Acts 2:1–41)
8. The Philippian jailer (Acts 16:25–34)
9. Lydia (Acts 16:11–15, 40)
10. Cornelius (Acts 10)
11. Roman centurion (Matthew 8:5–13, Luke 7:1–10)
12. Ethiopian/Nubian/Cushite eunuch (Acts 8:26–40)
13. The Samaritans (Acts 8:4–13)
14. Greeks (Acts 11:19–26)
15. New Testament letters—most are written to mixed audiences of Jews and Gentiles

Matthew 28:16–20

Matthew 28:16–20 is a helpful passage to consider, as it explains the scope of salvation and who can be saved:

The eleven disciples traveled to Galilee, to the mountain where Jesus had directed them. When they saw him, they worshiped, but some doubted. Jesus came near and said to them, "All authority has been given to me in heaven and on earth. Go, therefore, and make disciples of all nations, baptizing them in the name of the Father and of the Son and of the Holy Spirit, teaching them to observe everything I have commanded you. And remember, I am with you always, to the end of the age." (CSB)

This passage clearly paints a view of salvation as open to everyone, from any nationality or ethnicity. Yet Hebrew Israelites ignore the clear meaning and interpret the phrase "all nations" in this verse as referring to Israel alone. They will say, "We know that all 'all's don't always mean all." But we need to read verses like this in the context of the rest of the New Testament, and when we do, it clearly applies to the gentile, non-Israelite nations.

Matthew 10:5–6

Matthew 10:5–6 is a key text that Hebrew Israelites cite to support their claim that gentiles cannot be saved because Jesus instructs his disciples, "Don't take the road that leads to the Gentiles, and don't enter any Samaritan town. Instead, go to the lost sheep of the house of Israel" (CSB). In this passage, Jesus is sending out the twelve for the first time (compare Matt. 28:18–20 and Acts 1:8), so in context we understand that this is a training phase. Later, we see how Jesus instructs his disciples to spread the gospel to "all nations" (Matt. 28:18–20) and "to the ends of the earth" (Acts 1:8). Context matters.

Matthew 15:24

Another passage they espouse is Matthew 15:24, where Jesus tells the Canaanite woman, "I was sent only to the lost sheep of the house of Israel" (CSB). This woman is a Canaanite who met Jesus in the region of Tyre and Sidon (Matt. 15:21–22). The Canaanite woman's response is an affirmation of Jesus's claim in Matthew 11:21–22 that even gentile nations like Tyre and Sidon and Sodom and Gomorrah would have responded by faith if they had experienced the miracles he performed. If Jesus believes the Gentiles cannot be saved, why would he say that?

When Jesus talks about his mission as being only for Israel, he is referring to his particular role and God's priority in the redemptive plan; salvation comes first to the Jewish people. This is what he is to accomplish in his earthly ministry. Jesus was to go to Israel first so that the Israelites, as a nation, could embrace him. The Israelite response to God is dependent upon the disposition of their leadership and whether the people choose to follow Jesus as their Messiah instead of their leaders. Jesus mourns the Israelites' rejection of him and warns his disciples that Israel will respond like the fig tree in his parable (Matt. 21:18–22). He speaks here of Israel as a nation, not as the Northern and Southern Kingdom. While individual Israelites respond to the gospel positively, much of the nation rejects Jesus. Paul unpacks this in Romans 9–11, arguing that the gentiles are now grafted into the Lord's plan.

Israel's rejection was part of God's greater plan, the revelation of one of God's mysteries. This mystery of the gospel—that God's people would reject their Messiah so the gentiles would receive him—was something hidden in previous times (as Paul says in Ephesians 3). There were types and shadows hinting at what was to come, but the full understanding was concealed until the time of Jesus and the early church. This is why Jesus wouldn't allow his disciples to announce that he was the Messiah until it was time for him to be rejected (Matt. 16:20; Luke 9:21–22).

John 10:16 and Ephesians 2:11

In John 10:16, Jesus states, "I have other sheep that are not from this sheep pen" (CSB). Hebrew Israelites apply this passage to Ephesians 2 and argue that when Paul talks about the dividing wall of hostility, he is talking about hostility between the northern and southern tribes of Israel. In other words, they view Jesus as exclusively engaging the southern tribes and then eventually having other Israelites go into the world and seek after the scattered northern tribes. But it is important to remember that when Jesus came, he didn't treat Israel and Judah as two different nations or people, nor did the apostles.

Hebrew Israelites will argue that the phrase "remember, that ye being in time past Gentiles in the flesh" (KJV) in Ephesians 2:11 is evidence that there were Israelites who were in a "gentile state of mind" (meaning unbelief). What is significant is that saved gentiles in the New Testament are still referred to as gentiles, not something different. This is a clue that it is referring to an ethnic category, not a spiritual one. Whenever God changes someone's spiritual status or name, he doesn't continue to call them by the name as a general rule, but God typically names them and calls them based on their new status. If Hellenized Jews were redeemed from their former status, why are they still called gentiles in Ephesians 3 and Galatians 3 and the book of Acts? The Hebrew Israelites' interpretation requires this strange renaming. Yet it is clear that God saves across ethnic lines. The gospel is bigger than Israel—and so is the kingdom of Christ.

Jesus's Color in Revelation 1:14

Another key doctrine Hebrew Israelites uphold is that Jesus isn't white. They cite the KJV translation of Revelation 1:14–15 as proof:

His head and his hairs were white like wool, as white as snow; and his eyes were as a flame of fire; And his feet like unto fine brass, as if they burned in a furnace; and his voice as the sound of many waters.

In their view, "feet like unto fine brass, as if they burned in a furnace" is describing a dark skin color, while "his hairs were white like wool" describes the hair of Black people.

While I agree with their claim that Jesus is not white, it is difficult to show that Revelation 1:14–15 proves that he is Black. It's interesting that Hebrew Israelites view the imagery in what is clearly an apocalyptic book, a genre characterized by figurative language, as literal; yet in interpreting nonapocalyptic literature, where literal language is preferred, they adopt a more figurative interpretation. A closer examination of this passage makes it quite clear that the text isn't about skin color of any kind. This text is describing Jesus Christ's character and might (which Hebrew Israelites never focus on).

HEBREW ISRAELITE ARGUMENTATION

If you ever engage in a conversation with a Hebrew Israelite at camp, you'll notice that they tend to jump around a lot, and they don't develop any depth in understanding the passages they read. For the most part, they believe the key to understanding a verse isn't found in the verse's context, but in another verse from a different passage or section of the Bible. Seeing someone flip through multiple verses with speed and precision seems impressive—until you ask them to take a closer look at the passages they are throwing out at you.

In a discussion I once had with a Hebrew Israelite, he was discussing Jesus's and the apostles' relationship with the law. He was flipping through different verses to convince me that Jesus and the apostles kept the law, but when I tried to show him passages in Acts that would bring some context to the conversation, he ignored them and flipped to another verse. Then he began heckling me as an immoral person.

This hodgepodge approach is driven by a principle called "precepts," found in Isaiah 28:10: "For precept must be upon precept, precept upon precept; line upon line, line upon line; here a little, and there a little" (KJV). They believe this verse in Isaiah means that the correct way of understanding the Bible is by connecting one verse to another verse, even if the two verses are not related by context or meaning.

But that's not what this verse in Isaiah means. This is a prophecy, not a lesson in hermeneutics or how to interpret the Bible. Isaiah isn't trying to teach Israel that they should interpret the Scriptures solely through this one concept. Rather, it is a judgment oracle directed at the half tribe of Ephraim. The meaning of this judgment is somewhat debated, but most interpreters see it as a taunt of Ephraim.

All of this reinforces how the Hebrew Israelites tend to use the Bible and how their misinterpretation leads to poor argumentation. They adopt a very narrow view of Bible interpretation, and when you dialogue with them, you have a clear sense that if you aren't one of them and haven't been "awakened" to their teachings, you won't be able to understand the reasoning they espouse. They tend to reject interpretations that differ from their own and are not open to other understandings of the passage, no matter how much evidence you provide.

The Fulfillment of the Law

Hebrew Israelites are trained to anticipate and break down the common responses Christians give to the questions they pose. Here is an example of how a typical conversation between a Hebrew Israelite and a Christian concerning the Old Testament law might go:

> **Hebrew Israelite:** "Do you keep the laws, statues, and commandments?"
>
> **Christian passerby:** "No. As a Christian, I believe that I am under God's grace."
>
> **Hebrew Israelite:** "Well have you read Romans 6:1–2? 'What should we say then? Should we continue in sin so that grace may multiply? Absolutely not! How can we who died to sin still live in it?' (CSB). Now let me ask you this: What is sin?"
>
> **Christian passerby:** "Sin is missing the mark."
>
> **Hebrew Israelite:** "NO! Haven't you read 1 John 3:4: 'Whosoever committeth sin transgresseth also the law'?" (KJV)

At this point, you are being maneuvered into admitting that the law is the only place transgression is found. They are moving you to the question: if you are now only under grace, why does the New Testament still define sin as a transgression of the law?

The ease with which a Hebrew Israelite seemingly breaks down the Christian's answers and spouts off Scripture to support their own views is unsettling—and that's their strategy. But if we review this exchange closely, we'll see that the Hebrew Israelite has a fundamental misunderstanding of Jesus's relationship to the law. They often conflate the concept of *fulfilling* the law and *keeping* the law.

There are multiple uses of the word *fulfilled* as it pertains to Jesus. Jesus kept the law. The problem arises when Hebrew Israelites try to say that Jesus both did *and* fulfilled the law so that we can now do the law ourselves in its fullness. The teaching of Jesus and the apostles in the New Testament, by contrast, is that we now walk in Jesus's fulfillment of the law by way of the gospel through the law of Christ. It's helpful to have a clear understanding of what it means to say the law is fulfilled if you are going to dialogue with a Hebrew Israelite.

Consider these verses from Matthew 5. Jesus says, "Think not that I am come to destroy the law, or the prophets: I am not come to destroy, but to fulfil. For verily I say unto you, Till heaven and earth pass, one jot or one tittle shall in no wise pass from the law, till all be fulfilled" (5:17–18 KJV). What does it mean to fulfill the law? *The Eerdmans Bible Dictionary* defines "fulfill" as "temporally and spatially, the coming-to-pass of the days of one's life or of prophecies, promises, and intentions . . . nearly all biblical references to fulfillment, both in the Old and New Testament, can be understood on this basis."[27] In other words, fulfillment refers to something that was expected, through prophecy or promise, now happening and coming to completion. Yet this is not how the Hebrew Israelites understand "fulfill." They believe that "fulfill" means "to do."

Matthew 2:14–15 is a good example of why this interpretation is incorrect. It says that Joseph took Jesus and Mary to Egypt and remained there "until the death of Herod: that it *might be fulfilled* which was spoken of the Lord by the prophet, saying, Out of Egypt have I called my son" (Matt. 2:15 KJV). Did Jesus do anything in this passage? No. Yet Scripture was nevertheless fulfilled, even though he had a passive role (as a baby) in that prophecy coming to pass. Much of the prophecy surrounding the birth of Jesus is also like this. Fulfillment includes both participation and passivity in relation to the sovereign work of God.

R. T. France makes a similar point about the term "fulfill" in Matthew 5:17–18:

> It is therefore improbable that when he contrasts "abolish" with "fulfill" he is speaking simply about obeying the requirements of the law and the prophets. "Fulfill" (rather than "obey," "do," "keep") would not be the natural way to say that, and such a sense would not answer the charge of aiming to "abolish." In Matthew's gospel the verb *plēroō*, "fulfill," plays a prominent role, most notably in its ten occurrences in the formula-quotations where it denotes the coming into being of that to which Scripture pointed forward (whether by direct prediction or understood typologically). In Matt 5:17 πληροῦν "properly implies more than mere implementation or discharge."[28]

The key in all of this is understanding that fulfillment is not described as us now doing the law. Rather, we understand that Jesus fulfilled the law by his own doing and by giving us a fuller picture of what the law was given to accomplish. As Galatians 3:24 states, the law was our "schoolmaster" (KJV) or "guardian" (CSB) "until Christ came, in order that we might be justified by faith" (ESV). As Clinton E. Arnold explains, "The law was temporary, like a custodian, keeping people in check as a disciplinarian (3:23–24)." The Greek word here is *paidagōgos*, describing a slave in Hellenistic society who acted as tutor and guardian to children as well as imposing discipline. The slave also led the children to the school, overseeing activities and helping "to bring up the child."[29] Hence, the *paidagōgos* was a trusted member of the family and even sometimes had charge of homeschooling before group schooling became accepted.[30]

Jesus is the true teacher. That is why Titus 3:11–12 calls the incarnation of Jesus as the appearing (epiphany) of the grace of God instructing us to deny godlessness and worldly lusts. I don't know how much clearer you can get than Galatians 3:24 that the law was a guardian/tutor until Jesus Christ came and justified us. Verse 25 says that we are no longer under the guardian. Jesus fulfilled the law based on Deuteronomy 6:5 and Leviticus 19:18, which call for loving God and loving your neighbor both Jew and gentile. The Savior did both. Mark 12:31 says that there are not greater commandments than these.

The Purpose of the Law

All of this leads us to a better understanding of the purpose of the law, which is a key discussion point with Hebrew Israelites. Hypernomianism or attempting to keep the law isn't new to our day or unique to the Hebrew Israelites. The new covenant is filled with people who are committed to the law in a way that it wasn't meant to be kept. One of the questions you frequently get from Hebrew Israelites is whether Paul and the apostles kept the law. The best answer I can give to that is yes and no! They kept the law as Jewish men, but also made concessions where offense would have been taken because of the freedom and obedience that the gospel called for.

Paul demonstrates his understanding of Christians' relationship to the law in Acts 21:15–25. Here, Paul shares with the apostles "what God had done among the Gentiles through his ministry. When they heard it, they glorified God and said, 'You see, brother, how many thousands of Jews there are who have believed, and they are all zealous for the law'" (21:19–20 CSB). They then recommended that Paul demonstrate his own respect for the law by taking the Nazarite vow: "Take these men, purify yourself along with them, and pay for them to get their heads shaved. Then everyone will know that what they were told about you amounts to nothing, but that you yourself are also careful about observing the law" (21:24 CSB). He took this vow not because he had to but because he was going to be around Jews who didn't understand how the law related to the new covenant. He hoped that by becoming as one under the law—even though he wasn't—he could earn an audience with Jews who would otherwise reject him. He lives out his later instructions to love the weaker brothers by meeting them where they are (Rom. 14).

As the early church grew and gentiles began to vastly outnumber Jews, sensitively engaging Jews and meeting them where they were would become a challenge. We can see in Galatians and 2 Timothy that Judaizers—those who sought to impose Jewish religious and social customs on others—were a major problem in the church. The Judaizers of whom Paul speaks went far beyond respecting Israelite law keeping. They were working against the gospel, giving a meritorious quality to their law keeping as a means of both justification and sanctification. These Judaizers were deeply entrenched in Jewish culture, and Paul tended to have extremely sharp words for them—partly because of his devout background as an Israelite Pharisee of the strictest kind (Phil. 3:1–11). Paul goes as far as to say, "They want to be teachers of the law, although they don't understand what they are saying or what they are insisting on" (1 Tim. 1:7 CSB). This statement could just as easily have been made today in reference to the Hebrew Israelite movement.

Paul then makes a statement that helps us all as we navigate the intersection between the law and gospel: "But we know that the law is good, provided one uses it legitimately" (1 Tim. 1:8 CSB). Many Hebrew Israelites will accuse Christians of antinomianism—of teaching that we can do whatever we want. But that's a misunderstanding of the gospel of grace. In Christ, our relationship to the law has changed, but our relationship with Christ has not made us a people without law.

Correct Use of the Law

Even within Christianity, there are varying views on the law's usage. But the common thread is that the law was never meant to make one righteous. Here are a few of the purposes Christians see in using the law:

1. To provide moral structure (1 Tim. 1:9)
2. To reveal sinfulness (Rom. 3:9–25; 7:14–25)
3. To prepare us for the gospel (Gal. 3:24–26)
4. To display the holiness of God (Lev. 19:1–18)
5. To show the distinctiveness of Israel as a people (Lev. 20:26)
6. To draw the gentiles to Yahweh (Deut. 4:5–8; Isa. 49:6)

By no means is this an exhaustive list, but it contains the foundational role the law plays in the life of the believer to understand the gospel. Jesus's fulfillment of the law now gives us the ability to follow the Ten Commandments in a fuller way. The gospel isn't lawless but is God's lawful way of filling us with the true heart principles of the law of all of life. If you claim you are still under the law—as the Hebrew Israelites do—and also claim you are in Christ, you are not understanding the gospel.

One of the things that many Christians are weak in understanding, as well as most Hebrew Israelites, is the law of Christ. The law—the collections of rules and laws that God gave to the people of Israel as a rule of life—is no longer a requirement for believers in Christ (Rom. 6:14; 7:1–6; 2 Cor. 3:10–18; Gal. 2:19; Eph. 2:15; Heb. 8:13). Being "under" the law is covenant language, meaning you are under that old covenant with Israel. But now, covenantally, in Christ you aren't under the law.

Here Hebrew Israelites will argue and ask: is the law written on your heart yet? They think that having the law written on your heart means you can recite it without looking in your Bible, but that's not the correct meaning. Being written on the heart means that Jesus Christ—his desires, attitudes, and purposes—is now present in your heart and mind through the Spirit (Ezek. 36:25–27; Gal. 5:16–18). Hebrew Israelites believe that the new covenant doesn't come until the kingdom of God is fully here, something that will happen in the future.

What we need to understand is that the new covenant is governed by the law, but is not under it. Jesus gives us a new commandment: "I give you a new command: Love one another. Just as I have loved you, you are also to love one another. By this everyone will know that you are my disciples, if you love one another" (John 13:34–35 CSB). Paul repeats this in Galatians 6:2, saying it this way: "Carry one another's burdens; in this way you will fulfill the law of Christ" (CSB). Jesus, through his incarnational life, death, and resurrection, fulfills this law, his own law. It is essentially a restatement of his answer to the greatest commandment. Jesus was asked: "Teacher, which command in the law is the greatest?" He responded, "'Love the Lord your God with all your heart, with all your soul, and with all your mind.' This is the greatest and most important command. The second is like it: 'Love your neighbor as yourself.' All the Law and the Prophets depend on these two commands" (Matt 22:36–40).

Remember, the law of Moses had 613 laws. By contrast, the law of Christ, or the "law" of the New Testament, has about 1050 commands, yet it is one law with countless ways to apply it. Most camps hate their enemies and pray for their destruction, but Jesus says, "Love your enemies and pray for those who persecute you" (Matt. 5:44 CSB). Even with the law of Moses and the law of Christ, we would all fall short. As believers, we must grow into the new covenant through faith and grace. But this grace isn't a license to sin; it empowers us to confess, repent, and grow in Jesus.

As we dialogue with Hebrew Israelites, our greatest desire is to see them saved by the glorious gospel and walking in the freedom that comes from being in Christ.

CHAPTER 8

KEMETICISM AND THE GOSPEL

Vince Bantu

KEMETICISM IS on the rise both among celebrities and everyday people. Whether we interact with those who have totally embraced these ideologies or those who are dabbling, this chapter will help the reader develop a working understanding and apologetic for Christians who want to respond to this ideology.

Kemeticism is a revival of ancient Egyptian religious practices. The modern Kemetic movement gained popularity in the 1970s and has been on the rise in recent years. While the history of the movement is interesting, the focus of this chapter is an exploration of the interfaith dynamics between Christian (Ge'ez: *Nazrawi*) and modern Kemetic communities. For those new to this discussion, it is helpful to know that different terms are used by Kemetic communities. Let's begin by defining some of these key terms as they are used by this community:

- *Bisrat* (Ge'ez: "gospel")
- *Haymanot Ret'et* (Ge'ez: "orthodox theology")
- *Nazrawi* (Ge'ez: "Christian")
- *Nouda* (Coptic: "God")
- *Ruah Yahweh* (Hebrew: "Spirit of God," i.e., "Holy Spirit")
- *Shajeh* (Coptic: "Word," i.e. "Bible")
- *Urpeh* (Coptic: "church")
- *Yeshua* (Hebrew: "Jesus")

My first in-depth introduction to the Kemetic community was during my final years of graduate school. I got a call from a friend of mine who is a pastor in one of the most historical congregations in the St. Louis area. My friend asked me if I would talk to one of his elders in the *urpeh* (church) about a personal struggle he was having. When I spoke with this elder on the phone, he told me that his elderly father-in-law, himself an elder in the church for decades, had recently left the faith and began espousing a version of Kemetic belief. I got together with this elder and his father-in-law at a coffee shop, and we had a cordial conversation. The elderly man told me that he finally felt free from "lies" he had been told his entire life. He said that *Nazrawi* (Christian) beliefs are merely a copy of the ancient religion of *Kemet* (Egypt) and that the *urpeh* (church) is a white man's religion. Though he had no credible sources to back up his claims, he was nonetheless convinced enough to walk away from the *bisrat* (gospel) in which he believed for most of his life. I still pray for this man on a regular basis, and I hope you will as well.

While the Kemetic (or "conscious") community exists in a variety of beliefs and denominations, its emergence in the urban, Black community can largely be traced to the influence of an Afro-Panamanian leader named Ra Un Nefer Amen. Ironically, Black people like Amen were not warmly received in the white Kemetic Orthodox movement that has been active in the United States since the early-twentieth century. Amen started the Ausar Auset Society in 1973 in New York City. Amen was largely influenced by Hindu, Buddhist and traditional Kemetic (or Egyptian) religious teachings. He advocated a religious fusion of various traditions, healthy eating, and the belief that Christianity is a white man's imitation of Kemetic religion. Various branches of the Kemetic tradition have developed in the Black community since the work of Amen. However, they share some common beliefs that will be addressed in this chapter. The following remarks will not attempt to provide an exhaustive analysis of Kemetic theology, but rather will provide a *Nazrawi* (Christian) response to core Kemetic critiques of the *bisrat* (gospel). Despite the theological variety and disagreement between many of these groups (e.g. Hebrew Israelite, Kemetic, Muslim, Five Percent, Moorish Science Temple, etc.), they share two things in common:

1. Most if not all of their congregants have a Christian background either personally or in their family history.
2. They all view the gospel as a product of white supremacy.

Our focus here will not be a comprehensive analysis of Kemetic theology in its own right but rather a *Nazrawi* (Christian) response to two central propositions of the Kemetic community regarding the *bisrat* (gospel). The first claim is that the *bisrat* (gospel) is the white man's religion. The second is that the *bisrat* (gospel) is nothing but a copy of Kemetic religion.

INCORRECT ASSERTION 1: THE *BISRAT* (GOSPEL) IS THE WHITE MAN'S RELIGION

Kemetic communities are not unique in their claim that the teachings, worship, and ministerial witness of Christians who proclaim the *bisrat* (gospel) are foundationally a product of white, Western hegemony rooted in Greco-Roman imperialism. This is a regrettably common perception all across the world. In Black communities on the African continent and in the diaspora, this perception has often been the cause for Black *Nazrawi* (Christians) to reject the *bisrat* (gospel) and embrace a variety of new religious faiths. The following points will be made especially with Kemetic communities in view.

The Gospel Emerged from an Oppressed Minority Community

In addition to the revelation of the *Ruah Yahweh* (Spirit of God), the *haymanot* (theology) of the Christian *urpeh* (church) is principally built upon the *Shajeh* (Bible). Despite contentious historical, literary, and theological differences among biblical scholars, all agree that the New Testament books were written in the late first or early second centuries by Palestinian Jews who had accepted the teachings of the *bisrat* (gospel).[1] Palestinian Jews had struggled against Hellenistic Seleucid dominance and succeeded in creating the independent Hasmonean Dynasty following the Maccabean Revolt (167–160 BC). The Persian and Roman empires capitalized on internal strife, and each invaded Palestine in the first century BC until the Herodian Dynasty was established in 37 BC as a client kingdom of the Roman empire. Anti-Roman sentiment was widespread in Palestine during the time of Jesus. During the late first and early second centuries, a series of wars were fought in which Palestinian Jews unsuccessfully fought the colonial hegemony of the Roman Empire. The New Testament, therefore, was written by an oppressed Palestinian Jewish minority during this period of militarized rebellion.

The New Testament is full of anti-Roman, subversive discourse in which the empire is characterized as a prostitute (Rev. 17:1–18), Caesar worship is replaced by the lordship of *Yeshua* (Jesus) (Phil. 3:20), and systems of injustice common to the Roman empire are overruled by the norms of *Nouda* (God) (Phlm. 15–17).[2] Following the writing of the *Shajeh* (Bible), early *Nazrawi* (Christians) were severely persecuted by the Romans as they labored to defend the *bisrat* (gospel) against Greco-Roman philosophy and religion. *Nazrawi* (Christians) were often construed as "barbarians," and the *bisrat* (gospel) was associated with the poor and marginalized. In contrast, traditional Roman religion was prevalent among those in power, as demonstrated by this quote from Tatian the Syrian: "Be not offended with our teaching, nor undertake an elaborate reply filled with trifling and ribaldry, saying, 'Tatian, aspiring to be above the Greeks, above the infinite number of philosophic inquirers, has struck out a new path, and embraced the doctrines of Barbarians [i.e. Christians]."[3]

The Roman view of the *bisrat* (gospel) was rooted in the Roman view of Judaism, which was negative: "Then, too, there are those unhappy revenue-farmers—and what misery to me were the miseries of those to whom I owed so much!—had handed them over as slaves to Jews and Syrians, themselves peoples born to be slaves."[4] Therefore, it is inaccurate to say that the *bisrat* (gospel) came from the Roman Empire as a mechanism of imperialism; rather, the opposite is true—the *bisrat* (gospel) emerged from a minority group as a movement of resistance against Roman imperialism.

White Supremacy Is a Product of *Romanitas*, Not the *Bisrat* (Gospel)

Racism is not unique to the United States nor to the modern world. Racism has its roots in Greco-Roman philosophy, literature, and culture—or *Romanitas*. The Greek philosophers who laid the foundation of what would become Roman identity argued for social hegemony rooted in biological determinism:

> Now it's on account of these things that this, seeking to have more than the many, is said by convention to be unjust and shameful, and they call it doing injustice. But nature herself, I think, reveals that this very thing is just, for the better to have more than the worse and the more powerful than the less powerful. And it is clear in many places that these things are so: both among the other animals and in whole cities and races of human beings, the just has been decided thus, for the stronger to rule the weaker and to have more.[5]

Roman authors also made it plain that a central aspect of determining social superiority and inferiority was skin color: "Let the straight-legged man laugh at the club-footed, the white man at the black man."[6] As the *bisrat* (gospel) entered into Greco-Roman communities, many of these Roman pseudo-Christians embraced the racism of the Roman world and infected the *bisrat* (gospel) with it (much like many Western pseudo-Christians continue to do today).

However, such racism is explicitly rejected in the *Shajeh* (Bible). Indeed, while Black skin was frequently disparaged in Greco-Roman and other Near Eastern ancient civilizations, Black skin is the only skin color that is explicitly referred to in the *Shajeh* (Bible)—and it is highly valued![7] Dark skin was also esteemed in other communities in which the *bisrat* (gospel) took early root, such as Axum (Ethiopia). Thus, the racism that infiltrated Roman Christendom was a product of *Romanitas*, not the *Shajeh* (Bible).

The *Bisrat* (Gospel) Embraces All Cultures

From the beginning of *Nouda*'s (God's) salvation plan for humanity, he chose Abraham to be the father of the Hebrew people, through whom "all peoples on earth will be blessed" (Gen. 12:3). For this reason, *Nouda* (God) reminded Israel through his prophet Isaiah that "it is too small a thing for you [Israel] to be my servant . . . I will also make you a light for the Gentiles, that my salvation may reach to the ends of the earth" (Isa. 49:6). After *Yeshua's* (Jesus's) earthly ministry, the *bisrat* (gospel) spread from the early Jewish communities and began to include gentiles, the first of whom was a Roman soldier named Cornelius. When Peter, one of Jesus's closest disciples, heard that the *bisrat* (gospel) had been revealed to non-Hebrews as well, he realized that God was accomplishing his long-term plan to include the gentiles: "I now realize how true it is that *Nouda* (God) does not show favoritism but accepts from every nation the one who fears him and does what is right" (Acts 10:34–35).

As more gentiles were accepting the *bisrat* (gospel) and becoming *Nazrawi* (Christian), the question arose as to whether these non-Hebrew *Nazraweyan* (Christians) needed to assimilate to Hebrew culture through traditions such as circumcision. Peter, along with other apostles, led a council of *Nazraweyan* (Christians) in Jerusalem to communicate the truth of the *bisrat* (gospel): that being a *Nazrawi* (Christian) is about faith in *Yeshua* (Jesus), not specific cultural traditions (Acts 15:1–35). Rather than imposing cultural imperialism, the *bisrat* (gospel) accepts all people in their cultural specificity, which is a crucial part of *Nouda*'s (God's) creative intent. *Nouda* (God) created a diverse humanity as a reflection of his image. The *urpeh* (church) is a multicultural multitude that exists eternally in heaven in cultural distinctiveness (Rev. 7:9).

Paul and other early *Nazraweyan* (Christians) communicated the *bisrat* (gospel) to the Hebrews and Greeks using their cultural concepts (1 Cor. 9:20). An example of this was the apostle John's use of the Platonic term *logos* to refer to *Yeshua* (Jesus) (John 1:1–18). The concept of the *logos* was a Greco-Roman one; in calling *Yeshua* (Jesus) the *logos*, John was communicating the *bisrat* (gospel) using Greek concepts.[8] Likewise, even the Hebrew name for *Nouda* (*El*) borrowed from Canaanite religious practice.[9] Orthodox Christian theology is therefore one that embraces all cultures into the *urpeh* (church).

Human cultures are tainted with sin and therefore are also in need of redemption (Rom. 1:18–32). The relationship between human cultures and the *bisrat* (gospel), therefore, is a twofold process in which the *Ruah Yahweh* (Spirit of God) fills the body of Christ, purifying those elements of human culture that are against *Nouda*'s (God's) will and embracing those aspects of culture that are in line with the kingdom of *Nouda* (God).[10]

The *Bisrat* (Gospel) Was Global from the Beginning

The *bisrat* (gospel) is often thought of as the "white man's religion," and for understandable reason. Without question, white, Western people groups have made the loudest and most invasive expressions of Christendom, having a wider impact than other expressions of the *bisrat* (gospel). This has been the case since the Roman emperor Constantine syncretized the *bisrat* (gospel) with Roman religion and identity and the *bisrat* (gospel) became seen as a Roman religion. Foundational European leaders such as Clovis I, Reccard I, and Charlemagne likened themselves to Constantine, while the Crusades, the Inquisition, and the transatlantic slave trade were later extensions of a Western Christendom destined to conquer the earth in the name of *Yeshua* (Jesus).

While this Westernizing perversion of the *bisrat* (gospel) has dominated the popular image of the *urpeh* (church), it does not reflect the situation of the earliest *urpeh* (church). When the *Ruah Yahweh* (Spirit of God) came upon the believers at Pentecost, "there were staying in Jerusalem God-fearing Jews from every nation under heaven" (Acts 2:5). These earliest Jewish *Nazraweyan* (Christians) were from various ethnic groups from across the Roman and Persian empires. Acts later speaks of the first Nubian convert through the ministry of Philip (Acts 8:26–40).[11]

The *bisrat* (gospel) spread rapidly in the early years of its existence. *Nazraweyan* (Christians) were attested to exist in the Persian empire during the second century, at which time the *Shajeh* (Bible) was translated into Syriac, a dialect of Aramaic that was spoken by many *Nazraweyan* (Christians) in Roman Syria, Arabia, and Persia.[12] The *bisrat* (gospel) was also attested to have spread across the Indian subcontinent in the third century, and Armenia became the first nation to accept the *bisrat* (gospel) as a national religion at a time when the Roman empire was slaughtering *Nazraweyan* (Christians).[13] The African kingdoms of Makouria and Nobatia (Nubia) as well as Axum (Ethiopia) embraced the *bisrat* (gospel) as their national religion in alliance with the Egyptian church and in defiance of Roman Christendom.[14] The *bisrat* (gospel) spread across China from Persian missionaries along the Silk Road during the seventh century; there it was referred to as the *jingjao* ("Luminous Way"), and believers depicted crosses atop Buddhist lotus flowers.[15]

The fact that *Nazraweyan* (Christians) existed across the world before Roman imperial Christendom and were unaffected by or resisted Roman imperial Christendom makes the claim that the *bisrat* (gospel) is a "white man's religion" untenable.

The Theology of Imperial Christendom Is a Corruption of *Haymanot Ret'et* (Orthodox Theology)

The effects of Western, white, imperial Christendom are so pervasive that, even today, millions of people cannot separate the *bisrat* (gospel) from the corrupted, colonizing, enslaving version of Christendom that has been foundational to the Western world. However, any expression of the *bisrat* (gospel) that holds a particular culture as better than another is a corruption of the teachings of *Yeshua* (Jesus) and is therefore heretical.

The common assumption that the *bisrat* (gospel) is a white, Western religion is perhaps the single greatest stumbling block for people to accept *Yeshua* (Jesus) as Lord and Savior. For this reason, the *urpeh* (church) must vehemently and unapologetically denounce any expression of the *bisrat* (gospel) that prizes one culture over another and that assumes that the theology, worship, and ministry practiced in one particular cultural form is the only correct method. The *bisrat* (gospel) is a universal message of salvation realized in the person and work of *Yeshua* (Jesus), and it transcends and takes up residence in all cultures. If any culture could ever have claimed to have a monopoly on the *bisrat* (gospel), it would have been the Hebrews, as the original source of the *bisrat* (gospel) (John 4:22). However, the *Shajeh* (Bible) takes great pains to emphasize that *Nouda*'s (God's) salvation plan was for all of humanity and that *Nazrawi* (Christian) theology and worship cannot be confined to the Hebrew culture (Isa. 49:6; John 4:23; Acts 15:6–11; Rom. 2:28–29). Indeed, the *Shajeh* (Bible) expressly condemns any attempt at culturally assimilating non-Hebrew *Nazraweyan* (Christians) (Acts 10:15; Gal. 2:11–21).

Haymanot Ret'et (Orthodox Theology) Preceded Imperial Christendom and Has Persisted to the Present

The true practice of the church that characterized the earliest *Nazraweyan* (Christians) has never gone away; it has been present and active since the beginning. Western, imperial Christendom is only 1,700 years old; the true *bisrat* (gospel) has been practiced for 2,000 years. Yes, imperial Christendom is much louder than the true *bisrat* (gospel)—but that doesn't make it the authentic expression of the church (quite to the contrary actually; see Matt. 7:13–22). Even Malcolm X understood that the true *urpeh* (church) was present in Africa long before the beginning of white supremacist Christendom.[16]

Frederick Douglass articulated well the distinction between imperial Christendom and orthodox theology:

Between the Christianity of this land, and the Christianity of Christ, I recognize the widest possible difference—so wide, that to receive the one as good, pure, and holy, is of necessity to reject the other as bad, corrupt, and wicked. To be the friend of the one, is of necessity to be the enemy of the other. I love the pure, peaceable, and impartial Christianity of Christ:

I therefore hate the corrupt, slaveholding, women-whipping, cradle-plundering, partial and hypocritical Christianity of this land. Indeed, I can see no reason, but the most deceitful one, for calling the religions of this land Christianity.[17]

INCORRECT ASSERTION 2: THE *BISRAT* (GOSPEL) IS A COPY OF KEMETIC RELIGION

In addition to claiming that the *bisrat* (gospel) is a "white man's religion," Kemetic communities commonly assert that the teaching of the church is an unoriginal imitation of the ancient religion of *Kemet* (Egypt). They argue that the mythologies of Kemetic and the *bisrat* (gospel) religion are similar, and Kemetic religion, therefore, preceded the writing of the *Shajeh* (Bible); *Nazraweyan* (Christians) copied their beliefs from that of *Kemet* (Egypt).

The *Shajeh* (Bible) attests to several central figures who spent time in *Kemet* (Egypt), including Abraham, Moses, and Jesus. The common theory among Kemetic communities, therefore, is that these figures and those under their influence copied their belief system from traditional Kemetic religion. Kemetic communities further allege that aspects of Scripture such as the Ten Commandments, virgin birth, visit of the magi, identity of Joseph, baptism of *Yeshua* (Jesus), crucifixion, and resurrection are all reflected in traditional Kemetic mythology.

Apologists can contest this "copy" theory not only on the grounds of its historical inaccuracy but (more importantly) for its suppositional inappropriateness. Not only are many of the alleged "copies" between the *bisrat* (gospel) and Kemetic religion unsubstantiated fabrications, but this entire line of thought is a modern, Western argumentation that is alien to the Kemetic tradition this religion's practitioners claim to uphold. Apologists can refute this inaccurate claim with the following assertions.

Kemetic Religion Is More Similar to Other Ancient Religions than It Is to the *Bisrat* (Gospel)

Kemetic communities often argue that *Nazraweyan* (Christians) copied Kemetic religion, and that Kemetic religion itself was a completely original religious system. However, *Kemet* (Egypt) is among several other ancient societies that developed religious systems that influenced one another. When we compare *Nazrawi* (Christian) beliefs to those of ancient Kemetic, Indian, or Mesopotamian civilizations, we find that the *Nazrawi* (Christian) faith is far more distinct.

Kemetic civilization is one of the oldest human civilizations on earth, with evidence of hunter-gatherer societies stretching back to the tenth millennium BC and a unique religious system that is attested in pyramid texts and hiero-glyphic accounts as early as 2,400 BC. Other ancient societies that developed independently of *Kemet* (Egypt) and around the same time are India, Sumer, Assyria, and Babylonia. The religious systems that developed in these ancient civilizations are much more similar to one another than any of them are to the *bisrat* (gospel). Some of these similarities include:

1. Belief in a pantheon of gods, which are often seen to be patrons of spe-cific cities, vary in degree of importance, sometimes commit immoral acts, are often thought to be embodied in kings, sometimes experience family strife, and are often associated with elements of nature
2. Temple devotion, which involved providing the shelter, food, and drink that the deities are thought to require
3. Entrance into the afterlife—whose nature, if variously understood across antiquity, is based primarily on the deeds and lifestyle of the individual

We find an example of similar beliefs in the most prominent Kemetic god, Amun. Amun is first mentioned in pyramid texts during the twenty-second century BC and became fused with the sun god Ra as Amun-Ra during the twenty-first century BC. Many other ancient civilizations that were contempo-rary to *Kemet* (Egypt) also worshiped a sun god as one of the most prominent in a pantheon of deities, as in the case of the Babylonian god Utu/Shamash.[18]

Ancient religions also had frequent contact with one another and therefore influenced one another. This was certainly the case for Kemetic religion. During the seventeenth and sixteenth centuries BC, the land of *Kemet* (Egypt) was ruled by a Western Asian people called the Hyksos, who introduced significant elements of technology, culture, and religious practice into the region. Indeed, Kemetic people began to fuse Hyksos gods and goddesses with Kemetic ones. One example of this is the Mesopotamian goddesses Anat and Astarte, who are reported in the Kemetic source *The Contendings of Horus and Seth* to be daughters of Ausar (Osiris) and given as allies to Seb (Seth).[19] Anat and Astarte were worshiped by Kemetic people long after the Hyksos dynasty ended, as they are found in temple inscriptions in Memphis, Tanis, and Avaris as late as the twelfth century BC.[20]

Another example of influence through outside contact is the vast cultural and religious exchange that occurred for centuries between *Kemet* (Egypt) and its southern neighbor Cush. These two empires often traded, intermarried, and conquered one another, resulting in countless examples of interreligious fusion. One such example is the prominent Cushite lion-god Apedemak, who is attested in Kemetic temples from the late second millennium BC, where he was worshiped alongside the Kemetic goddess Isis.[21]

During the Ptolemaic and Roman occupations of *Kemet* (Egypt), the Kemetic people often adopted Greek and Roman religions and fused them with traditional Kemetic deities. A prominent example of this is the fusion of the Kemetic goddess Auset (Isis) with the Greek goddess Serapis, whose personalities were interchanged and worshiped simultaneously in Kemetic temples that exhibited both Kemetic and Greek architectural influences.[22]

The Majority of the "Similarities" Are Fabricated by Modern Kemetic Communities

Modern Kemetic communities as well as other conspiracy theorists who specialize neither in biblical studies nor Egyptology have claimed that the *Shajeh* (Bible) copied the claims of traditional Kemetic religion and is therefore illegitimate. However, the claims of Kemetic and *Nazrawi* (Christian) religion are much more different than they are similar.

Proponents of Kemetic religion make many comparisons between Yeshua (Jesus) and the Kemetic god Heru (Horus).[23] Heru has been attested in Kemetic religion since the Pyramid Texts of the twenty-fourth century BC and is associated with various forms, backstories, and cultic practices. During the Old Kingdom period, Horus was thought to be the brother of Ausar. However, during the New Kingdom period, the "younger Heru" story became one of the most popular mythologies in Kemet. Proponents of Kemetics claim that this story is the "source" of *Nazrawi* (Christian) claims about Yeshua (Jesus).

According to Kemetic mythology, Heru was born of Ausar and Auset, who originally ruled over a paradise they had created. Ausar's brother Seb killed Ausar for having sex with Seb's wife Nephthys. Before Auset could resurrect Ausar, Seb had Ausar's body cut to pieces and scattered. Nephthys and Auset found all of Ausar's body parts except his penis and reassembled Ausar's body. Auset flew over his body and drew his semen into herself to become pregnant with Heru, and then Ausar descended into the underworld to reign as Lord of the Dead. Isis bore Heru in a Nile swamp and hid him from his uncle Seb until he became an adult. Heru then challenged Seb for rule of Kemet, and the supreme god Ra decreed that the two must compete in a series of competitions. Heru emerged victorious, but Ra denied Heru's kingship. Auset therefore disguised herself as a beautiful woman and told Seb that her husband had been killed by his brother, who then denied her son the throne. Seb vowed to find and banish this man, at which point Auset revealed her true identity. Ra gave the throne to Heru because of Seb's vow. Heru then restored prosperity to *Kemet* (Egypt) and later had four sons.[24]

Even a cursory reading of Kemetic sources on Heru reveal the striking dissimilarities between the Kemetic skygod and the biblical account of *Yeshua* (Jesus):

- Heru is one god of many, whereas Jesus is the one and only son of *Nouda* (God).
- Heruis under the authority of Ra, whereas *Yeshua* (Jesus) holds all authority.
- Auset is a goddess, whereas Mary is a human.
- Auset enacts her own conception through assembling a corpse, whereas Mary conceives through the *Ruah Yahweh* (Spirit of God).
- Heru is born in a swamp, whereas Yeshua (Jesus) is born in a manger.
- Heru's goal is to attain the throne of *Kemet* (Egypt), whereas *Yeshua's* (Jesus's) goal is to attain the salvation of humanity.
- Heru *almost* died as a child in an assassination attempt from his uncle Seb, whereas Yeshua (Jesus) voluntarily laid down his life as an adult for the propitiation of sins.

Even New Testament scholars such as Bart Ehrman—a noted atheist who does not ascribe to the belief system advanced by the Gospels—rejects the Heru-Yeshua conspiracy theory as historically unsubstantiated absurdity.[25]

Being Older or Unique Was Irrelevant to Traditional Kemetic Religion

Modern Kemetic communities who attempt to discredit the gospel misunderstand the religion they claim to practice in two fundamental ways. First, ancient Kemetic religion does not see itself as better than other religions, and second, ancient Kemetic religion did not care whose religion was older.

It is a modern deviation from traditional Kemetic religious worldview to claim that this religion is theologically superior to, truer than, or better in any way than the *bisrat* (gospel) or any other religion. Kemetic religion, like all other ancient religions, was influenced by and influenced other belief systems. Ancient religion was much more pragmatic than dogmatic; in other words, ancient peoples cared less about specific theological doctrine than the practical benefits of patronizing various gods for financial, political, or health benefits. For this reason, Kemetic religion never saw their belief system as mutually exclusive to others.

We find frequent fusions of Kemetic religion with religious cosmology that entered *Kemet* (Egypt) from later civilizations, demonstrating that ancient Egyptians desired to alter their theology in favor of outside belief systems. For example, the Mesopotamian goddess Astarte was interchanged with Auset in Kemetic iconography, and the two were interchangeably depicted suckling the baby Heru.[26] Indeed, most of the depictions and statues of Isis suckling an infant Heru come from the Ptolemaic period of Kemetic history, and the artistic styling of these statues was influenced heavily by Greek motifs.

It was during this time of Greek colonial rule in *Kemet* (Egypt) that the younger Heru became more prominently worshiped than the original, older Heru from the twenty-fourth century BCE Pyramid Texts.[27] Therefore, the Auset-Heru motifs that modern Kemetic communities claim the *bisrat* (gospel) copied were themselves heavily influenced by Greeks. Indeed, during the Greek Ptolemaic rule of *Kemet* (Egypt), the Kemetic people worshiped Heru as a synthesis with Greek gods such as Heracles, Apollo, Eres, and Harpocrates.[28]

Much of the modern argumentation surrounding Kemetic religion and the *bisrat* (gospel) centers on the fact that Kemetic religion came first. Yet Kemetic religion did not prioritize antiquity. Ancient people did not think this way. When they encountered a new god or religion, they readily incorporated it into existing practice. If they saw a particular god as profitable or beneficial, they accepted it and fused it with existing gods. There was never a sense that what came first was somehow better.

Egyptian Nazraweyan (Christians) Presented Their Faith as Distinct

Most ancient religions, including traditional Kemetic religion, believed in worshiping multiple gods from multiple cultures and presented their gods as compatible with other gods. *Nazraweyan* (Christians), on the other hand, insisted on worshiping only *Yeshua* (Jesus) and insisted their faith was distinct from all others.

The *bisrat* (gospel)—like the Hebrew beliefs from which it emerged—was unique in the ancient world for insisting that its Way was the only way. One of the earliest Kemetic *Nazraweyan* (Christians), Pachomius, rejected the traditional religion of his native Thebes. His biography claims that the presence of the *Ruah Yahweh* (Spirit of God) in Pachomius caused Nile gods (crocodiles) to flee from him and caused him to vomit pagan sacrificial wine.[29] The exclusivism of the *bisrat* (gospel) was very uncommon in the ancient world. It is for this reason that the Romans persecuted *Nazraweyan* (Christians): Romans did not have anything against *Yeshua* (Jesus), but they were offended that *Nazraweyan* (Christians) claimed that *Yeshua* (Jesus) was the only one worthy of worship.

Proponents of traditional Kemetic religion never saw the *bisrat* (gospel) as a copy but as a nuisance precisely because they couldn't copy it like they could all other religions.[30] Greeks and Romans never persecuted traditional Kemetic religion—they absorbed it. On the other hand, they persecuted Kemetic *Nazraweyan* (Christians) fiercely for their *unique* insistence on being the only truth.[31] Romans did not persecute traditional Kemetic religion because it posed no threat to their polytheistic worldview. However, the Romans—the ancestors of the white man, the very people that modern Kemetics claim to be the source of the *bisrat* (gospel)—did persecute Kemetic *Nazraweyan* (Christians).

CONCLUDING REMARKS

Most modern Kemetic communities who claim that the *bisrat* (gospel) is a "white man's religion" are not aware of or ignore the fact that, following the Council of Chalcedon in AD 451, the dominant Roman Christendom persecuted the unique expression of the *bisrat* (gospel) that developed in *Kemet* (Egypt). Because the *Nazraweyan* (Christians) of *Kemet* (Egypt) refused to accept the Roman church's definition of Christology, the Roman church—backed by the Roman Empire—began to systematically persecute the Kemetic *urpeh* (church).[32] There had already been a long-standing tradition of the Kemetic *urpeh* (church) withstanding persecution for their faith; Kemetic *urpeh* (church) leaders such as Athanasius suffered Roman persecution for their defense of the doctrine of the divinity of *Yeshua* (Jesus), against the Roman emperors Constantine and Constantius, and Kemetic *Nazraweyan* (Christians) were subjected to Roman persecution for their refusal to worship Roman gods during the first three centuries of the *urpeh* (church).[33] By contrast, Kemetic citizens who upheld traditional belief assimilated to Ptolemaic and Roman religion by fusing Kemetic and Greek gods in a manner consistent with ancient religion. When the *bisrat* (gospel) entered Kemet, however, the growing church resisted Roman paganism and oppressive Roman Christendom. The pagan religion of *Kemet* (Egypt) sold out; the Kemetic *urpeh* (church) fought for their freedom. Part of the reason for this was the inherent aristocracy built into traditional Kemetic religion. Salvation in the afterworld (or Field of Reeds) depended on one's ability to purchase amenities needed for the gods and preservation of the dead. For this reason, traditional religion was practiced largely by the wealthy. However, the *bisrat* (gospel) represented empowerment for the poor; not only was wealth not required for becoming a *Nazrawi* (Christian), but entrance into the church often entailed gaining employment, housing, reading ability, and a community for all regardless of social status. As the *bisrat* (gospel) flourished

among Kemetic people, the minority who practiced the traditional religion—
which at that point had become fused with Greek religion—was primarily
the wealthy, who often persecuted the lower-income *Nazrawi* (Christian).[34]
Therefore, African people have had a long history of resisting the oppression
of European Christendom and pagan religious practices among our own communities through the power of the *bisrat* of Yeshua.

CHAPTER 9

BLACK WOMEN AND THE APPEAL OF THE BLACK CONSCIOUS COMMUNITY AND FEMINISM

Sarita T. Lyons

Restore the joy of your salvation to me,
and sustain me by giving me a willing spirit.
Then I will teach the rebellious your ways,
and sinners will return to you.
—Psalm 51:12–13 (CSB)

AFRICAN AMERICAN women are facing a threat in disguise. The Black conscious community claims to offer women a path to self-knowledge, community, and acceptance, and the feminist movement promises women power, autonomy, and freedom. But instead, both offer women a lifeless lifeboat that denies God's sovereignty, goodness, and purpose for his creation. Urban apologists must fight to reclaim their disillusioned and disoriented daughters by teaching God's purpose and love for women, by confessing the failures of the church to live out real Christianity, and by showing women the joy and freedom gained in rooting their identity in the one who already came to rescue them, the only true source of life, Jesus Christ.

I know what it's like to be a Black woman who left the church and came back to Jesus. I went from being a young girl who was almost expelled from a Philadelphia public school for passing out Bible tracts and teaching Bible study during recess to being a young woman on a college campus who wouldn't willingly attend church or read the Bible for two years. The night Jesus delivered me, I didn't know this Scripture, but it was the prayer of my heart: "Restore the joy of your salvation to me, and sustain me by giving me a willing spirit.

Then I will teach the rebellious your ways, and sinners will return to you" (Ps. 51:12–13 CSB).

I know there are other Black women who are desperate for cultural identity, sick of misogyny, and tired of begging for a seat at a table where God has already prepared a place for them. I understand that having those frustrations and hurts can make one vulnerable to being tossed into a raging sea of confusion, only to be picked up by a "lifeboat" that cannot save. This illusion of a "lifeboat," though Black and beautiful and smart and sincere, is taking on water because there are holes in the boat that we cannot see. These holes are distortions of God's Word, rejections of God's will, and fantasies of counterfeit freedom. If women do not abandon ship and cling tightly to God's Word, they will drown in the very lies they believed would save them.

This chapter is a call for the church to defend the faith against ideologies from two specific groups: the Black conscious community and feminism. Both of these groups cast Christianity as a detriment to the dignity, equality, and flourishing of Black women. Both of these groups have influenced Black women to rethink their womanhood in similar ways. The goal of this defense is to warn the church about how these two groups appeal to Black women, to expose efforts to redeem one's racial or gender identity outside of Christ as idolatrous, and to show that the dignity of Black women is affirmed in Scripture.

THE LIFELESS LIFEBOAT

I proudly attended a Historically Black College and University (HBCU) and still cherish my years there. However, during this season of my life, I began to question everything I'd ever believed about Christ. My desire to learn my cultural identity and be empowered as a Black woman led me into the lifeless lifeboat of Kemetic and Yoruba teachings. My introduction to the conscious community was a shock to my system. I had never heard the things they taught. Adam Coleman describes the conscious community as a "nebulous entity," some of which have specific belief systems, but the majority of which have "no formal creed or organization . . . these include the Hebrew Israelites, Moorish Scientists, Egyptian (Kemetic) spiritualists, and practitioners of African mysticism."[1]

Initially, I was desperately trying to engage in syncretism by blending my Christian beliefs with these practices, but "no one can serve two masters" (Matt. 6:24). I attended lectures, which led me to attend an African dance class, engage in meditation and kundalini yoga, and finally to sit at the feet of a "Baba"[2] who meticulously unraveled my thin belief system with intellectual lies about the Christian faith. Even when I would push back, I was no match for the well-studied information about ancient Kemet, and the introduction to the Yoruba Orisha was fascinating. I was told that my male and female deity types were Ogun and Oshun.[3] While I didn't know to call myself a feminist, as "a daughter of Oshun," I certainly put my femininity on a pedestal. The conscious community often promotes the idea that the Black woman is a god, which is another iteration of some radical feminist thought. I felt like a superhero: powerful, magnetic, beautiful—but tricked. I believed my Christian parents had good intentions but bad information. The new ideologies I was encountering were framing Jesus as an appropriation of Egyptian religions and a stolen legacy of African people.

I was vulnerable to these lies due to a recent breakup with a boyfriend, the void of not knowing my heritage, and painful church hurt from male leadership. The new community I found appeared to fulfill my needs. I became part of a community of Black folks who were spoken-word artists, called me sistah and queen, gave me "conscious books," and taught me how to naturally care for my body, wrap my head, eat healthy, and smudge away negativity with sage. Together we laughed, cried, and talked about everything that I loved—except Jesus. In the conscious community, I saw images of Black men who were strong, outspoken, well read, and appeared to have high respect for Black women. I was a young, lonely, and biblically illiterate Christian who had not been prepared to encounter people who rejected the Bible but knew more Scriptures than I did. I was on this lifeless lifeboat, reading tarot cards and cowry shells; I performed rituals to the "gods," built altars to the ancestors, bathed in honey, buried meat in the ground, and put cake in a river as an offering.

My story is not unique. Many other Black women are on lifeless lifeboats, and they need the church to point them to the true ark of safety, Jesus Christ. Effective urban apologists must strategically anticipate the stumbling blocks the devil uses to deceive. Apologists must point to the superiority of Scripture and sensitively apply truth to the tangible and psychological effects of racism and sexism.

THE APPEAL OF THE BLACK CONSCIOUS COMMUNITY

There are many reasons the Black conscious community is appealing to African Americans today. When discussing these appeals, we tend to think broadly about the ways the movement appeals to both men and women.

We hear the familiar attractive aspects of the movement, like knowledge of self, returning to our roots, resisting white supremacy, and being engaged in spiritual practices indigenous to our ancestors prior to slavery. However, what we don't often discuss are the nuances of how Black *women* may be drawn to the Black conscious community. While the diversity among Black women makes it impossible to speak for or categorize them all, it is still relevant to explore some special considerations for Black women when considering the appeal of the Black conscious community. Below are six considerations for the church that speak to the psychology and needs of some Black women that make the Black conscious community appealing.

Dignified and Divine

"Sistah," "queen," and "god" are three of the most common ways Black women are addressed or named in the Black conscious community. These titles ascribed to Black women are powerful affirmations, and they often consciously or unconsciously serve as a healing balm for the wearied Black female soul. All Black people know the pain of living in a world where there is always a threat of being called a "nigger," but to be Black and a woman renders you vulnerable to people cursing you with other damaging names like "ho," "bitch," "trick," and "dyke." For many, it doesn't matter if it is logical, historical, or factual—being named sistah, queen, and god can have a psychological impact that is refreshing and alluring. I remember the first time a Black man who was not my biological brother called me "sistah," it made me feel protected. Isn't that what brothers are supposed to do—protect? In a world where many women are accustomed to men approaching them disrespectfully, making comments about their body, or viewing them as a potential sexual conquest, being referred to as "sistah" initially brings a sigh of relief for a woman who is constantly navigating the effects of rape culture while also offering the nonsexual closeness that all people need.

The Black conscious community also refers to Black women as "queens," a reminder to our community and the world that African men and women were once royalty and should be viewed with dignity today. Despite the implausibility that every ancient African woman was a queen, calling all Black women "queens" today serves as a self-esteem boost, dignifies the history of Black women, and changes the narrative that Black women are accustomed to hearing about themselves in a white supremacist and gender-oppressive world.

The Black conscious community is known for teaching that Black women are to be valued, respected, and consulted because in Ancient Kemet (Egypt), there were female monarchies. Ife Jogunosimi writes,

In ancient Africa, the woman not only had a special place within the context of the family but often ruled nations wielding much power. One only has to look at the ancient nation states of Egypt, Kush, and Ethiopia to see women in positions of leadership and power.[4]

Interestingly, Jogunosimi used the Bible—a book mocked and despised by most in the conscious community as nonaffirming of Blackness or womanhood—as evidence of African queens. Jogunosimi writes, "Further references to Meroe and the lines of queens named Candace can be found in the New Testament of the Holy Bible . . . In the book of Acts 8:26–28 . . . ."[5]

Lastly, the Black conscious community has touted the Black woman as god. Joseph Gibson believes that there is archaeological, mythological, and documentary proof of the Black woman being depicted as god inside and outside of Africa.[6] Some also attribute the title of god or goddess to Black women based on Egyptian women having been deified as goddesses.[7]

It should be noted, that like in all groups—even within Christianity—people do not always live up to the values they espouse. Duplicity and imperfection are traits of a sinner and evidence of why we need a Savior. However, imperfection is more harshly judged in the Christian community than in the Black conscious community (or anywhere else). While no groups are perfect, the Christlessness of these groups is what leaves them powerless to overcome sin and to live up to their ideals to love and respect Black women. Therefore, it is important to know that the Black conscious community is not the utopia and safe haven for women that one might fantasize it to be. Like other groups, in my experience, the Black conscious community has been guilty of disrespecting, ignoring, abusing, sexualizing, and sleeping around with their "sistahs," "queens," and "gods."

However, there is something significant for the church to learn from this appealing aspect of the Black conscious community as we evaluate not only a biblical apologetic but also an appropriate practical response to Black women who are disheartened by the church and find a "home" in the Black conscious community. Aside from the "Black woman is god" lie, because no person is God but Jesus,[8] we must assess how some churches have done a disservice by believing the only thing worth filling Black women with is doctrine and not dignity.

The labels "sistah," "queen," and "god" have been a part of the conscious community's efforts to restore the dignity of Black women that has been systematically attacked since African people were stolen from their homeland. Malcolm X said, "The most disrespected woman in America is the black woman. The most unprotected person in America is the black woman. The most neglected person in America is the black woman."[9] However, Black women should not have to leave the church in order to be respected, treated as an equal, or to have their African history celebrated. The Black woman does not have to feed her esteem with platitudes of being a "queen" in the twenty-first century or pretend that every Black man in the conscious community is a safe "brother" just because he calls her "sistah," nor does the Black woman need to feel powerful by the delusion that she is a god.

However, the church must understand why those names hit home. The church must also evaluate why many Black women don't feel seen, valued, or significant in the church when the Head of the church died and was resurrected to redeem and esteem her life. As I will discuss later, Christ affirms the dignity of all women, and being a Christian doesn't mean Black women have to divest from all the wonderful African history that is theirs. It is not counterproductive for the church of today to do more of what many traditional Black churches did in teaching and affirming the worth, abilities, necessity, and contributions of Black women and girls.[10]

Additionally, affirming the beauty of male and female relationships (Christian siblings) outside of romance or marriage should be the norm of the church. Black women need Christian brothers, and brothers need Black Christian sisters in the body. It is important for the church to teach and prepare men and women to love one another as siblings, to be a safe place for one another, to defend, care for, and communicate with one another as brothers and sisters.

The Black conscious community should not be where Black women learn their heritage, experience brotherhood and sisterhood, and are affirmed. All these things must happen in the church and be seen as cooperative with and not in competition with the gospel. The church does not have to dress up Christianity to be appealing to Black women; the church just has to practice true Christianity, embracing Black women as fellow image bearers (Gen. 1:27), beloved by God (1 John 4:10), called by God (Eph. 2:10), siblings in the family of God (Rom. 8:29), corulers with man in the earth (Gen. 1:28–30), members of the royal priesthood of believers (1 Peter 2:9), and worshipers whose African tribe will be in heaven around Jesus's throne (Rev. 7:9–10).

The Spiritual vs. Religious Appeal

A common attraction to the Black conscious community for Black women, specifically millennials, is the DIY ("do-it-yourself") spirituality.[11] Some Black women have been drawn to African spirituality to avoid what is perceived as a rule-following, authority-driven, self-limiting, controlling, and condemning religion. Luna Malbrox, a former church attender, said, "But even though more young Black people are leaving organized religious institutions, that doesn't mean we aren't spiritual. Steadily, it seems like when we move away from Christian church, we move towards less organized spiritual practices based on traditional African spirituality."[12] The move is from institutionalized religion to a self-defined "African" spirituality.

Another woman who left the church said, "The Church is oppressive for a lot of Black women . . . But these African traditions empower women. They are empowering you to have a hand in what you're doing—to create your own magic."[13] In fact, outside of the connection to Africa, the freedom to self-select practices from an African spiritual smorgasbord reveals that many women are motivated to practice African spirituality for personal fulfillment rather than out of adoration for a particular deity or a desire to cultivate a spiritual life that would effect systemic change in the world. For instance, "Modern black witches are practicing Yoruba-based faiths, with a few Millennial touches. They build altars to ancestors so they can seek their advice on everything from romance, professional advancement, casting spells using emoji to help banish depression, surround themselves with crystals in the hope that they will relieve stress, and burn sage to cleanse their apartments of negative energy."[14] For many, this is a "live your best life," "do you," "boss-chick," "it's all about me" mentality masquerading as African spirituality.

These DIY spiritual freedoms and options position practitioners as Lord of their own lives (the Black woman is god), encouraging them to serve themselves above all else. This DIY or Burger King spirituality invites you to "have it your way" by promoting self-discovery, creativity, nonconformity, and a lack of accountability to leadership. Unlike the Kemetic practices that elevate the ideals of the god MAAT,[15] many in the Black conscious community do not function under any specific order or morality-driven value system. Instead of offering allegiance to or even understanding specific African spiritual practices, syncretism is the common path in the Black conscious community. Personally, I was taught and simultaneously engaged in Kemetic practices and Yoruba practices, mixing rituals, divination, altar building, language, and clothing from both cultures. Some of what is happening with the practice of African spirituality is the mixing of various beliefs, practices, and cultures. Black communities are increasingly celebrating "entrepreneur spirituality," where syncretism and self-creating is viewed as freeing and historically African. I distinctly remember asking for instructions regarding some of the practices I was exposed to and I was told, "Ask the ancestors for help; they will guide you." Often what I witnessed were people experimenting with the spiritual world, and for many, that is appealing.

The use of African spirituality for self-centered aims seems disrespectful and counterintuitive as a brand of African culture. What is imperative for the church to know is that some women may have encountered a very legalistic, nonrelational, restrictive religious experience in the church. A lack of clear teaching on Christ and women's equality with men in Scripture, as well as missed discipleship experiences, left gaps in a Black woman's church experience that made Christianity feel oppressive instead of empowering. There is no greater means of freedom, transformation of the personal life, and reordering of the entire world than what Christ provides. The assessment the church must make is whether or not we are transmitting that truth clearly and lovingly for Black women. It is important for the church to consider the ways we can improve our engagement of Black women based on their unique needs, prior hurts, and the intersectional complexities of being a Black woman in America.

In addition to strengthening our engagement and teaching, we must never forget that the world's system continuously promotes independence, nonconformity, and autonomy as the aim of the human life. Some of the attraction to the Black conscious community is the permission some sects grant to connect to Africa or attain knowledge of the self without many moral expectations or calls for change (other than shedding colonialism and resisting white supremacy). The gospel—not just the so-called social gospel—mandates justice, equality, love of neighbor, humility, and impartiality. Black women can be Christian, retain a plethora of cultural expressions, be empowered, and resist white supremacy all at once because those things are not antithetical to the Christian faith. The Black conscious community is not the curator of culture and justice. God is.

Women Empowered as Spiritual Leaders

Black women are also drawn to the Black conscious community because they will be welcomed not only as "queens" but also as spiritual leaders. Given some of the real exclusion women have experienced in the church, African spirituality is attractive to many because it easily affords women leadership roles, gives them a voice, and encourages them to use their gifts and passions to serve themselves and others. The freedom and flexibility to practice spirituality outside of the boundaries that are believed to be set by men in the church and not God have been an appeal.

Black women can be initiated into the Yoruba priesthood; instead of being prophetesses in the church, they are reading tarot cards and cowrie shells, communing with ancestors, leading rituals, and engaging in other types of divination. A Maryland group called "Dawtas of the Moon," open to both men and women, is led by a high priestess who oversees the group and performs the rites.[16]

It is imperative for the church to provide a biblical apologetic for womanhood, allow women to serve in leadership, hear their voices, receive their gifts for the body's upbuilding, and affirm Christ's love for women in Scripture (addressed later in this chapter). This encouragement for the church is not to compete with African spirituality because Black women like these things, but because it is biblical and therefore the right thing to do. Black women should not be leaving the church because they don't believe there is a place for them due to race or gender.

The Influence of Pop Culture

There may have been a time in the not-so-distant past where a Black woman calling herself a witch would have been shocking; however, as Malbrox writes, "Millennials have rebranded witchcraft as cool."[17] The rate at which we see millennials embracing witchcraft is in large part due to pop culture, which has found ways to incorporate elements of African spirituality into art.

Dr. Ernest Grant, a Pastor in Camden, New Jersey, said,

> [West African spirituality] moved into the mainstream in early 2016 when acclaimed artist Beyoncé released her Grammy-winning album, *Lemonade* . . . she (Beyoncé) drew upon the imagery of one of the most revered orishas [deities] in the Yoruba pantheon, Oshun. In her video *Hold Up*, she dawned the fluorescent yellow dress of the goddess of love and fertility who's often depicted as wearing the same garb.[18]

Beyoncé has also used her influence to echo sentiments in support of the Black conscious community's declaration that the Black woman is god. During the 2016 MTV Music Video Awards, she performed a rendition of "Don't Hurt Yourself" and said, "When you love me, you love yourself. Love God herself."[19] Though Beyoncé does not call herself a god, she does put *God* in the feminine form, representing both the feminist ideology of God being a woman and the Black conscious community ideology of the Black woman being divine. Similarly, Erykah Badu has hinted at the Black woman being god in her song "On and On," saying, "If we were made in his image then call us by our name. Most intellects do not believe in God, but they fear us just the same."[20]

Syncretism reaches a wide audience through pop culture. It can be theologically confusing to Black girls and women to see mixed messages from their idols, like Beyoncé dressing as an African goddess when in the past she professed to be a Christian. As mentioned before, I initially thought I could safely engage in both Christianity and African spirituality, but I eventually leaned more into African spirituality and away from Christ. Some self-described Black witches say they still attend church and believe that Christianity and African witchcraft are complementary and not mutually exclusive, saying things like, "The Bible ain't nothing but a big old spell book."[21] Seeing one's pop culture icons weaving African spirituality into their art and performances makes it more attractive.

While Christians should avoid overspiritualizing entertainment, it is imperative that the church talk through pop culture with its members, stay abreast on the latest trends in culture, and teach the congregation how to judge all things through a biblical lens. Christian women may consider their diet from pop culture to be merely entertainment, but it is important for the church to communicate that we are always being "edutained," not merely entertained. Helping Christian women think through what the world is teaching them while entertaining them is vital, as well as providing opportunities through preaching, teaching, and discipleship to process the tendency to blindly consume entertainment. Our liberty in Christ affirms that we don't need to condemn all music, but Christians should be strategic and guarded as we celebrate and enjoy artistic diversity.

Black Women Are Beautiful

Some Black women may be attracted to the Black conscious community for their celebration of Black women's beauty and their rejection of standards of beauty normed around whiteness. White beauty was always glorified throughout history, while Black women have been called ugly and unfeminine. "Black is beautiful" is a more commonly celebrated truth in the Black conscious community, and Black women are more likely to hear affirmations for their physical appearance; commonly rejected Black phenotypes such as coarse and kinky hair, dark skin, wide noses, big lips, and wide hips are celebrated.

Unfortunately, microaggressions around Black women's physical appearance occur in churches as well. The whitewashing of Christianity has been discussed more frequently than the whitewashing of biblical womanhood. A simple google search of "biblical womanhood" doesn't lead to many images of Black women. It is also difficult to find images of women of the Bible who aren't portrayed as white. Images of white women are used on a majority of mainstream Christian networks, women's conferences, Bible teachings, women's ministry advertisements, and books. This is ironic, as Vince Bantu points out, because "The 'typical' Christian of the twenty-first century is not a white man [or woman], but an African woman."[22] Identifying our "sheroes" of the faith as people of color is just one example of the color-correction needed surrounding biblical womanhood in the church.

While I agree that true self-esteem is not found in the self but is rooted in the person and work of Christ, we must not overlook the systematic way in which Black women's physical features and presence have been rejected, mocked, or rendered invisible in some churches. Black women who have been members of majority white churches almost never see Black beauty affirmed or incorporated into the life of the church. We are so conditioned to equate white-ness with rightness and whiteness with beauty that we have cooperated with white supremacy in the exclusion of the Black woman as a symbol of beauty and as something to be esteemed. The church should not glory in external features, but it also should not elevate or showcase one image of womanhood and beauty over another. Women of color do not need to be written into the redemptive narrative to boost their self-esteem; Black women should be seen in the redemptive narrative because we are already there!

Black Women Are Heard and Accepted

Black women have found solace in the Black conscious community for more than just spiritual practices. Many Black women are praising these communities for creating a safe place of belonging for Black women to talk about their trauma from racism, sexual abuse, misogyny, and homophobia. One woman said, "Witchcraft serves as a safe haven for some LGBT youth who don't feel welcome in the Church (and) the number of online posts by and about LGBT witches attests to the overlap between queer and witch communities."[23] Empowerment is a major theme within the Black conscious community, and a notable feature of the Black Witch Convention is that it was ". . . replete with talk of sexual trauma, suppression, and self-acceptance, it felt like group therapy. Women cried or spoke in trembling voices as they described their experiences of abuse."[24]

It is important for the church to take notice of the fact that the Black conscious community, for many Black women, represents a hub of advocacy around intersecting issues of race, gender, sexuality, and feminism. One might suspect that Black women are primarily drawn to the movement around racial identity, but the appeal and the fight for equality is multifaceted. Many Black women go to the Black conscious community to find a place of escape from the judgment, exclusion, or condemnation that many feel in church from people who are not equipped to deal with mental health issues, grief, trauma, and LGBTQ concerns in a healthy and Christ-centered way.

The church may consider staffing and services that address mental health issues, providing trauma-informed care from lay leaders to pastors, as well as deferring to experts when a need is beyond the scope of expertise in the church. Additionally, even when referrals are necessary, building a community of compassionate care, support groups, and safe spaces for women to talk and share outside of traditional Bible studies or women's ministry could prove beneficial.

The church also has to be more equipped to engage with the LGBTQ community and with individuals who struggle with same-sex attraction. The church hasn't known how to address the issue holistically without feeling like they've abandoned biblical sexuality, so struggling individuals often find it difficult to find love and compassion among Christians. It is imperative for politics and issues pertinent to Black women to be engaged biblically and sensitively from the pulpit. Opportunities for discipleship and support should be given for more private matters that aren't always appropriate to work through in small groups with men present. This also highlights the importance of having Black women on staff and in positions of leadership at the church who can engage Black women personally in ways that may not be possible for male leadership.

THE APPEAL OF FEMINISM

In our postmodern world, feminism is a difficult word to define. Most people see feminism as the belief that women are equal to men, or as Sarah Bessey defines it, "Feminism simply consists of the radical notion that women are people too."[25] Bell Hooks defines feminism as "a movement to end sexism, sexist exploitation, and oppression."[26] These definitions of feminism explain why women like Chimamanda Ngozi Adichie say "We should all be feminists."[27]

In the late 1960s and 1970s, Black women sought to expand the feminist movement to include issues highlighting the triple oppression of Black women—racism, sexism, and poverty—which was ignored by middle-class white feminists. Angela Davis says, "It is no longer permissible for white women to justify their failure to struggle jointly with women of color by offering such frail excuses as, 'We invited them to our meetings, but they just don't seem interested in women's issues.'"[28]

From this desire to make women's liberation movements inclusive of Black women's concerns, Black feminism or womanism developed.[29] "Womanist" (or "womanism") is a term coined by Alice Walker to mean a person or movement that critically analyzes the intersection of sexism and anti-Black racism.[30]

Walker also used the term "womanist" to refer to women who love other women, whether platonically or sexually.[31] As there are various derivatives of feminism (like evangelical feminism[32]), so it is with womanism. For example, womanist theology focuses on the Black woman's experience in theology, highlights how Black women have been left out of both feminist theology and Black liberation theology, celebrates Black women's experiences with God, and aims to combat oppression of women in church practice.[33]

WARNING: FEMINISM IS NOT JUST EQUAL RIGHTS FOR WOMEN

On the face, it may seem difficult to find fault with a philosophy whose goal is to remove Black women from oppression and the shadows of theology. Not all feminists or womanists reject God, biblical womanhood, or the authority of Scripture, and it would be unfair to treat them as a monolith. However, feminist ideologies (the umbrella term I'm using for this discussion) have evolved beyond simply promoting equality for women. Feminism has had a hand in shaping gender and sexual ethics, abortion views, disdain for gender roles and leadership structures in the family and church, and even a call to question the biblical image of God as male.[34]

Bessey exclaims, "Jesus made me a feminist."[35] However, the various agendas of feminism could render that statement extremely misleading for Christian women. As Mary Kassian points out in her book *The Feminist Mistake*, feminism "proposes that women find happiness and meaning through the pursuit of personal authority, autonomy and freedom."[36] However, those pursuits are in opposition to the Lordship of Christ. Kassian explains that the historical development of feminism can be traced back to three consecutive decades and stages:[37]

- Stage One: Naming Self (1960–1970)
- Stage Two: Naming the World (1970–1980)
- Stage Three: Naming God (1980–1990)

She further explains:

Feminism began with the deconstruction of a Judeo-Christian view of womanhood (the right to name self); progressed to the deconstruction of manhood, gender relationships, family/societal structures, and a Judeo-Christian worldview (the right to name the world); and concluded with the concept of metaphysical pluralism, self-deification, and the rejection of the Judeo-Christian deity (the right to name God).[38]

Many women are proud to call themselves feminists because of the movement's righteous activism and resistance against the discrimination and oppression of women in society. Many goals and perspectives of feminism are not only compatible with true Christianity, but they are also a justice mandate of Christianity (Isa. 1:17; Psa. 82:2–4). Even so, it is clear from careful study of feminist ideologies that they promote much more than equal rights for women or activism against the oppression of women. It is important to know that how groups define the oppression of women is not the same.[39] When there is an attack on the legitimacy of God, the authority of the Word of God, or a rejection of manhood and womanhood as defined by God, the church must engage with caution. The desire to name oneself and name the world dismisses God's role as Creator of the world and of people. You can't name (define) a world or even yourself if you had no hand in making either. God gave identity and purpose to everything he made. A clearer picture of what some feminist ideologies encourage women to do is to rename themselves and rename the world, rejecting the name (definition) God originally gave it. Further, seeking to name God is blasphemous, because God has already named himself (Ex. 3:14).

A BIBLICAL RESPONSE TO FEMINISM

Paul warns us that our fight is not against flesh and blood (Eph. 6:12). This is not a battle between feminists and nonfeminists or feminists and the church. Satan is much too crafty for us to draw the battle lines there. We need to call out the real enemy, who desires to sift our hearts from belonging completely to the Lord. The devil is the father of all lies (John 8:44). He is not concerned with women's rights. He'll use women's movements and failures of the church to cast doubt on God's goodness and diminish his right to be Lord in our lives.

Feminist ideologies have been dropped into women's hearts like a sweet-smelling and slowly dissolving bath bomb, infusing women with the belief that the Bible's teachings of womanhood should bow to their own definitions of womanhood and equality. Yet, spiritually speaking, these ideologies do not oppose men; they oppose God. Adopting feminist ideologies may not initially change one's faith in God, but if a woman stays on this "lifeless lifeboat," it will undoubtedly carry her far away from the faith and eventually sink her. But it will not defeat God (Deut. 11:25).

God Created Woman with Inherent Dignity and Equality

Feminist arguments against a biblical picture of womanhood stem from the influence of early church leaders who had sexist attitudes toward women.

Nancy Tuana points out, "Gratian, a twelfth-century Benedictine monk, often considered the father of canon law, was the primary proponent of the position that women lacked a soul and were not created in God's image."[40] These views relegated women to "second class" citizens in churches. However, if we see God's heart toward women in Scripture, we'll see that nothing is further from the truth.

Created in the Image of God (Gen. 1:26–27)

The divine tribunal decided to create humanity (male and female) in the image of God. The law of first mention is key to understanding God's design and plan for women throughout Scripture. The law of first mention is a hermeneutical tool suggesting that when God says something for the first time, he sets a standard for how we are to understand that word, principle, or topic when it later appears in Scripture. The first mention of "femaleness" affirms her as an image bearer of God. This is woman and man's most significant identity marker at creation.

To be created in the image and likeness of God does not mean we *are* God, as goddess mysticism and some in the conscious community have claimed.[41] Rather, we are God's representatives, together showing the world who the triune God is through our gender similarities and differences. As image bearers, we can show off God's commutable characteristics, like the fruit of the Spirit (Gal. 5:22–23), being forgiving, just, gracious, righteous, etc. As an image bearer, it is vital that our primary and most core sense of self be rooted in God. To know yourself, you must know God. If you don't know God, you can never fully know yourself.

What, then, has become of women's ability to reflect the image of God, even after sin? R. Kent Hughes says, "The image of God still persists, in sinful men and women, though marred and sometimes even caricatured—and a witness against itself. Nevertheless, the image of God that we all bear is wonderous and holds eternal potential."[42] Women must reject feminist ideologies that encourage them to rename themselves as a form of self-esteem, instead walking in an identity that reflects the nature and character of God. Self-naming is not an "upgrade" to God's design for womanhood. Hannah Anderson says,

> Even as we begin to find our sense of identity in him, we can quickly be tempted to want to actually *be* God. We can develop a sense of self that convinces us that we are stronger, more capable, wiser, and more powerful than we actually are. We can believe that categories are meant to be broken, that nothing can contain us, that we are limitless. In other words, we can begin to confuse our created identity with God's identity as our Creator.[43]

Created from Man's Rib: A Picture of Gender Equality (Gen. 2:21–22)

In Genesis 1:26–28, God creates man and woman in his image. God blesses them and calls them to be fruitful, to multiply, and to fill and subdue the earth. This is a clear picture of equality as they are made corulers over his creation. However, God forming woman from the man's rib is theologically significant in the discussion of equality as well. God removes one of Adam's ribs and uses it to literally build a woman. R. Kent Hughes notes that "woman's creation out of Adam is the basis for her equality."[44] Matthew Henry remarks that woman was "not made out of his head to top him, not out of his feet to be trampled upon by him, but out of his side to be equal with him, under his arm to be protected, and near his heart to be beloved."[45] At creation, the woman is built with the same material as man, the same bone and the same flesh. This prompts Adam to rightly identify their equality—"bone of my bone and flesh of my flesh"—but also to rejoice at their undeniable differences by calling her "Woman."

God Created Woman with Unique Callings
Called to Be a Helper (Gen. 2:18)

Perhaps one of the most distained callings given to a woman by God among feminists is "helper." Even women in the church often bristle when they read that woman was specifically created to be a helpmate to man. However, if we truly understood how powerful this calling is, we'd quickly repent for turning up our noses and learn to walk in the power of this identity.

The Hebrew word *ezer* appears twenty-one times in the Old Testament. Twice it's used to refer to the woman Eve (Gen. 2:18, 20), three times it refers to Israel's appeal for military help (Isa. 30:5, Ezek. 12:14; Dan. 11:34), and in sixteen instances, it refers to God as the helper of his people.[46] The second Hebrew word, *knegdo*, means the woman was a "corresponding" or "suitable" helper. Woman's role as an *ezer* does not imply inferiority or subordination; it refers to her ability to aid the man with military-like strength, act as a rescuer, and help in the way God helps his people. Women should draw strength from the matriarchs in the faith and use them as examples of how to live out this powerful calling. Here are some examples of *ezer* women from the OT and NT:

- Midwives Shiphrah and Puah refuse to kill the baby boys born to Hebrew women (Ex. 1:8–21).
- Jochebed saves her son Moses by putting him in a basket on the river-bank (Ex. 2:3–4).
- Zipporah performed a circumcision (male duty) to save her husband Moses from God's wrath (Ex 4:24–26).

- Rahab, a prostitute, strategically helps Israelite spies by hiding them in her home. She also negotiates the salvation of her family (Josh. 2:1–21; 6:17, 25).
- Abigail intervenes to save her household from being killed as a result of her husband's foolishness and to save David from vengeful bloodshed (1 Sam. 25:3–35).
- The daughters of Zelophehad appeal to Moses to receive their father's inheritance. Their appeal becomes the basis for the law to be changed benefiting other women (Numbers 26:33; 27:1–11).
- Ruth gains attention from Boaz because of her noble character and helps her desperate mother-in-law find peace (Ruth).
- Deborah is a prophet, wife, judge, and military strategist who organizes the battle plan against Jabin and takes the honored place beside the military leader Barak in battle (Judg. 4:1–14).
- Huldah was a prophet whom the high priest Hilkiah and King Josiah requested to interpret the book of the law. Her interpretation led to religious reform in Judah (2 Kings 22:1–20).
- Joanna, Susanna, Mary Magdalene, Martha, and many other women used their financial means to help support Jesus's ministry (Luke 8:2–3).
- Mary Magdalene was the first person Jesus called to proclaim the good news of his resurrection (John 20:16–18).
- Lydia was a businesswoman who provided a meeting place and money for the new Christian church in Philippi (Acts 16:11–15, 40).
- Priscilla and her husband Aquila were coworkers in ministry with Paul, planting churches. The church in Ephesus met in their house, and she and her husband taught and corrected Apollos's doctrine. They also risked their lives for Paul (Acts 18:24–26; Rom. 16:3–5).
- Phoebe was a deacon and benefactor for gospel ministry (Rom. 16:1–2).
- Euodia and Syntyche were coworkers in ministry with Paul (Phil. 4:2–3).
- Mary, Tryphena, Tryphosa, and Persis "worked very hard in the Lord" for the sake of the church (Rom. 16:6, 12).
- Junia ministered with Paul and was commended among the apostles for her faithfulness and character (Rom. 16:7).
- Lois and Eunice, Timothy's grandmother and mother, had great faith and taught Timothy the ways of the Christian faith (2 Tim. 1:5).

Called to Have Powerful Influence (Gen. 3:6)

Influence is an unseen power at work behind the scenes. It is defined as "the capacity to have an effect on the character, development, or behavior of someone or something, or the effect itself."[47] When used for good, influence can empower ministers, advance the gospel, and make the name of God great in the earth.

While our first striking example in Scripture of a woman's influence appears negatively, it nonetheless shows just how powerful her influence is. God gave Adam clear instructions about what tree not to eat from, but the Bible tells us, after the woman ate the fruit, she gave it to her husband "and he ate it" (Gen. 3:6 CSB). That is astounding! No questions asked, no "Honey, I don't think this is a good idea," and no spiritual leadership from Adam. Some women have used this portion of Scripture as evidence that in a "patriarchal Bible," women are painted as tricky seducers who are guilty for the failures of men. In her book *Clothed with the Sun*, Joyce Hollyday writes, "And of course, she is the weak one, the tempted one, the one whose deficiency gave sin a toehold in the world. The implication is that all would have been perfect had woman not come along and spoiled it."[48] This instance certainly was negative; it was a downright deadly use of influence. Nevertheless, it reveals that God has given women a certain power.

Feminists would have us believe that the Bible is highlighting a woman's inherent weakness. To the contrary, Genesis 3 highlights an *abuse* of power rather than a *lack* of it. In all superhero movies, when the superheroes first discover their powers, they are often depicted inadvertently burning up neighborhoods, breaking glass windows, running into walls, and generally wreaking havoc. Then someone like a mentor comes alongside them, with either a similar power or knowledge of their powers, to train them to respect, control, and to direct their powers for good.

Perhaps the church has misunderstood this powerful influence as well, leaving even church men to come to horrible conclusions about women. Both men and women can misuse and abuse power, which is why we are admonished, "Do not get drunk on wine. . . . Instead, be filled with the Spirit" (Eph. 5:18). Wine is both literal and metaphoric—what is more intoxicating than power? However, when the power to influence is under the control of our mentor, the Holy Spirit, it is an amazing, God-glorifying gift that should be celebrated and respected by men and women alike. If women understood their power and allowed the Holy Spirit to fill their lives, that power could be submitted to God and used for good and not evil, to build instead of destroy, and to give life instead of death. This is the true picture of meekness—power under control.

As women, we need not feel powerless, but we must leverage the power of influence wisely. God responded to Eve's misuse of power with discipline, but even that was done with grace and redemption in mind. Eve was the woman who influenced her husband to sin, and she was also the woman whose womb God would use to bring life into the world. Her misuse of influence was not the end of her story. Paul tells us, "No discipline seems pleasant at the time, but painful. Later on, however, it produces a harvest of righteousness and peace for those who have been trained by it" (Heb. 12:11). What a harvest of righteousness was produced through Eve, this "life giver"! Women are a major component of God's redemption plan. What harvest of righteousness will women let God produce through those who use their powerful influence for his glory?

Called to Willingly Receive Male Leadership (Gen. 2:23; 3:2)

From the beginning, our foremother displayed receptivity, contentment, and satisfaction with God's choices for her life. Eve willingly received a name from Adam (Gen. 2:23), which is a major stumbling block for feminists, who put a high value on self-naming. There is no record of Eve arguing with Adam about the name "Woman" or "Eve." She did not question him, suggest another name, or express displeasure with his decision.

Instead of this representing another instance of patriarchy—men dictating a woman's identity and destiny with blind submission—the woman's receptivity may be evidence of two things: she trusts God, and she willingly receives from a man who sees, knows, and appreciates her. Adam naming woman was not an arbitrary or frivolous decision; it is Adam's way of bearing witness to what God had done in creating woman. Hughes says, "God had honed Adam's naming powers; the man spontaneously declared, 'She shall be called Woman (*ishshah*) because she was taken out of Man (*ish*).'"[49] This was no casual or insignificant naming ceremony. "The sound play celebrates their relationship. Because man and woman had perfect unity prior to the fall, him naming her was not a sign of dictatorship but intimacy—he saw the woman for who she was, an equal yet a softer (*ishshah*) version of himself."[50]

Women willingly receiving male leadership does not mean a woman must follow or submit to any man at any time. It does not mean that women don't have a voice or can't critique and question men. Nor does it mean that men should never be willing to receive leadership from a woman. However, it does point to the woman's God-given calling to exercise a meekness and humbleness in receiving leadership from men—to put willingly her power under control.[51]

Male Leadership in the Home

Genesis does not let us in on the conversation Adam had with Eve when he relayed God's command not to eat from the tree of the knowledge of good and evil, but it is implied that God gave him the responsibility to communicate these instructions to her. This responsibility does not suggest that God ordained male dominion of women. However, this prefall reality does demonstrate that man was given a spiritual responsibility without subjugation. In fact, anytime women in the church or home are called to follow a man, they are ultimately following him as they are following Christ (1 Cor. 11:1). God hasn't called women to follow men off a cliff or into sin, but to follow in submission and obedience to God.

Feminists and others with egalitarian views of Scripture have tried to persuade women to reject God's intention for male leadership despite the creation order and other clear biblical references to male headship (1 Cor. 11:2–16; Eph. 5:21–33; 1 Tim. 2:11–15; 3:1–7; Titus 1:6; 1 Peter 3:1–7). Feminist theology would argue that a traditional reading of these texts perpetuates patriarchy and the continued oppression of women. However, we must be cautious if the call to liberate women involves the rejection of Scripture; that's not liberation at all, it's bondage. Men leading the way in the creation order of mankind is just one picture of the leadership role God intended men to have. It does not mean that women can't lead anything (the Bible testifies to this fact in the Old and New Testaments), and it doesn't mean any man can lead any woman (Eph. 5:21; 1 Peter 3:1–4). However, it does show God's intention for a man to lead his own bride (wife) and to lead Christ's bride (the church).

The New Testament not only affirms male leadership in the home but also shows the serious call of being a husband. Men are called to lead their wives, and that leadership should reflect the way that Christ leads and loves his church. Not only does this Christlike leadership for husbands come with authority; it also comes with a call to sacrifice and die (Eph. 5:25). Husbands are called to love their wives as they love themselves (Eph. 5:28). This directive implies men already love themselves; however, in their role as a husband, they should honor, provide for, and care for their wives with the same enthusiastic love that they would ordinarily reserve for themselves. Husbands are called to lead, but they are instructed in Scripture on how that leadership must function. Husbands should not be harsh with their wives (Col. 3:19). Husbands should be understanding toward their wives; they should honor and appreciate them as co-heirs with them in grace, so that their prayers will not be hindered (1 Peter 3:7).

Male Leadership in the Church

In evaluating the state of Black women in the church, Pastor Eddie Lane says,

As one who is committed to the principle of equality of men and women in the home and church in terms of spiritual gifts in the body of Christ, I am troubled by the aggressive pursuit of the kind of equality that has little regard for the distinctive role and function of men and women . . . In my view, access and equality must not be understood to mean that there are no distinctions to be made from a biblical perspective . . . It is important to note here that respect for male leadership in the home and in the church is not an argument against the leadership of women in other areas beyond these two contexts.[52]

To Lane's point, men and women in the church unfortunately have restricted the argument around access to church leadership to pastoral roles. While many people take issue with the interpretation of Scripture that prohibits female pastors, I find Paul's instructions to be clear and consistent with God's message of male headship in the home and in the church throughout Scripture. "Whoever aspires to be an overseer desires a noble task. Now the overseer is to be above reproach, faithful to his wife. . . . He must manage his own family well. . . . If anyone does not know how to manage his own family, how can he take care of God's church?" (1 Tim. 3:1–5).

A mindset that I believe is highly influenced by feminist thought (especially since there is a premium put on the self-defined agency of women) is the notion that women should be able to do anything a man does with the same fruitfulness because of her talent or giftedness. But God allowing good to come from a nonideal situation is not a stamp of approval from God—neither is a woman's ability to outperform a man in a particular ministry capacity. We see throughout Scripture that God frequently used people for kingdom work who were not highly gifted, but they were called by God. I call this issue "The Competency over Calling Debate." A woman may be able to get the job done just as well as a man (or in some cases, better than a man), but ability without authority is a moot point in God's kingdom.

I love and highly respect many pastors who disagree with my view as too conservative, and I know many pastors who view the freedoms I see in Scripture for women to minister, teach, and serve as leaders in the church as too liberal. We are reading the same text and seeing different things, and we may never all agree. There are things in Scripture that I'm still working through, studying, and asking the Lord to clarify—most Christians are wrestling with the Bible on a multitude of topics. This is not a hill worth dying on because the debate regarding female pastors is not a core issue of the faith. There are weightier theological issues more central than this. Ultimately, men and women should humbly ask themselves, "Are my views mostly shaped by feminist ideologies, culture, sexism, church tradition, my own will, or a deep desire to interpret Scripture with integrity and the help of the Holy Spirit (despite the fogginess of our own human understanding)?"

God loves women and has called women to do amazing things in the kingdom for his glory. Limiting the discussion of women's service or leadership in the church to the role of pastor is unfortunate and damaging. In my opinion, the church has so exalted the role of pastor and preacher that we've treated the other gifts and callings in the body as inferior. No one gets excited if someone says, "I've been running from the Lord, but I sense in my spirit a call from God to clean the church bathrooms." The role of pastor has been the coveted position, despite the warnings of strict judgment that pastors will face (James 3:1; Heb. 13:17). Unfortunately, the pastor often holds a position of unbridled and unshared power.

Idolizing the calling that the Bible reserves for men has inevitably boxed women in, sat them down, and shut them out. Women who have undoubtedly strong prophetic, leadership, teaching, and preaching gifts are left to either question the legitimacy of their gifts, not use the fullness of their gifts, or go against Scripture and misuse their gifts in an egalitarian context that grants them permission. Women need pastors to see, affirm, and communicate that there are many important avenues in ministry for a woman to effectively edify the body with her gifts and callings. What God has put in women should not be squandered; it should be properly nurtured and directed through clear teaching, discipleship, and pastoral care. I encouraged the church in an article I submitted for Dr. Eric Mason's book, *Woke Church*,

> It is incumbent on leadership to reevaluate areas where women have been relegated to serve that are not based on biblical prohibitions but rather on cultural practices that may be extensions of sexism and misogyny. Black women should be affirmed to serve in greater capacities than the traditional roles of children's ministry, choir and hospitality. The goal is to release women for expanded Titus 2 and Great Commission mandates. Women can serve communion, teach men and women in appropriate settings, lead ministries and small groups, be theologians, seminary professors, apologists, deacons, evangelists, and missionaries, read Scripture, pray in public, be involved in social justice, develop curriculum, provide counseling, be trained for leadership, work on church staff, and speak on various platforms where they should be compensated like male speakers.[53]

Jesus Affirms the Dignity and Purpose of Women

It is imperative that every Black woman knows that everything she needs is fulfilled in Jesus. Where man fails, Jesus is victorious. Where man tears down, Jesus lifts. The Scripture is replete with examples of Jesus's love, protection, and affirmation of women, which was revolutionary during that time:

- Jesus regularly addresses women in public, which was not the norm for a man to do in antiquity (John 4:27; 8:10; Luke 7:11–13; 8:48; 13:12).
  - At a well, Jesus has a conversation with a Samaritan woman who is an outcast. After her conversation with Jesus, she becomes an evangelist to her people (John 4:4–42).
  - Jesus saves a woman caught in adultery from being stoned by forcing her male accusers to acknowledge that they are not morally superior to her (John 8:1–11).
  - Jesus commends Mary for choosing to sit at his feet (the position male disciples took) and listen to his teaching rather than remaining busy with the serving tasks as her sister Martha does (Luke 10:38–42).
- Jesus protects women from unwarranted divorce, which would likely leave them poor and vulnerable. Jesus answers questions about divorce by pointing the Pharisees back to creation as the standard for how to view marriage and challenged the culture's notions that women were the property of men who could easily be dismissed (Matt. 19:1–9).
- While the culture values women based on their ability to birth children, Jesus defines those who are "blessed" as "those who hear the word of God and obey it" (Luke 11:27–28).
- Jesus identifies men and women who obey his Father as his real family, reframing the priority of earthly parents, children, and siblings (Mark 3:32–35).
- The community of a woman with chronic bleeding rejects her as unclean, but Jesus is not repulsed in the least; he heals her and praises her faith (Luke 8:43–48).
- Jesus commends a poor widow for her sacrificial gift of two small copper coins. In Jesus's eyes, her gift is greater than what the rich were giving (Luke 21:1–4).
- Jesus rebukes pious men who call Mary's worship wasteful when she pours expensive oil from her alabaster flask over his head and feet. Jesus defends her, calling her worship "beautiful" and saying that "wherever the gospel is preached throughout the world, what she has done will also be told, in memory of her" (Mark 14:3–9).

- Jesus tells parables highlighting women (Luke 15:8–10; 18:1–8). Using women in parables demonstrates that Jesus does not treat women as invisible. Jesus highlights women in his teachings and affirms their lives.
- Jesus heals a woman with a disabling spirit, and she praises God. When the male ruler objects to him healing on the Sabbath, Jesus calls him a hypocrite and reminds him that this woman is a "daughter of Abraham" (Luke 13:10–16).
- Jesus is tender and compassionate to Martha and Mary when Lazarus dies. He offers words of comfort, cries with them, and then raises their brother from the dead (John 11:1–44).
- Jesus stops to address female mourners before his crucifixion, displaying selfless compassion despite his own suffering (Luke 23:27–31).
- Jesus commissions Mary as the first witness to proclaim news of his resurrection to the disciples, even though the testimony of a woman was not considered sufficient proof in court at this time (John 20:17).
- Jesus rebukes his disciples when they argue about who would be the greatest in the kingdom and calls them to a posture of childlike humility (Matt. 18:1–4; Mark 9:33–37).
- In the upper room prior to his death, Jesus models servant-leadership, a model that undoubtedly impacts how women should be treated by men (John 13:1–17).
- Jesus acknowledges the spiritual agency of women. He does not minimize or condone their sins, but lovingly confronts and covers women. He recognizes a woman's personal choice and individual freedom (Luke 7:44–50; John 4:16–18; 8:10–11).

Despite the clear evidence that women are given dignity, affirmed, and loved by Jesus in Scripture, women have not always encountered this picture of God's love for women in their relationships with men. Many women can relate to the character Sophia and her famous speech in the movie *The Color Purple*, "A girl ain't safe in a family of men. But I never thought I'd have to fight in my own house. I loves Harpo. God knows I do. But I'll kill him dead before I let him beat me." All women have a Harpo in their lives, whether it's a literal person or a system of oppression.

The good news is that women don't have to save themselves or depend on a lifeless lifeboat, because Christ has already died to save them. I see Jesus as the multidimensional model of male perfection. No matter how men have failed you, no matter who your Harpo is, Jesus redeems that painful situation and ransoms your heart. It is imperative for the church to course correct and be an example before the world of how to live out Jesus's love for women in tangible ways.

THE CHURCH MUST FIGHT FOR THE DISILLUSIONED AND DISORIENTED DAUGHTER

The disillusioned and disoriented daughter is the baby that is conceived when false teaching and church failure collide. Black women need the church—men and women, laypeople, and leaders—to step up to the pulpit and step out into the community to tackle issues that impact the lives of Black women. The church, not the feminist movement, should lead the way in solving problems such as sexual abuse, rape and exploitation, domestic violence, inadequate access to healthcare, prenatal care, unequal pay, occupational segregation, the criminalization of Black girls from K-12, cycles of single parenting, poverty, unsafe neighborhoods, the mistreatment of women who struggle with same sex attraction, and much more. It is reprehensible for the church to go to war in support of pro-life values but play the pacifist when it comes to issues that affect Black lives outside the womb.

Even if the church has theological disagreements with some of the ideologies, beliefs, and practices of the conscious community and the feminist movement, we must listen to them, engage with them, and be open to learning from them. As the church, our faith and convictions cannot be so fragile that we would refrain from sitting with, talking to, and sacrificially serving people different from us. We have to go outside the safe bubble of the local church and touch people, love people, and fight for their needs, because that's what Jesus did. We don't make Jesus attractive if what people see the church doing is having conferences about biblical womanhood, writing books on social justice, podcasting, and posting Scripture on social media but never crying out against Black women's pain and suffering and never helping to meet their needs. The church must "learn to devote themselves to good works, so as to help cases of urgent need, and not be unfruitful" (Titus 3:14 ESV). Jesus met pressing needs, he listened to people's pain, and he intervened, whether they were his followers or not. That's what made Jesus attractive; that's why many women followed him. The Bible does more than affirm women's identity; it also calls us to imitate Jesus, who came to preach the gospel to the poor, heal the brokenhearted, bring sight to the blind, and set the oppressed free (Luke 4:18).

The church must also confess and repent of the various ways it has injured women, including sexual predation by leaders and laymen, mishandled domestic violence reports where women are forced to share blame with their abuser, and the absence of accountability and church discipline for men. Apologists who respond to feminism must also be prepared to answer for the church, whose behavior has often left women vulnerable to feminist rhetoric. Christian men must proactively and unwaveringly protect the dignity of Black women with the same conviction as they protect who can stand in the pulpit. Christian men should not be known more for telling women what they can't do than for mobilizing women to do all that they can do. I am not suggesting that the church revise Scripture, but it may need to revise its manmade bylaws to include women in influential positions of leadership so that the body can be blessed by women's wisdom, perspective, and expertise. There are many churches and leaders who have already answered this call, and we all should praise God for them. However, there is a history of hypocrisy that opens the door for feminist thinking to lick the wounds the church created.

Based on anecdotal data I've collected from my own experience and the women I've counseled and ministered to in private practice and in the church, women aren't fighting for a feminized church. Black women being seen and loved, having a voice and a place at the table of leadership, does not feminize the church any more than God creating woman feminized the world. The presence of women brings balance. Having balance in the world, church, and home means that the God-given uniqueness of women stands side-by-side with the uniqueness of men and is given equal value.

It is not good for man to be alone, so God made the woman (Gen. 2:18). Every wonderful and godly characteristic of women should be embraced as necessary for the flourishing of all people and seen as a requirement for properly reflecting the nature and heart of God. When women are submitted to Christ, they enhance every person and every environment they grace. Women not only help, women enhance. A woman submitted to Christ will bear fruit (evidence) in her life of God's sanctifying work. A woman submitted to Christ is prudent (Prov. 19:14), industrious (Prov. 31:13–18), wise and understanding (Prov. 24:3–4; 31:26), compassionate (Prov. 31:20), courageous (Est. 4:16), strong and dignified (Psa. 46:5; Prov. 31:17, 25), modest (1 Tim. 2:9–10), kind (Prov. 31:26), committed in prayer (Luke 2:36–38), trustworthy (Prov. 31:11–12), valuable (Prov. 18:22), fruitful (Prov. 31:31), discerning (Ex. 2:7; 1 Sam. 25:33), praiseworthy (Prov. 31:28–30), beautiful (Prov. 31:30), humble (Luke 1:38), generous (Prov. 31:20; Rom. 16:1–2), hospitable (2 Kings 4:8–10), a disciple maker (Matt. 28:19; 1 Cor. 11:1; 1 Thess. 2:8; Titus 2:3–5), blessed (Luke 1:45), faithful (1 Tim. 3:11), and a committed colaborer for the gospel (Phil. 4:3). The presence and contributions of godly women are unmistakable.

What Black women bring to the table for the glory of Christ makes demons shudder; and that is why there is such a formidable attack on our lives.

In an effort to fight for the disillusioned and disoriented daughter, it is imperative for men and women to remember that a woman is a full human being as an individual. Her identity, worth, and purpose are not contingent on being in a relationship with a man; Christ defines her. Women are justified, sanctified, and affirmed by Christ alone. It is also imperative that men and women realize that to be dependent on Christ, secure in Christ, and satisfied in Christ does not mean that Black women can't desire and be pursued for healthy relationships with men. A woman's focus on Christ and contentment with her life are not signs that she is disinterested in men or wants to live life without men. In fact, I have found that many intelligent, accomplished, gifted, and faithful Black women appreciate and desire strong, godly, Spirit-filled male leaders. Many women support men leading their families, communities, and churches. Many women don't want to be the primary spiritual leader of the home; women don't want to be the only disciplinarian because of an absentee father; women don't want the pressure of being the sole financial provider. Women love and appreciate men who have vision, focus, and spiritual discipline. Women appreciate men who are tough but tender, have strong convictions, and are compassionate. While women's main source of affirmation comes from Jesus, women are encouraged as wives or sisters in Christ when men affirm and support their callings, whether they are stay-at-home moms, Bible teachers, professors, doctors, or CEOs of companies. Women desire men who can commit in relationships and value marriage; women want men who worship and work; and women want men who pray more than they play video games. If a man has to demand submission and demand respect, or if at any time a man has to pound his chest and remind a woman that he is the man, then he likely has not done what God has commanded him to do (Eph. 5:25, 1 Peter 3:7). Godly women, empowered by the Spirit and submitted to Christ, have less challenges submitting to male leadership when the man gives her something honorable to submit to. If we want to combat the feminist influence in the church, I propose women become serious students of God's Word, root their identity in Christ, and confidently see the beauty of their God-given femininity. I propose that Christian men become leaders worth following. We must come together as churches to fight for the disillusioned and disoriented daughters.

It's time for warfare! The church must call out the false teachings and attacks on the faith that have emerged from the Black conscious community and feminist ideologies. The "lifeboats" women are climbing into are offering "healing" to women by rejecting or attempting to revise God, his Word, and his plan for women. These groups, like wolves in sheep's clothing, are capitalizing on the church's disinterested posture and sluggishness to stand against racism and sexism, and they are overpromising and under-delivering the identity, freedom, and power that is only found in Jesus. Both the Black conscious community and the feminist movement are trying to end what they believe are the most dangerous forms of oppression and domination. The Black conscious community says, "Don't be dominated by the white man"; the feminist movement says, "Don't be dominated by men"; but the real problem is refusal to be dominated by God! We will always be ruled by what we exalt. To exalt God does not make light of our struggle; it just sees God as Lord over our struggle. However, God can't be Lord over our struggle if we don't first make him Lord over ourselves!

In order to keep Black women from drowning in a sea of confusion, the church must affirm Black women as beloved, called, and valued image bearers of God. The church must teach the truth of God's Word fearlessly and uncompromisingly to bring clarity to God's design for womanhood and to celebrate the powerful role women have as joint heirs in Christ. The church must courageously and prophetically call out forms of toxic masculinity and sexism hiding out as complementarianism, as well as challenge systems of white supremacy that demean and devalue Black women's intellect, body, and spirit. The church must pray to demolish strongholds, listen to Black women, lament with Black women, love Black women, and unleash Black women for kingdom ministry in the home, church, and world.

It is time for warfare! Ephesians 6:11 tells us to "put on the whole armor of God, that you may be able to stand against the schemes of the devil" (ESV). First Timothy 6:12 implores us to "Fight the good fight of the faith." First Corinthians 15:57 says, "But thanks be to God! He gives us the victory through our Lord Jesus Christ." If we believe this is true, then the church will not wave the white flag of surrender in the fight for the Black woman. If we believe this is true, then the church must come against any lifeless lifeboat that dares to carry Black women away from the truth, waging war under the blood-stained banner of Christ—the true Ark of Safety!

CHAPTER 10

INTENTIONALLY ENGAGING BLACK MEN

Eric Mason

IN MOST black churches, men make up just 25 percent of the congregation. Black men are searching for value and identity, and they're not finding it in the church. We as a community need to be intentional in how we engage black men. If we don't, black religious identity groups will.

Buying a house can be an amazing accomplishment. It's a blessing to come into your own space, feel like it's yours, and know that you can make changes to it without getting permission first. But sometimes a homeowner can personalize the house so much that it loses its value. Many times, the only one who loves the home is the owner. And if the owner favors a décor style that is from another era, it will be hard to sell. Potential buyers won't be able to see themselves in it.

Many churches have become like these over-personalized houses. They've made their customs and traditions their main identity and refused to adapt to changing culture. Traditionalism prioritizes cultural patterns that people refuse to change at the expense of ministry. Black church culture is beautiful; however, like any expression of culture, it has to adapt contextually if it is going to connect with younger generations in this new mission field. My purpose in writing this chapter is to draw attention to black men who haven't been able to see themselves represented in the culture these churches have created. To put it bluntly, many churches aren't losing men; they've simply never *had* them.

When we first started our church, Epiphany Fellowship, the men made up about 50 percent of the congregation. About a dozen years later, we'd gained a few more men, but the number of sisters (black women) had grown exponentially. And not only did they grow numerically, but the women were more economically stout, educated, and further along in life than the men in the congregation. The women were engaging other women and men with the gospel and bringing new people to church. We were seeing growth among our women, but not among the men.

So my elders and I drafted a plan to pour into the men of our church in an effort to aid their growth. We felt this was a state of emergency, one that even the sisters could recognize. Many of the black women in our ministry desired to find a black spouse, but there weren't enough men in the church for them to marry. So our focus became engaging our men, developing them in both doctrine and life skills in a more intentional way.

Over the past thirty years, many churches have seen something similar to what we experienced—a growing gap between the number of black men who attend and the number of black women.

A CALL FOR MEN IN PUBLIC WORSHIP

Scripture calls men to be willingly present in public and private worship gatherings. Paul says in 1 Timothy 2:8, "Therefore, I want the men in every place to pray, lifting up holy hands without anger or argument" (CSB). The word translated "men" here (ἀνήρ, *anēr*) refers to adult males, not people in general.[1] Paul doesn't use the Greek word *anthropos* (ἄνθρωπος, "man" or "person"), and there is a reason for this. Paul seems to be expressing his desire for men to show public submission to Jesus Christ in the context of local gatherings of the church. Consider that in this verse, where Paul explicitly calls out the men, Paul is resuming and concluding a section about prayer he began in 1 Timothy 2:1–2. In 1 Timothy 2:3–7, Paul writes about God's concern for all people as the motive for prayer.[2] But now, in verse 8, Paul is making it clear he wants the men specifically to be visible in worship.

In passages like 1 Timothy 2 and 1 Corinthians 11, Paul isn't attempting to mute the place and voice of women in the gathering. Scripture shows that women have been significant supporters of the gospel movement. Luke 8:1–3 shows women financially supporting and serving Jesus's ministry. In the book of Acts we read of women like Mary the mother of Jesus (Acts 1:12–24), Tabitha (also known as Dorcas; Acts 9:36–43), Mary the mother of John Mark (Acts 12:6–19), Rhoda (Acts 12:6–19), Lydia (Acts 16:11–15, 40), Damaris (Acts 17:16–34), and Priscilla (Acts 18:1–28), all of whom played a strategic role in gospel mission, from miraculous answers to prayer to financial support, church planting, missions, and evangelism.

The New Testament is filled with examples of women serving publicly and behind the scenes. Yet here in 1 Timothy 2:8, Paul wants to highlight the importance of men in the church's gatherings. Paul challenges the men about their anger and their arguing, and he addresses the women who have been a distraction in the gatherings. He calls for the men to take the lead in prayer and worship to ensure that nothing negatively impacts the worship expression and experience.

This is a timely word for the church today. We need to see the absence of black men from the church as a 9-1-1 emergency. There is no quick fix for this; societal issues and internal factors, the incarceration rate of black men, the school-to-prison pipeline, pastor worship, the lack of community engagement, and the sins predominant among men are among the major issues we must tackle. Undoubtedly, the cults and false ideology groups discussed in this book seem to inordinately attract black men. While the numbers in these groups still fall short of the number of men in the black church, their branding makes it appear that they are growing—and men are the primary demographic behind that growth.

I want to be clear that the black church has done more for black America than any other group in history. The church's powerful investment in historically black colleges, banks, the arts, economic development, and the civil rights movement cannot be replaced or denied. But something is happening in the black church today. We're seeing a comprehensive attack on the black man: an attempt to discredit, disenfranchise, and destroy him. In 1 Timothy 4:1–2, Paul warns, "The Spirit explicitly says that in later times some will depart from the faith, paying attention to deceitful spirits and the teachings of demons, through the hypocrisy of liars whose consciences are seared" (CSB). Paul is speaking of spiritual warfare—and today, we're seeing this warfare manifest as a war on black men.

In their landmark work *Adam Where are You? Why Most Black Men Don't Go to Church*, Dr. Jawanza Kunjufu and Dr. Jeremiah Wright Jr. offer an astounding analysis of the male population crisis in the church:

> For the male population, if we combine the 70 adult men with the 29 male youth, the 99 men now represents 25 percent of the total population of 390. The combined female population of 291 represents 75 percent of the population of 390, which means that the average Black church is made up of 75 percent females and 75 percent adults and elders. I sincerely believe that for the Black Church to grow, develop and thrive, it has to increase its percentage of males and youth.[3]

CHURCH MEMBERS ON THE ROLL IN BLACK CHURCHES[6]

	Total	Urban	Rural
Average Total	390	479	171
Average Adult Men	70	90	30
Average Adult Women	199	240	88
Average Total Youth	101	120	54
Average Male Youth	29	35	16
Average Female Youth	77	91	38

According to the numbers in this chart,[4] the average black church is made up of seventy-five percent females and seventy-five percent adults and elders. For the black church to grow, develop, and thrive, it has to exponentially increase its percentage of men.[5] What needs to change for this to happen? I believe we must become more missiological in our thinking and practice. We need to view ourselves as cultural outsiders, working to pierce our way into a context that, though familiar, is far from the kingdom.

Sadly, many churches in the city are still in maintenance mode, keeping programs running and maintaining the status quo. In many ways, we have become ingrown and irrelevant to the surrounding culture. One solution is to move away from pastor-centered ministry to a more gospel-centered and Christ-centered ministry. Another solution is to become more missiologically driven, able to intentionally engage black men—especially those attracted to identity groups. In order to engage these men, we must meet them where they are and understand what they need.

WHAT DO BLACK MEN NEED?

Spiritual Fathers

Everyone is aware of the general cultural problem of fatherlessness in the black community, but there is also a massive need for the church to have a community of men who are *spiritual* fathers. These spiritual fathers should fit the character qualifications outlined in Titus 2: they must "be self-controlled, worthy of respect, sensible, and sound in faith, love, and endurance" (2:2 CSB). Paul calls Timothy and Titus "his true sons in the faith" because of his role in their spiritual development and their respective ministries (1 Tim 1:2; Titus 1:4).

Being a spiritual father is one of the most valuable roles a man can fill in the body of Christ. Paul says to the Corinthians, "Even if you had ten thousand guardians in Christ, you do not have many fathers, for in Christ Jesus I became your father through the gospel" (1 Cor. 4:15). The term the NIV translates as "guardian" here refers to a slave who would accompany a child on his way to school. Although respected by the child and responsible to teach him manners, this guardian was more than just a teacher; students might affectionately refer to or treat special teachers like their guardian as "fathers."[6] Galatians draws on this same idea with regard to the law (3:24–25). Both of these "tutors" were supposed to point the student (the disciple) to Jesus.

Spiritual fathers must avoid the mistake of trying to *be* Jesus for the person they disciple; they are playing a valuable role in helping other men grow spiritually. And while the role of spiritual father isn't an office in the church, it is a great way to create and maintain a relational lifestyle of discipleship. Because of the state of the world we live in and the very real "daddy deprivation" issues that exist, we need older men who are willing to invest in and help restore our younger men.

Malachi 4:6 gives us the principle behind older men instructing the younger generation: "And he will turn the hearts of fathers to their children and the hearts of children to their fathers" (CSB). John the Baptist used his ministry to reconnect his own generation with the Abrahamic covenant in order to ultimately point people to Jesus. In this work, the focus is on restoration. The Lord goes on to say in this passage, "Otherwise, I will come and strike the land with a curse" (CSB). This serves as a warning to us. When generations of men are disconnected from their fathers (both physical and spiritual), spiritual chaos will ensue.

My spiritual sons are those who have a deep, vested interest and commitment to the ministry and vision of the church and the kingdom. They must have a unity of mind, commitment, and kingdom passion, and they must be teachable. A call to full-time ministry is not necessary, but there should be a deep-seated kingdom alignment.

Biblical Literacy and Intellectual Engagement

In an era of information, memes, and urban legends, biblical literacy is a must. We cannot assume that people understand the faith. Many men who are caught up in black identity movements and cults will tell you that they were Christians. But when you dig further into what they mean, they tell you they grew up in the church and considered themselves Christian because they went with their family. Rarely can they identify a time when they trusted Jesus, when they were discipled, when they were taught Christian doctrine, or when they served in the church. Many of these men didn't leave Christianity—they just left the spiritual nest of their Christian home.

I have a family member who joined the Nation of Islam. He told me that his main reason for joining was that it seemed to reflect his sense of care for the world, and it seemed to provide practical answers to real issues—or at least the rhetoric he heard sounded that way. This common experience points to a problem with our current preaching of the gospel. It is impossible for us to preach the word of God by the power of the Spirit and not show that the gospel is sufficient to answer the questions of life, the soul, and the world. In our preaching, we must provide insight into *how* to change, and the church must develop clear mechanisms for discipleship. We must build men like Ezra, who "determined in his heart to study the law of the LORD, obey it, and teach its statutes and ordinances in Israel" (Ezra 7:10 CSB).

The ministry I lead approaches discipleship as multifaceted: through the pulpit, in small groups, at Wednesday night Bible study, in our men's ministry, through outreach, in living out daily life together, and much more. In each of these areas, we strive to teach the body the fundamentals of following Christ. The author of Hebrews reinforces the importance of teaching those basics: "Therefore, let us leave the elementary teaching about Christ and go on to maturity, not laying again a foundation of repentance from dead works, faith in God, teaching about ritual washings, laying on of hands, the resurrection of the dead, and eternal judgment" (Heb. 6:1–2 CSB). Paul and the apostles repeatedly taught some of these same basic doctrines and practices in order to stabilize the churches they planted. They did not assume those who had responded to the gospel knew these basics or understood how to put them into practice. They intentionally discipled.

One of the basic beliefs and practices the early church leaders taught was sexual purity: "For it seemed good to the Holy Spirit and to us to lay upon you no greater burden than these essentials: that you abstain from things sacrificed to idols and from blood and from things strangled and from fornication; if you keep yourselves free from such things, you will do well" (Acts 15:28–29 NASB). Sexual faithfulness to God is one of the basic beliefs that must also be taught today.[7] It involves practicing restraint outside of marriage and enjoying freedom with one's spouse.

Black men need more than most of our pulpits and Bible studies currently offer them. Black men need to know Christology, ecclesiology, sanctification, historical theology (global, not just Western), apologetics, spiritual formation, bibliology, and theology proper. Men don't like to be caught off guard in the street, and they'll jump on board with whatever will best equip them.

Unfortunately, the church at large has dropped the ball on this. We've not made in-depth scriptural education a priority. This era of bibleless pulpits—where the Word is mentioned but not expounded upon—is going to catch up with us in this generation. To avoid this, we have to preach the gospel *and* explain its implications.

Community and Brotherhood

Black men aren't Westerners; rather, they are Africans whose past culture has been largely forgotten. One part of African culture that many Africans hold dear is captured by the South African philosophical concept known as *Ubuntu*. Michael Battle explains *Ubuntu* as follows:

> Westerners may find Ubuntu—an African concept of personhood—a strange word with perhaps an even stranger meaning. Emphasizing the communal and spiritual dimension of human identity, the concept of Ubuntu (pronounced oo-BOON-too) of necessity poses a challenge to persons accustomed to thinking of themselves as individuals.
>
> Ubuntu is an African concept of personhood in which the identity of the self is understood to be formed interdependently through community. This is a difficult world-view for many Westerners who tend to understand self as over and against others—or as in competition with others. In a Western worldview, interdependence may be easily confused with codependence, a pathological condition in which people share a dependence on some-thing that is not life-giving, such as alcohol or drugs. Ubuntu, however, is about symbiotic and cooperative relationships—neither the parasitic and destructive relationships of codependence nor the draining and alienating relationships of competition.[8]

Whether we understand it or not, black people in the western hemisphere still innately operate this way. When we find ourselves saturated by the major-ity culture, we tend to herd to each other. When we are the only black people in a white space, we tend to feel the invisible eyes of all black people saying, "Make us look good!" We naturally feel the need for others to get a glimpse into our world through their experience with us.

Today, we're increasingly seeing men turning to isolation and secrecy, even the extroverts. Not only does this seem to defy our innate needs as men of African descent, but it's also cautioned against in Scripture. Proverbs 18:1 says, "Whoever isolates himself seeks his own desire; he breaks out against all sound judgment" (ESV). The NET Bible study notes indicate that "the 'one who has separated himself' (cf. KJV, ASV, NASB) is not merely anti-social; he is a problem for society because he will defy sound judgment. The Mishnah uses this verse to teach the necessity of being part of a community—to teach that people have social responsibilities and need each other."[9]

One of the first lessons I learned from a mentor was that the foundation for trust and comradery is relationship. Relationship can take you anywhere. Pastoring in Philly, I've learned that Philly folks always let you know where you stand with them—particularly men. They tend to keep a deep relational distance from those they view as outsiders. The Philly community views every new person with contempt or suspicion. However, once you are in, you are family, and you will find an unflinching loyalty that will last a lifetime. They expect to receive the same loyalty from you.

Churches need to make more effort to develop relationships with men. They have to build community in which men can get connected. As a first step, we need men who are already in the church to make a concerted effort to engage with any man who comes to church, whether he comes on his own or is brought there by a girlfriend, wife, buddy, or child. We can use this innate sense of connection to people of African descent in the West to help black men, as a group, see redemptive community. The gospel calls all Christians together; we need black men to feel free to connect as well.

CORE CULTURAL CONCERN ENGAGEMENT

The family member who joined the Nation of Islam, as well as several friends who are involved in NOI, has said that the NOI was appealing because they are concerned about the social concerns in the world. I've heard similar reasoning from men in other black ethnocentric groups, and there is a growing sense today that the church is no longer concerned with the needs of black men.

Dr. Carl Ellis Jr. introduced me to the concept of core cultural concerns. The black church developed core cultural concerns as an outflow of its understanding of the gospel and theology—an outworking of the gospel in the church. Dr. Ellis traces the history of core cultural concerns and how they relate to African American identity:

In the 18th and 19th Centuries, these core values led us to be involved in taking the gospel to the rest of the African diaspora and beyond. These values also became the basis of the great cultural movements of the 20th Century, namely, the Civil Rights Movement and the Black Consciousness Movement. These cultural core values themselves were the products of

African American Christian theology, yet the dawning of the 20th Century saw the abandonment of most of them by the church. Yet, they were rediscovered and redefined by those who were hostile to Christian theology. This resulted in the steady decline of the church's theological influence in African American culture.

The arrival of the 21st Century has seen the general abandonment of our historic cultural core values, facilitating the outbreak of today's African American cultural crisis, namely, the loss of African American identity. We have gone from Afro-centric to ghetto-centric, from Black consciousness to self-sabotage, from social progress to nihilistic regress, from pro-Black to anti-Black, from true spirituality to thug spirituality.[10]

According to Ellis, three of the primary core cultural concerns are survival, refuge, and resistance to oppression.[11] And these are still the concerns of many black men today. To reach black men, we must intentionally seek to meet the needs of black men, applying the gospel in a comprehensive way so that they can build environments where they feel empowered to thrive and transcend these core concerns. We have to develop ministries that engage the mind, body, and soul. As a church we have to create invigorating environments for men to be stimulated intellectually—everything from libraries within our churches with relevant resources to fellowships that gather around social interests. We can also engage men through athletic ministries like flag football, basketball leagues, going to the range, and exercise.

CONCLUSION

As we conclude, I want to offer a word of hope. At the soul level, the greatest need of black men is the gospel, and the church has an opportunity to apply the gospel to the darkest places of men's lives. We must engage the reality that many men live under the pressure of being feared. Consider this eye-opening quote from Elijah Anderson:

33 percent of young black men in their twenties are under the supervision of the criminal justice system—in jail, in prison, on probation, or on parole. This astounding figure must be considered partly responsible for the widespread perception of young black men as dangerous and not to be trusted. This kind of demonization affects all young blacks—those of the middle class, those of the dwindling working class, as well as the street element.[12]

This cycle of fear must change. And for that to happen, we have to engage men at the soul level. We have to engage them with the content of the gospel (1 Cor. 15:1–3) *and* with the scope of the gospel (Rom. 1:16). All of this is possible because the gospel is sufficient and able to satisfy any concern. The gospel is the answer to the needs of all people, including today's black men.

CHAPTER 11

BLACK ATHEISM

Adam Coleman

God of our weary years; God of our silent tears
Thou who has brought us thus far on the way
Thou who has by thy might; Led us into the light
Keep us forever in the path, we pray
Lest our feet stray from the places, our God, where we met thee
Lest our hearts, drunk with the wine of the world, we forget thee
Shadowed beneath thy hand; May we forever stand
True to our God; True to our native land
—"The Black National Anthem" by James Weldon Johnson

BLACK CHRISTIANS are walking away from God at an alarming pace. Some are turning to Black religious identity groups. Others are signing off from religion altogether, instead claiming that God does not and/or cannot exist. Urban apologists can use sound reasoning to engage these Black atheists with the truth that God does exist and that he alone provides the foundation for their personal value.

I'll never forget the day my sister said to me, "Adam, I'm an atheist now." To say that I was shocked would be an understatement. If anything had been a constant in our childhood, it was being in the church pew on Sunday morning. But when my sister went off to college, that all changed. My sister and a circle of friends she met at school adopted the view that Christianity is just a bunch of fairy tales for people who don't know much about how the world "really" works. Her drift into atheism, along with the lifestyle changes that followed, eventually began to drive a wedge between her and the rest of our family. Sadly, my sister's story is becoming more and more common today.

Quite frankly, too many of us are under the mistaken impression that this does not happen in our community. Many in the African American context still take for granted the conviction that we as a community believe in God, particularly the God of Christianity. Yet according to the Pew Research Center, on the matter of religious engagement, the fastest-growing religious group among African Americans is the "unaffiliated"—those who identify as nothing in particular, agnostics, or atheists.[1]

There is a great deal of controversy surrounding the appropriate way to understand atheism. Atheism, classically defined, refers to the belief that there is no God (or gods). However, many atheists today take exception to that rendering and suggest atheism is better framed as a *lack of belief* in a God (or gods).[2] In this chapter, I take atheism to be a belief that there is no God (or gods). However, the responses we will explore are applicable to any form of atheism that includes or implies the nonexistence of God (or gods) as a feature of reality in one's worldview or perspective. I use the term "Black atheism" to denote the strain of atheism among people of African descent—whether they be continental Africans or Africans of the diaspora—that is often characterized by the culture and concerns of those communities.[3]

THE RISE OF BLACK ATHEISM

Philosopher John Mbiti observed that "Africans are notoriously religious," and a prominent feature of African religion is "God as the ultimate explanation of the genesis and sustenance of both man and all things."[4] This has held true as a characteristic of the community of Africans of the diaspora: we believe in God. Pew Research studies show that 83 percent of African Americans profess a strong belief in God.[5] Black atheism, therefore, is a cultural aberration. While the denial of God's existence has traditionally been taboo in our community, atheism is nevertheless a latent challenge to Christianity that merits our attention.

During the Great Migration, an estimated six million African Americans relocated from the rural South to northern states, particularly the urban centers.[6] Accompanying this population shift, an artistic, social, and intellectual movement known as the Harlem Renaissance broke out in New York City, with residual expressions surfacing in other cities.[7] Black atheists today would argue that challenges to religious thought were already present in aspects of African American culture like the Blues before this period. However, during the Harlem Renaissance, humanism and atheism found a louder voice in the works of Claude McKay, Langston Hughes, Zora Neale Hurston, and others. Frustrations about the African American predicament seem to have been the impetus behind the amplification of these voices.[8] The potency of these frustrations is perhaps best captured by James Baldwin, who was a product of the Harlem Renaissance. In his iconic *The Fire Next Time*, he opines, "If the concept of God has any validity or any use, it can only be to make us larger, freer, and more loving. If God cannot do this, then it is time we got rid of Him."[9]

Today there are those who hope to take up the Black atheist mantle and broaden its reach in our community. Some of the leading spokespersons of Black atheism like Sikivu Hutchison, Mandisa Thomas, and others are using their platforms to recruit actively for atheism, particularly among millennials. Organizations like "Black Atheists of America" have even made in-roads on college campuses.[10] Atheism has also gained a silent cultural presence through public figures like Ta-Nehisi Coates, who have not overtly forwarded the cause of atheism yet maintain influence as thought leaders in our community.[11]

CHALLENGES POSED BY BLACK ATHEISTS

Generally speaking, Black atheists come to the table offering two streams of critique against God and Christianity. First, they claim that belief in God is an outdated, irrational relic of our community's past. While belief in God—particularly through the lens of Christianity—has traditionally provided emotional, social, and civic support for our community, they argue that it is a false belief that should now be abandoned for a more rational worldview—atheism. Dr. Anthony Pinn, professor of humanities at Rice University, is a prominent spokesperson for atheism in the Black community. In his book *Writing God's Obituary,* he puts it this way: "Theism produces sloppy ways of thinking because it doesn't necessarily respect reason but instead favors fiction."[12]

Second, the Black atheist would cite the church, and Christianity more broadly, as a culprit behind our oppression, or at least an irredeemable accomplice to the forces against us. As such, Black atheists argue that Christianity is a morally inadequate worldview that is unfit to move our community forward. In this manner, Black atheists often look to employ reason and morality as a two-pronged attack against Christianity. Those engaging in urban apologetics should be prepared to counter these kinds of objections.

Challenge 1: Does God Exist?

In response to the first atheist critique—that theism is built upon a foundation of emotion, "sloppy thinking," etc.—I will draw upon the insights of seventeenth-century Ethiopian philosopher Zera Yacob. Zera Yacob struggled with the same kinds of concerns that have driven so many to embrace atheism.

He too questioned whether God existed. Yet in the midst of his crisis of faith, Yacob followed the path of reason toward affirming God's existence.

Yacob was raised in a Christian community during a time of serious religious and social unrest in Ethiopia. Seeking to escape the volatility of the times and threats to his life, Yacob fled and lived in a cave. During his time of voluntary exile, Yacob wrestled with existential questions concerning the nature of man, morality, rationality, the ongoing slave trade, the reality of evil, and the existence of God. In 1667, the ideas Yacob developed during his time in exile were compiled in a work titled *Hatata*—the Ge'ez word for "inquiry."[13]

Zera Yacob has been regarded as a pioneer of Enlightenment thinking in Africa, in part because his work *Hatata* features a heavy emphasis on the centrality of reason.[14] In addition, a number of ideas attributed to individuals like Rene Descartes and Immanuel Kant are present in Yacob's *Hatata*, which was developed independent of and in some cases prior to the works of those European Enlightenment thinkers.[15] In chapter 3 of *Hatata*, Yacob grapples with the reality of evil in the world, particularly the evil humans inflict on one another, and questions God's existence. However, while reflecting on the Psalms, he comes to realize that God is indeed the best explanation for why anything exists. At various points in *Hatata*, Yacob alludes to features of the world that he takes to be indicative of an intelligent Creator. In the following passage, he appears to draw these insights together into one centralized expression of his reasons for affirming the existence of God:

Later on I thought of the words of the same David, "Is the inventor of the ear unable to hear?" and I said: "Who is it that provided me with an ear to hear, who created me as a rational [being] and how have I come into this world? Where do I come from? Had I lived before the creator of the world, I would have known the beginning of my life and of the consciousness [of myself]. Who created me? Was I created by my own hands? But I did not exist before I was created. If I say that my father and my mother created me then I must search for the creator of my parents and of the parents of my parents until they arrive at the first who were not created as we [are], but who came into this world in some other way without being generated. For if they themselves have been created, I know nothing of their origin unless I say, "He who created them from nothing must be an uncreated essence who is and will be for all centuries [to come], the Lord and master of all things, without beginning or end, immutable, whose years cannot be numbered." And I said "Therefore there is a creator, else there would have been no creation. This creator who endowed us with the gifts of intelligence and reason, can he himself be without them? For he created us as intelligent beings from the abundance of his intelligence and the same one being comprehends all, creates all, is almighty."

—Zera Yacob, *Hatata*[16]

To follow the steps of Yacob's reasoning toward a Creator, we must take into account his overall approach to gaining knowledge. In chapter 5 he says, "Indeed, he who investigates with the pure intelligence set by the creator in the heart of each man and scrutinizes the order and laws of creation, will discover the truth."[17] Thus, a guiding principle for Yacob is the centrality of employing reason and observations of the natural world to attain truth. This accords with Romans 1:20, which states, "For since the creation of the world God's invisible qualities—his eternal power and divine nature—have been clearly seen, being understood from what has been made, so that people are without excuse."

In that vein, Yacob incorporates three aspects of the natural world and human experience—namely order, rationality, and dependence—into framing his "inquiry" about God's existence. He seems to understand them as being three effects that require a single cause. In the passage from *Hatata* cited above, Yacob uses a series of questions to highlight these three effects in his search for an ultimate cause:

1. *Order*: Who is it that provided me with an ear to hear?
2. *Rationality*: Who created me as a rational [being]?
3. *Dependence*: Where do I come from?

We will follow in Yacob's footsteps and explore his three effects in the following order: dependence, order, and rationality (DOR). These effects will provide a framework for the evidence that God exists. We will see how these effects are actually three guideposts pointing to God's existence, and we will thus debunk the atheists' claim that belief in God is contrary to reason.

The Problem of Dependence

The centerpiece of Yacob's pursuit of truth is the question, "Where do I come from?" In search of a reason for his own existence, Yacob ultimately arrives at the explanation for why anything exists at all. Yacob conveys this in chapter three of *Hatata* as he essentially makes a cosmological argument for God's existence. Cosmological arguments often include two stages:

1. Establishing that some foundational cause (first cause) or explanation for everything exists.
2. Discerning what that foundational cause or explanation is like.

Great thinkers going back to Plato and Aristotle have contended that some feature of reality, like cause and effect in the world, points to the existence of a foundational cause.[18] Zera Yacob inferred that this first cause is God. Among the variations of cosmological arguments defended by philosophers today, the Leibnizian Contingency Argument is perhaps one of the more popular ones. We will take a few moments to employ the Leibnizian Contingency Argument as a tool to sketch out the first stage of the cosmological argument Yacob raises to address the "problem of dependence." In a brief treatment of the second stage of the cosmological argument, we will draw from Yacob's insights about order and rationality to deepen our understanding of what the First Cause of the universe is like.

German mathematician and philosopher Gottfried Wilhelm Leibniz—who, among other things, is credited for independently discovering differential and integral calculus—published works during the late seventeenth and early eighteenth centuries in which he too explores the mystery of existence. Yacob and Leibniz are on the same quest to make sense of why things exist—or as Leibniz puts it, "Why is there something rather than nothing?"

The concept undergirding Yacob's inquiry can be seen as a version of what philosophers call Leibniz's "principle of sufficient reason" (PSR). The PSR, succinctly stated, is, "Everything that exists has an explanation for its existence."[19] From the outset, Yacob dismisses the notion that he could be the reason for his own existence since it would be logically impossible for him to exist before he existed in order to create himself. Yacob then widens the scope of his search for an explanation. He first looks to his parents, then his parents' parents, then his ancestry going back to the first humans, and then finally to the physical material of which those first humans consisted. In each case, Yacob encountered the same problem. It seemed that for every cause, the question could be asked, "Why does that exist?" and one would always have to appeal to yet another cause. If so, then one could potentially explore an infinite number of *dependent* causes that owe their existence to other causes while never getting to the bottom of why the totality of things exists. To solve this problem, Yacob concluded that there must be another type of entity that is fundamentally different from these kinds of causes: something that is *independent* in that it does not owe its existence to anything beyond itself.

Leibniz's work offers philosophical language that adds depth to the important distinction Yacob made. Leibniz recognized that everything that exists falls into one of two categories: they are either *necessary* or *contingent* entities. As philosopher Dr. William Lane Craig explains in *On Guard: Defending Your Faith with Reason and Precision*, necessary entities are the kinds of things that exist by a necessity of their own nature: it is impossible for them to not exist. For example, some philosophers believe that abstract objects like numbers exist in this way. On the other hand, it is possible for contingent entities to not exist; they therefore need a reason beyond themselves to explain why they do in fact exist.[20] For example, planets, people, computers, and this book are all contingent things.

This distinction between contingent and necessary things helps us make sense of how dependent and independent entities exist. Entities that depend upon something beyond themselves to exist *lack a necessary nature*: they are contingent. By definition, an entity that *has a necessary nature* does not depend on something beyond itself in order to exist. By virtue of their own nature, necessary entities *"cannot not exist."*[21]

This contrast between contingent and necessary things provides a framework for resolving the problem of dependence that Yacob puts forth. Whereas Yacob and the other potential causes he considers are contingent entities, the range of these contingent things that exist could ultimately be explained if—at the foundation of it all—there is a necessary entity with the capacity to bring them about. According to Yacob, that entity is God.

Leibniz's Contingency Argument

Let's take a more detailed look at Leibniz's Contingency Argument, which can be summarized in the following steps:

1. Everything that exists has an explanation of its existence—either in the necessity of its own nature or in an external explanation.
2. If the universe has an explanation of its existence, that explanation is God.
3. The universe exists.
4. Therefore, the explanation of the universe's existence is God.

Volumes have been written about the various ways in-depth defenses can be provided in support of each premise of this argument.[22] For now, we will briefly survey key elements of each and see why many philosophers take this to be a powerful argument for the existence of God.

Premise 1: Everything that exists has an explanation of its existence—
either in the necessity of its own nature or in an external explanation.

There are a number of reasons to accept premise 1 as being more plausibly true than not. First, as we encounter things in our everyday experience, we have a rational expectation that they have explanations for their existence. Indeed, the idea that things can pop into being from nothing or exist for no reason flies in the face of our deepest intuitions about how the world works. In this sense, human experience and our intuitions about the world point to our first premise having a sort of self-evidence to it. Second, to reject premise 1 would significantly undermine science, which revolves around discovering what exists and how things happen in the natural world. The whole field of modern cosmology, for example, is aimed at discovering an explanation of the universe.[23] Also, for things to come into existence or occur for no reason would do away with the order and consistency in nature that scientists rely upon to make observations. Third, there is nothing irrational about Yacob's question, "Where do I come from?" The question of human origins has been a fixture of profound philosophical discourse for ages. This search for origins is undergirded by the common notion that the nature of a thing has something to do with the kind of explanation needed to account for it. Fourth—as we have seen from exploring Zera Yacob's and Leibniz's analyses of what best explains why things exist—things can be understood as belonging to one of two categories: necessary and contingent entities. Ultimately, it is reasonable to affirm that things have reasons for their existence. Surely it would be a gross display of hypocrisy for atheists to deride Christians for supposedly lacking reasons to believe in God while maintaining that the universe exists for no reason.[24]

Premise 2: If the universe has an explanation of
its existence, that explanation is God.

Premise 2 of our argument is probably the most controversial one. Nevertheless, there are solid reasons for affirming it. Atheists commonly respond to the Contingency Argument by contending that the universe simply has no explanation. As atheist philosopher Bertrand Russell asserted during his famous dialogue with Frederick Copleston, "I should say that the universe is just there, and that's all." But this response is logically equivalent to premise 2—it is impossible for Russell's response to be true and premise 2 to be false. In other words, the two statements stand or fall together. Carefully consider the following statements:

a. *If atheism is true, the universe has no explanation of its existence.*
b. *If the universe has an explanation of its existence, then atheism is not true.*

It would be logically inconsistent for the atheist to assert statement A while denying statement B. Yet, in comparing statement B to our second premise, they are in substance saying the same thing. Therefore, when the atheist claims the universe has no explanation, they are by default conceding premise 2: if the universe has an explanation of its existence, that explanation is God.[25]

We can also affirm premise 2 on other grounds. What kind of explanation could be the cause of the universe? Obviously, it would need to be something apart from the universe in some sense. Scientists generally use the term "universe" to refer to nature in its entirety, as in all of time, space, matter, and energy. Therefore, the explanation of the universe must possess qualities such as being timeless and exceedingly powerful—as Yacob surmises—as well as being spaceless and immaterial. With respect to things that are timeless, spaceless, and immaterial, Dr. William Lane Craig notes, "There are only two sorts of things that could fit that description: either an abstract object like a number or else an unembodied mind. But abstract objects can't cause anything. That's part of what it means to be abstract. The number 7, for example, can't cause any effects. So the cause of the existence of the universe must be a transcendent Mind, which is what believers understand God to be."[26]

A personal cause would also make sense of how there could be a timeless cause that produces a finite effect like the universe.[27] Thus, it is plausible that this cause would have to be "personal," as in having a mind with the capacity to reason, to have intentions, and to act upon what it wills to do. An analysis of the qualities an explanation of the universe would need to have points us to a timeless, spaceless, immaterial, unimaginably powerful, and personal "Cause," which Christians refer to as "God."

Premise 3: The universe exists.

With that said, we move from the most controversial premise to the least: the universe exists. For any sincere seeker of truth, this premise is obviously more plausible than asserting the universe's nonexistence. After all, if this premise were false, there would be no universe to question the existence of and no human beings like us around to question it. Therefore, the three premises of this Contingency Argument taken together bring us to the conclusion that logically follows:

Conclusion: The explanation of the universe's existence is God.

In examining the dependent nature of the universe, we have encountered our first guidepost pointing to God. Yet for Yacob, the mere existence of the universe is not the only piece of evidence to take into account in affirming

God's existence. He weaves his observations of order in nature together with his insight about rationality to build his analysis of what the explanation of his existence would have to account for.

Order and Rationality

At various points in *Hatata*, Yacob marvels at how the universe isn't thrown together haphazardly; things in nature function in a particular way. For example, in chapter 10 Yacob says,

> I was admiring the beauty of God's creatures according to their orders, the domestic animals and the wild beasts. They are drawn by the nature of their creation towards the preservation of their life and the propagation of their species. Moreover, trees in the fields and plants which are created with great wisdom grow, bloom, flourish, produce the fruit of their respective seed according to their orders and without error . . . All things are great and admirable, and all are created with great wisdom.[28]

It is plausible that this notion of orderliness, reflected in how beings function, is what Yacob has in mind when he asks, "Who gave me an ear to hear?" and that it informs why he construes the Ultimate Cause as a Creator throughout his discourse on God's existence. Perhaps Yacob did not approach his doubts of God's existence empty-handed but rather looked to order in the world as an indicator of divinity that helped him navigate his crisis of faith. Nearly four hundred years after Yacob's time, scientists and philosophers are still finding examples of order in nature—such as the fine tuning of the universe, information carried in the genetic code, and the mathematical structure of the physical world—that are indicative of an Intelligent Creator.

Furthermore, as Yacob ponders what sort of being the Cause of the universe must be, he notes, "This creator who endowed us with the gifts of intelligence and reason, can he himself be without them? For he created us as intelligent beings from the abundance of his intelligence and the same one being comprehends all."[29] In light of our ability to reason, Yacob sees it as more likely that rational beings like himself come from a rational source rather than a nonrational one. Has Yacob made a valid inference here? In his recent work *How Reason Can Lead to God*, Dr. Josh Rasmussen provides an analysis of the foundation of reality in which he describes power as "the capacity to produce an effect." Dr. Rasmussen notes that cognitive powers are a very different type of capacity than the ability to bring about physical outcomes.[30] As Yacob's question "Who created me a rational [being]?" seems to indicate, an ultimate cause that only explains what we see in the physical world doesn't quite capture the big picture of reality. Rationality has to be accounted for and any proposed cause that merely produces physical effects will not suffice. As modern atheist philosopher Thomas Nagel contends, "The existence of consciousness seems to imply that the physical description of the universe, in spite of its richness and explanatory power, is only part of the truth."[31] Yet, in our analysis of the Contingency Argument, we find God to be the Cause who has the mental properties needed to account for rational beings in the world.

Yacob takes it a step further, suggesting that our cognitive abilities point to a God who is not only personal but also relational. He writes, *"God did not create me intelligent without a purpose . . . that is to look for him and to grasp him and his wisdom in the path he has opened for me and to worship him as long as l live."*[32] If such is the case, then we find ourselves with a necessary Being who is timeless, spaceless, immaterial, unimaginably powerful, personal, and also relational. Again, this necessary being is who Christians call "God."

Notice, we arrive at this conclusion not through some appeal to emotion, wishful thinking, tradition, or indoctrination. Having briefly explored Yacob's three effects—dependence, order, and rationality (DOR)—we have evidence and reason to support theism. The cosmological argument is a sound deductive argument, meaning the premises are more plausibly true than their negation, and the conclusion logically follows from them. In addition, order in the universe and rationality serve to broaden our base of evidence even further. Thus, as it was with Zera Yacob, evidence and critical thinking have pointed us to the existence of God.

Challenge 2: Do Black Lives Really Matter?

Having established that there are rational grounds for affirming God's existence, we turn to that second challenge Black atheists raise—the moral implications of "The Struggle." The history of Africans in the West affords atheists a vast array of injustices to cite as evidence of real-world obstacles that God is unable or unwilling to subdue on our behalf—if he exists to subdue them. Truly, "We have come over a way that with tears has been watered," as "The Black National Anthem" reminds us.[33] Upon arriving in the "new world," enslaved Africans found themselves ensnared in a web of commerce and conquest. Their experience was in essence a dismemberment of the soul as their oppressors employed false narratives and racial categories to sever personhood from persons. As former enslaved person John Jacobs lamented, "To be a man and not to be a man—a Father without authority, a husband and no protector—is the darkest of fates."[34]

The scope of this chapter does not permit me to recount every step of our journey through slave auctions, forced labor, whippings, children "sold down the river," emancipation without compensation, lynchings, cross burnings, church bombings, Jim Crow, redlining, beatings in Selma, Bull Connor in Birmingham, the lingering economic legacy of protracted systemic injustice, and a host of other hurdles. Yet, while we are a people who have faced a plethora of challenges, the entirety of our struggle can be captured in one fundamental question: What does it mean to be human?

Our moral apprehension toward racism—humans being treated like cattle, denial of basic human rights, and so on—presupposes that those who are harmed by these things have value. By "value" I mean in the moral sense: the attribute that has to do with something or someone having a certain degree of dignity and informs what it means to treat them accordingly.[35] This is a natural connection for us to make. For ages, philosophers have explored the relationship between value and ethics. The value question is a hinge upon which ethical questions turn.

Objective or Subjective Value?

If humans have no value, any sense of moral obligation to respect the dignity of others and treat them right or any expectation for them to do likewise toward us would be without foundation. Therefore, in order to press this objection, atheists must assume that humans have value in some sense or another. An important question then arises: is human value best understood as being "subjective" or "objective"?

By "subjective" I mean dependent upon people's opinion or stance. For example, if I say chocolate ice cream is better than vanilla ice cream, that would be subjective. Suppose someone replies, "You're wrong. Vanilla ice cream is better." We could argue about which flavor is better, but that would be pointless, right? There is no fact to which one might appeal because it is just a matter of opinion. By "objective" I mean independent of people's opinion or stance in the same sense that 2+2=4 is correct regardless of what anyone thinks about it.[36]

If human value boils down to subjective opinions, whose opinion should we go by? We can certainly assign value to ourselves, but it takes more than that to support a robust system of ethics. I imagine my enslaved forefathers on the auction block appraised their worth in measures far greater than the price any merchant could secure for their purchase. Between the slave trader and enslaved person, who was "right" about the enslaved person's worth? If human value is subjective, the answer is neither. In principle, it would not be possible for either of them to be right since value is just as much a matter of opinion as me saying chocolate ice cream is better than vanilla—albeit with greater consequences.

In keeping with our deepest intuitions about human value and the morally significant experiences to which I alluded, I would suggest that human value is objective. Generally speaking, when protestors chant "Black lives matter!" they do not merely mean, "Black lives matter to me" or "Please adopt our subjective opinion that Black lives matter." They are making a more forceful claim. They are saying something more like, "It is a fact that Black people have equal value to others and should be treated as such." As we have seen, for atheists to hold the view that humans have no value or merely have subjective value kills their own argument from the start. In order for the atheist's contention to have any teeth, they must presuppose that humans have objective value.

God and Human Value

Worldviews are not created equal in terms of their ability to account for human value and the moral implications thereof. I contend that whereas theism has the resources to provide an objective foundation for human value, the same cannot be said for atheism. This argument from human value can be summarized as follows:[37]

1. If God does not exist, then objective human value does not exist.
2. Objective human value does exist.
3. Therefore, God exists.

Premise 1: If God does not exist, then objective human value does not exist.

By taking God's moral nature into account, we can demonstrate that Christianity affords a solid foundation for objective human value.[38] First John 1:5 says, "This is the message we have heard from him and declare to you: God is light, and there is absolutely no darkness in him" (CSB). In this verse, the word "light" denotes concepts like moral goodness, glory, and truth. Notice the verse does not say that God merely *has* light; it says God *is* light and there is no darkness in him. In other words, God himself is the pure essence of what it means to be good. Similarly, 1 John 4:8 states, "Whoever does not love does not know God, because God is love." God is not merely loving—God *is* love.

Furthermore, James 1:17 informs us, "Every good and perfect gift is from above, coming down from the Father of the heavenly lights, who does not change like shifting shadows." Thus, God himself, given his perfect and unchanging moral nature, is a viable foundation and reference point for objective moral values.[39]

According to Genesis 1:26–27, this same God—the essence and foundation of moral value—looked to himself to be the blueprint for mankind as he created us in his image and likeness. Upon completing his creative work, God declared that everything, including us, was good; in doing so, God conferred value on all mankind. Thus, human value is an objective fact of reality that is grounded in the nature, will, and decree of God. But what if we take God out of the picture? What objective basis remains for human value?

One of the common ways we gain self-understanding is to consider where we come from. For atheists who see reality in strictly naturalistic terms, we are essentially physical stuff that happens to be arranged in a particular way. So, what can the story of matter tell us about our moral worth? If the Standard Cosmological Model (the Big Bang) or something like it is correct, then it all began around fourteen billion years ago. Once upon a time the universe popped into existence from nothing, by nothing, and for nothing.[40] Now, it should go without saying that "nothingness" cannot have intentions; there were no plans laid for or value assigned to us as the universe came into being. Therefore, if atheism is true, gazing into the rearview mirror of our universe's history in search of value is an empty pursuit. If we cannot look to the origin of the natural world to find an objective foundation for human value, is there anything about nature itself that can account for it? I would argue the answer is no for a number of reasons.

While scientists can conduct experiments and make observations about how much something weighs, how dense it is, how it interacts with other forms of matter, and so on, moral worth is not something we can examine or measure in a test tube. Just think about it. What instruments would scientists use to ascertain how many units of moral value I have in my left hand? Perhaps that question sounds a bit silly, but it illustrates a fundamental point: moral worth is not a natural feature of matter. Through the sciences we have access to the kinds of natural facts I just alluded to, which are essentially descriptive of the world as it is. However, moral facts, like the proposition that humans have objective value, are fundamentally different from natural facts in that they are prescriptive; they impose upon us notions of how things ought to be. As atheist philosopher J. L. Mackie argued—given that objective moral values would be "qualities or relations of a very strange sort, utterly different from anything else in the universe"—on an atheistic worldview, one would be rational to take this as evidence that such values do not exist.[41]

Some suggest that the theory of evolution can save the day. Through natural selection and random mutation, we evolved into conscious creatures with communal tendencies and the capacity to feel empathy toward others.

Our communal nature and empathy gave rise to cooperative behavior, which helped humans survive: notions of human value are an outworking of our evolutionary history.[42]

It is true that things like empathy and cooperative behavior for the sake of the herd can be observed within the animal kingdom. However, an overview of human history with all our schisms, isms, and wars would suggest that nature has not instilled a species-wide conception of who we ought to include in our herd. Rather, it seems to reflect a broader story of natural selection in which "survival of the fittest" is ultimately the name of the game. In a world of limited resources where survival is the highest ethic, it would be perfectly rational to consider a notion of objective human value to be, at best, a useful fiction. When the rubber meets the road, however, human value has to take a back seat if and when the survival of our herd is at stake—whoever we take our herd to be.[43] After all, commenting on the social implications of evolution and the dynamic between races in his day, Charles Darwin, the father of the theory of evolution himself, predicted, "At some future period, not very distant as measured by centuries, the civilized race of man will almost certainly exterminate and replace the savage races throughout the world."[44] It appears that, if our sense of value really is a byproduct of our evolutionary history, we still find ourselves coming up short in our search for objective moral worth.

Some atheists might add an extra wrinkle in their model of morality to say that objective moral values exist in a similar sense that abstract objects like numbers exist, and we have evolved with rational faculties such that we can identify them. If that is true, voila! We can have moral value and keep God out of the picture. Still, this sort of explanation for moral values seems to miss the mark. If the universe has always existed without a cause or popped into being from nothing—and by chance the forces of nature worked together to form atoms, elements, molecules and then later, down the road, created us through an unguided process of evolution—it would be an extraordinary coincidence that these moral values were floating around as part of immaterial reality for all this time and we happened to develop in just the right way to accurately perceive them. That scenario is highly improbable to say the least.[45]

Aside from that, even if it could be shown that valuing fellow humans is an outworking of evolution, it is widely recognized among philosophers that attempts to deduce human value from such observations is to commit the is-ought fallacy. The mere fact that something is a certain way in nature does not mean that it ought to be that way.[46] For example, some species of sharks eat their young. Just because that is the case in nature, does that mean we ought to do the same thing? Obviously not.

For reasons like these, one can reasonably affirm that if God does not exist, there remains no grounds for objective human value. With that said, we will proceed to defending premise 2.

Premise 2: Objective human value does exist.

As explained earlier, for the atheist's moral indictment against God to have any real weight, they must presuppose that humans have objective value. Therefore, just by raising the objection, they have already conceded the second premise of our argument. Nevertheless, for those who would deny premise 2, we can appeal to what philosophers call "moral intuitions" to make our case.

Moral intuitions are not merely feelings but rather an awareness or deeply ingrained knowledge that something is good, bad, right, or wrong.[47] Because these intuitions are a fixture of how we make sense of our moral experience, we can employ them as tools for helping atheists see that premise 2 is more likely true than not.

Consider this scenario. Suppose you are on a cruise ship and the captain says over the loudspeaker, "I have good news and bad news. The bad news is our cruise ship is sinking and we won't make it to our destination unless we get rid of some of the weight we're carrying. The good news is, by my calculations, all we have to do is either throw twenty-five chairs overboard or twenty-five people overboard. I've decided to let the passengers choose which course of action we take." Now, if humans have either no value or merely subjective value, then there is no reason to think someone has actually done anything wrong if they give fellow passengers the boot. However, no one in their right mind would think it is justifiable to start chucking people into the ocean. Why? Because our deepest intuitions point toward it being more rational to affirm people truly have value and should not be treated with less care than furniture.

Lest we think this scenario is purely hypothetical, there is a historical parallel that demonstrates the real-world consequences of getting the value question wrong. On September 6, 1781, the British ship Zong set sail from West Africa to Jamaica, carrying over 400 enslaved persons. Prior to departure, the Zong's owner, James Gregson, had his shipment of enslaved people insured, which was common practice. After a few months at sea, the crew of the Zong found themselves in a desperate situation: they were off course and did not have enough water for the remainder of the voyage. In addition, both enslaved persons and crew members were dying of disease. Facing a grim dilemma, the ship's captain, Luke Collingwood, made a fateful decision. On November 29, 1781, Captain Collingwood ordered his crew to get rid of some of the "cargo" Gregson had insured. Thus, over the course of the few days that followed, the crew of the Zong threw 131 Africans overboard to their deaths. When the Zong arrived in Jamaica, Gregson filed his insurance claim for the monetary damage he "suffered" for the slain Africans. Initially Gregson received pushback from the insurance company, who objected that the Zong was found to have had a sufficient amount of water upon arrival in Jamaica. Gregson was awarded his insurance money after the courts upheld his claim. However, that decision was eventually overturned on appeal.[48]

For abolitionists like Olaudah Equiano and Granville Sharp, the Zong Massacre, as it came to be known, was a glaring example of the depraved nature of the international slave trade. They used this incident to fuel the public outcry against the slave trade as they petitioned for its abolition.[49] To agree with the abolitionists' conviction that what Captain Collingwood and the Zong crew did was objectively wrong is to agree with premise 2 of our argument: humans have objective value.

Conclusion: God exists.

From the two premises, it follows that God exists. Thus, this argument from human value illustrates how the moral challenges of our history do not point away from God but rather point toward God—particularly the God of Christianity. In fact, the biblical worldview has supplied African people with at least two streams from which to draw objective value.

First, the steadfast commitment to anchoring human value in God undergirds much of the progress we have made as a people. For example, this conviction was a source of personal resistance against the psychological assault of slavery. In the introduction of Clifton Johnson's book *God Struck Me Dead*, Dr. Albert Raboteau, Professor Emeritus of Princeton University, puts it this way: "Amidst a system bent on reducing them to an inferior status, the experience of conversion rooted deep within the slave converts' psyche a sense of personal value and individual importance that helped to ground their identity in the unimpeachable authority of almighty God."[50]

Furthermore, a biblical account of God-given worth was a significant undercurrent of the abolitionist movement. The biblical framework afforded African Americans the ideological common ground and moral currency, if you will, by which they advocated for themselves to the predominant culture. This theme echoed throughout the speeches and writings of some of the most prominent voices for African American freedom like J. W. Loguen, Medgar Evers, Dr. Martin Luther King Jr., and others.[51] Consider how former enslaved person Rev. Leonard Black employed the biblical concept of humans being made in God's image in his polemic against slavery:

Is man to be considered a mere ox, to be bowed up and stall fed? Has he not a mind capable of rising higher and higher in all that is expansive, pure, and holy? Has he not within him a spark of pure Divinity, which when he is surrounded by high and ennobling influences, is fanned into a light so bright as to lead us to respond to the glorious truth, Man is indeed made in the Image of God? Do you talk of selling a Man? You might as well talk of selling immortality or sunshine.[52]

A crucial takeaway from how the concept of being made in the image of God intersects with our history is that human value is ultimately a theological matter with serious implications. The success of the abolitionist and civil rights movements was to a significant degree due to them being predicated on an account of human dignity that aligned with God's truth. In light of the societal pressures we face today, we would do well to not lose sight of that lesson from our past.

Secondly, one way to gain insight as to what something is worth is to consider what someone is willing to pay for it. In John 15:13 Jesus says, "Greater love has no one than this: to lay down one's life for one's friends." The centerpiece of the gospel is that Jesus paid the price for our sin by laying down his life. What declaration of human value could be greater than God incarnate on the cross giving his life for mankind? He then defeated death through his resurrection so that we can enjoy eternal fellowship with him.

Christians' claim of Jesus's resurrection is defensible via historical evidence and rational inference. There are a number of historical facts surrounding the resurrection that are widely agreed upon by Christian and non-Christian scholars as being historically credible.[53] Examples of these facts are:

1. Jesus died by crucifixion at the hands of the Romans.
2. The disciples had experiences that they believed to be encounters with the bodily risen Jesus of Nazareth.
3. The apostle Paul converted to Christianity.
4. James, the brother of Jesus, converted to Christianity.
5. Jesus's tomb was found empty.

Keep in mind that these are not faith statements. Nearly all scholars working in fields related to early Christianity, New Testament studies, and so on agree that the first four of these statements are historically factual. Also, a strong majority of scholars agree on the historicity of the empty tomb.

When historians evaluate the historicity of an event, they gather data then use certain criteria to determine which hypothesis best explains the facts. Time after time, naturalistic hypotheses about what happened to Jesus after his burial have failed to account for the five historical facts I've laid out. Theories that Jesus did not actually die, the disciples stole the body, witnesses experienced mass hallucinations, and so on have all come up lacking when put under scrutiny in the academic community. However, there is one hypothesis that adequately meets the criteria to account for these facts. It is the explanation the church has stood on for nearly 2,000 years: God raised Jesus from the dead.[54]

The resurrection of Jesus is significant in rounding out our response to atheism. The Contingency Argument, order in nature, rationality, and the human value argument are powerful pieces of evidence by which we can rationally affirm the existence of God. The resurrection then takes us a step further in that it moves us from merely affirming *that God exists* to clarifying *who God is*. The Creator of the universe, who is the essence and foundation of the moral value in which our human worth is grounded, revealed himself to mankind in the person and ministry of Jesus Christ. Therefore, our ancestors who stood on the biblical worldview to maintain God-given dignity, fight oppression, and press on from being commodities to building communities did not do so based on a convenient lie. They were well within their rational rights to hold to the unchanging hand of the God of the Bible, who had brought them a mighty long way!

CONCLUSION

While atheists like Anthony Pinn would have us believe that the time for "God's obituary" is upon us, one can reasonably say that the reports of God's death at the hands of atheism have been greatly exaggerated. Atheism threatens not only to steal away the "souls of Black folks" but also to replace a sound moral framework with an atheistic system of ethics that ultimately cannot account for the objective human value any community needs to flourish and remain steadfast against oppression.

The reality is that we cannot build a strong community on a foundation of weak ideas. If we are to move forward as a people, we cannot do so with an atheistic worldview that does not provide solid answers to life's most profound questions. As we have seen, the affirmation of God's existence is not an irrational "feel-good" belief or immoral impediment to our people. The Contingency Argument, order in nature, rationality, human value, and the resurrection are signposts of reason and evidence which point to the true and

living God. Christians have these and other cogent arguments for the biblical
worldview at our disposal such that we should be emboldened to confront the
deception of atheism with the light of truth. Our commitment to doing so will
have both eternal and immediate implications for our community. By God's
grace may we rise to the call.

PART 3

TOOLS FOR URBAN

APOLOGETICS

CHAPTER 12

PHILOSOPHY AND WORLDVIEWS

Brandon Washington

EVERYBODY HAS a worldview that informs their beliefs and decisions. If urban apologists hope to engage in fruitful conversations—especially with members of Black urban identity cults—they must first understand and assess their neighbors' worldview. Philosophy provides us with the basic tools to evaluate a belief system according to its truthfulness, coherence, and existential viability.

Everyone is a *philosopher*. I make this claim without cynicism. If philosophy is defined as "thinking critically about questions that matter," then, strictly speaking, everyone is a philosopher; there are no exceptions.[1] Our ideas are grounded in philosophy's three essential subcategories: metaphysics (being and reality), ethics/value theory (behavior and aesthetics), and epistemology (knowledge).[2] When we read the news and try to determine what's real, evaluate human worth in order to make moral choices, or navigate contradictory messages from teachers to discover what is true, we are engaged in philosophical reasoning and decision-making. Unfortunately, we make these decisions without much, if any, deliberation. This chapter is dedicated to helping you think well as you examine the world around you.

A casual approach to thinking occurs for several reasons, but intellectual indifference is the one most relevant to this essay. Philosophizing is increasingly shelved and treated as a nonessential skill.[3] Anti-intellectualism and the adulteration of truth inhibit top-shelf thinking. Even within some Christian contexts, rigorous pondering is treated as antithetical to biblical faith.[4] This trend cannot be ignored. We are growing more stymied by a disregard for intellectual endeavors. Despite the urgent need to do so, few are equipped to contemplate the essential matters of life.[5] The upshot is disconcerting; everyone is a philosopher, but few are vigilant.

I am aware that many will read my claims and assume I am calling everyone to become a caricature of Socrates—I am not foisting such a life upon you.

I concede that there is a difference between vocational philosophers and the general population, but it is a difference in degree, not in quality.[6] While the vocational philosopher may dedicate notably more time and energy to thinking well, they have no monopoly on it![7]

All human beings are responsible for reasoning soundly; for Christians, it is a divine calling—an act of worship.[8] Our intellectual life is indivisibly linked to our discipleship. We have therefore inherited the imperative to serve as apologists.

By and large, the Black identity cults addressed throughout this book pride themselves on their intellectual prowess. Many of them measure their scholarship by comparing themselves to confessing Christians. They tout themselves as sophisticated alternatives to the Black church. Their posturing further obliges us to lean into our calling as intellectual missionaries. We must contextually serve the urban community and engage non-Christian worldviews for the sake of the gospel; sound reasoning is essential to the Great Commission. Our evangelistic responsibilities compel us to become intellectuals for the kingdom.[9] To that end, Paul charges us to "destroy arguments and every lofty opinion raised against the knowledge of God," and to "take every thought captive to obey Christ" (2 Cor. 10:5 ESV). Thus, this essay is a brief primer dedicated to philosophy's usefulness in evaluating and responding to worldviews. I will emphasize a sound understanding of truth, knowledge, and the laws of logic as tools for assessing objectionable ideas and their implications.

WHAT IS A WORLDVIEW?

A concise survey of worldviews can be thorny because the term has been politicized and because its popular connotations may distract from its philosophical worth.[10] A worldview is a scheme of foundational beliefs that serves as the lens through which we receive and interpret reality.[11] Wittingly or unwittingly, everyone has a worldview. It may or may not be very good, and many of us inherited it without much consideration. Despite this, we all possess a system of beliefs that we assume is true, and it operates as the filter through which we assess new information and experiences.[12]

Our worldview determines how we perceive the world, so we are obligated to appraise and maintain it.[13] Just as our bodies need nutrition, water, and regular exercise, our minds need good ideas, time to reflect, and regular bouts of vigorous thinking.[14] Blatant neglect of this responsibility is willful self-delusion and potentially self-destruction. Imagine going through life with poorly prescribed eyeglasses when you have unrestricted access to an optometrist who can restore your sight.[15] Doing so is both irresponsible and unnecessary. Assessing your worldview is at least as important as having your eyes examined.

Since worldviews are comprised of truth claims, which are subject to the laws of logic and the standards of truth, we can deliberately examine our ideas and determine whether or not we have good reasons for believing them.[16] This is a philosophical venture.[17] This essay will stress three nonnegotiable attributes of a credible worldview. They are:

1. Truth: A credible worldview must be comprised of true foundational beliefs.
2. Logical Coherence: The true beliefs must be logically consistent with one another.
3. Existential Viability: The true, consistent beliefs must be practically livable.[18]

These three criteria serve as the legs that keep a worldview upright. As with a three-legged stool, if any or all of them fail, it cannot bear weight; those who rest upon it will fall.[19]

EVALUATING A WORLDVIEW

This book addresses urban sects that are antagonistic toward the historic Christian faith. Each one contends that they possess a coherent scheme that appropriately informs how we should understand the world. Simply put, they are worldviews. They have core doctrines that inform their perception of the world, and they prescribe certain actions. Consequently, we must evaluate their tenability.

I have had my share of experiences with the lure of groups that are antagonistic to Christianity. Throughout my adolescence in the late 1980s and early 1990s, I was a Nation of Islam (NOI) sympathizer. I was not merely drawn to them; I was pushed. The NOI stood in contrast to a public schoolteacher with whom I regularly engaged during my childhood. She was an Anglo American woman who would occasionally share her ill-informed thoughts regarding ethnicity. For me, the final straw landed when she explained that African Americans did not know their African names because "they forgot them." She asserted that American slave owners graciously came to the rescue by bestowing surnames upon their slaves. She held that "African Americans couldn't take care of themselves, so someone *more capable* did."

The schoolteacher espoused an ethnic hierarchy regarding human worth and intellect. It was a fundamental aspect of her worldview—specifically, her anthropology: her view of humankind. Even as a child, I recognized that her words were absurd. Her intercultural illiteracy was the most offensive aspect of these dialogues because she genuinely believed her assertions were true. To this day, I am mending the wounds she inflicted in her role as a teacher of early-adolescent children.

That schoolteacher left me longing for dignity. The NOI became the fount of my self-respect. I was drawn to persuasive, well-dressed Black male leaders who appeared to be bold thinkers. They were the antithesis of the teacher. According to Elijah Muhammad, my dignity derived from my identity as the "Original Man."[20] While the Black man is the divine creation of Allah, the white man is the corrupt handiwork of an evil, rebellious scientist named Yakub.[21] I know; it's bizarre! But this creation story is vital to the NOI's anthropology and, thus, essential to their worldview.[22]

Even as a child, I wrestled with the implications of NOI beliefs. They uphold that because the Black man is original, the white man is derivative. Since a copy is always inferior to the original, the white man is a lesser being—lower than the Black man.[23] I was eventually struck by the implications of this view: if I believe the NOI's story, my worth comes at the expense of someone else's. They were giving me unfounded superiority instead of appropriate self-esteem. Such an act flies in the face of universal human dignity.[24]

I now have philosophical categories for the struggles I had as a twelve-year-old boy. Applying the three criteria of credibility—true, coherent, viable—I contend that both the schoolteacher and the NOI espouse indefensible worldviews. Failing only one of the criteria is enough to disqualify them, so it is fascinating that both the teacher and the NOI managed to fail all three!

First, both worldviews are built upon self-lauding, verifiably false representations of human history. The teacher's claim regarding forgotten African names and the NOI's allegations regarding the origin of "the white man" are plainly fabricated. The need to confront such patently false claims is annoying—to say the least! Having said that, history does not lend itself to the views of the teacher or the NOI. Hence, they fail to meet the first criteria: true foundational beliefs.

Second, both espouse an ethnic hierarchy and consequent contradictions regarding human nature. The teacher treated Anglo Americans as innately virtuous and African Americans as inept. The NOI merely inverts her behavior by glorifying Black people at the expense of all others, particularly white people. At the cost of racial unity, they fixate on legitimate ethnic distinctions and shamefully pejorative stereotypes. Each champions shady anthropology that denies some group of humans their dignity, but they hyper-dignify themselves.[25] Treating one ethnicity as inferior to another undermines innate human equality which results in inconsistent views of human worth. This forges erratic ethical theories, so it is rife with ethical contradictions. Any attempts to articulate it will expose its innate incoherence. (Twentieth-century defenses of "separate but equal" policies serve as quintessential examples of this absurdity.)[26] Conflicting views of humanity result in an internally incongruous or self-refuting worldview! Therefore, both the teacher and the NOI fail to meet the second criteria: logical coherence.

Third, both worldviews result in—and even sanction—ongoing ethnic division and conflict. If you try to live them out, conflict is inevitable and extreme. They do not lend themselves to reconciliation and mutually sacrificial esteem. You may momentarily benefit from the dissension, but eventually it escalates beyond your control and results in destruction. So, both the teacher and the NOI fail to meet the third criteria: existential viability.

In contrast, when we apply the three criteria of philosophical credibility to the Christian worldview, we find that it meets each one. Christian anthropology is grounded in the doctrine of the *imago dei* (Gen. 1:27). As a human being, I am created in God's image and likeness. I am his vice-regent. This role is not unique to me; I share it with *all* human beings. Under God, we are equal in worth and dignity. Accordingly, injustice, both *from* me and *toward* me, is objectively wrong. Such a view is true, coherent within the Christian worldview, and existentially viable for all humanity.[27] This is only one example of Christianity's supremacy over competing worldviews; simply put, it is uniquely equipped to explain our world and ourselves.

TRUTH

A book with Christian apologetics as its theme should be fixed on *truth*. Before considering whether Christianity is true, we must first determine what truth is.[28] This is not merely a matter of semantics. The discussion regarding truth must include its definition and defense because the concept of objective truth is no longer taken for granted.[29]

Annually, *The Oxford English Dictionary* chooses a "Word of the Year." It is selected because of a measurable uptick in its use and cultural acceptance. In 2016, *post-truth* was their word of choice.[30] They define post-truth as an adjective that denotes "circumstances in which objective facts are less influential in shaping public opinion than appeals to emotion and personal belief."[31] If the growing use and acceptance of this term are reliable gauges, then the culture is progressively denying the existence of *absolute* truth.[32] We are descending toward *cognitive relativism*. This has resulted in sayings like, "What's true for you is true for you, and what's true for me is true for me." But does this stand up to examination? Is it even remotely viable?

Relativism versus Absolutism

Relativists contend that truth is specific to an individual or an isolated group.[33] So, a person or a clan can decide what is true without regard for objective facts. Chaos will inevitably result from such a view.

Imagine the horrors of a world in which the answers to math problems are dictated by the whim of an individual. If 2+2=4, then my feelings on the matter are irrelevant. The answer is absolute, not relative. So when a stray voice contends that 2+2=5, they are making an objectively false claim. Even the relativist hopes that a team of engineers comes to objective mathematical conclusions before erecting a bridge over a river. If any of them is motivated by subjective feelings, the bridge's infrastructure may be compromised—resulting in disastrous consequences.

This idea is not restricted to the sciences. Ethics, the study of right and wrong behavior, is built upon objective standards.[34] We have moral absolutes.[35] When I contend that murder is wrong, I am expressing what is objectively true. It is not my sentiment. Remote tribal cultures have come to the same conclusion without consulting me because the prohibition against murder is objective and available to all who ponder the matter carefully.[36]

The Correspondence Theory of Truth

The *correspondence theory* is the most obvious and widely held understanding of truth.[37] As its name implies, the correspondence theory asserts that truth is that which "accord[s] with reality."[38] Essentially, a statement is true if, and only if, it agrees with reality. For example, when I assert that I have a wife and two children, my statement is true only if my wife and two children are objectively real. If they are mere figments of my imagination, then my assertion does not correspond to the actual state of affairs and is, therefore, false.[39] There must be a one-to-one correspondence between my statement and the objective facts. My contentions are true only if they align with the external world. Such a view of truth does not allow me to live according to an invented reality. Instead, it compels me to discover reality, and my assertions must conform to it. This is key because reality is absolute, not relative. If my declaration corresponds to reality, then it will be correspondingly absolute—true for everyone.

For example, if the lordship of Christ is objectively *real*, then my avowals regarding his lordship are objectively *true*. Those who are denying his lordship are making assertions that conflict with reality, so their assertions are false.

As a junior in college, I took a philosophical ethics class in which we applied the correspondence theory in a discussion regarding morality. The first-semester freshman philosophy major seated next to me boldly proclaimed that the correspondence theory was "ridiculous." "We make our reality," she asserted, "so truth is relative; it is what we make it. Even if we have contradictory beliefs, they are both true." She was advocating for *cognitive relativism*.[40]

When the class ended, I pressed her to answer a few questions. I asked, "So you are contending that there are no absolute truths?" She replied, "Yes." I followed up by asking, "When you make that contention, do you believe it is absolutely true?" Obliviously, she replied, "Yes!" She did not understand my line of questioning until I quipped, "So it is *absolutely* true that there are no *absolute* truths?" Her view is self-defeating. She was making an absolute claim against absolute claims. Philosophers refer to her fallacy as *self-referential incoherence*.[41] Moreover, she depended *upon* the correspondence theory while rejecting it! Upon realizing this, she was visibly crestfallen but promptly abandoned her erroneous position.

Unfortunately, the freshman's error is not uncommon. Harry Frankfurt addressed those of her ilk when he wrote,

> In any case, even those who profess to deny the validity or the objective reality of the true-false distinction continue to maintain without apparent embarrassment that this denial is a position that they do *truly* endorse. The statement that they reject the distinction between true and false is, they insist, an unqualifiedly true statement about their beliefs, not a false one.[42]

Adroitly, Frankfurt underlines the silliness of *truly* believing that there are no *truths*. Believing that something is true while simultaneously rejecting the existence of truth is the equivalent of wholly resting your weight upon a crutch while sincerely denying the existence of crutches.

The correspondence theory is foundational. Any coherent conversation requires that our claims accord to reality. Otherwise, our dialogues are nothing more than unintelligible sentiments. When engaging people of other worldviews, we are not merely exchanging opinions. We are conveying ideas that we genuinely believe correspond to the world around us. When we are sharing the gospel, we are functioning as purveyors of objective reality. We do not preach it as merely "true for us"—it is true for everyone.

KNOWLEDGE

Knowledge is "justified true belief."[43] If a claim is defensible, and it is true, and I believe it, then I have knowledge. For instance, I am sitting at my desk on a Tuesday as I write this essay. I genuinely believe today is Tuesday. I have been locked in my office for a long time and I may have lost track of the date, so I consult my reliable calendar; it verifies my belief regarding the date. It is, in fact, Tuesday. This scenario is an example of knowledge because:

1. The calendar credibly affirms that today is Tuesday (justification).
2. It is a fact that today is Tuesday (truth).
3. I believe it is Tuesday (belief).

If I were to walk out to the common area of my office to proclaim what day it is, I would be conveying what I know. I possess all the ingredients of knowledge, so my message is more than a mere opinion. I can preach today's Tuesdayness and confidently engage those who disagree.

As an apologist, you should not limit yourself to merely believing the trueness of Christianity. You are to appeal to the reasons for your belief and shamelessly cite them as justification. You must "always [be] prepared to make a defense to anyone who asks you for a reason for the hope that is in you" (1 Peter 3:15 ESV). This is an imperative! You are not sharing an opinion; you are sharing knowledge. So you are not to merely tell people what you believe; you are to tell them why you believe it! This contributes to them knowing the truth for themselves.

It may be helpful to consider what knowledge is by illustrating what it is not. It is possible to believe something that is true, but in the absence of justification, such a belief is *not* knowledge.[44] In high school, I received a perfect score on a multiple-choice history exam—even though I had not studied. I guessed the answer to roughly ten out of the twenty-five questions. I started by eliminating the answers that I knew were false, then I chose one of the two or three remaining options at random. (I'm sure I'm not the only one who has done this.) Somehow, despite probability, my conjectures were correct. However, they were not knowledge. If I were forced to retake the exam, failing is as likely as passing. My answers were true and, to varying degrees, I believed them. But they were not knowledge because I had no credible justification for my answers. While they were educated guesses, they were guesses nonetheless.

Epistemology—the study of knowledge—weighs what we know and our justification for knowing it.[45] If you are reading this as a Christian, I can honestly say that you believe what is true. But as an apologist, you are to discover and delve into Christianity's evidences and rationality. Arm yourself with justification for your faith. Doing so will allow you to convey knowledge instead of blind hope. Knowledge is epistemologically superior to hopeful speculation.

Recognizing knowledge as "justified true belief" is relevant to the apologist because we are claiming that our worldview conforms to reality, and many essential details can be known. If so, then we should equip ourselves to provide justification for our beliefs. An erroneous and yet popular view of religious belief avows that we cannot know the essential doctrines of our faith. Faith and knowledge are often pitted against one another under the woefully false assumption that faith is, by definition, blind. Such a contention presumes that once a person has justification for their faith, it becomes inadequate—or even impotent. This understanding of the relationship between faith and knowledge is both unbiblical and irrational.

The Bible is the chief obstacle for those who insist on digging a trench between faith and knowledge. The Scriptures are not subtle when calling us to be advocates of truth (Phil. 1:7, 16; 1 Peter 3:15; Jude 3). Such a charge would make little sense if we cannot know and reason regarding essential aspects of our faith. Paul's encounter with philosophers in Acts 17:16–34 was an intellectual display for the record books. He engaged both Epicureanism and Stoicism as he parlayed a defense of the gospel among thinkers who prided themselves on new information (Acts 17:21). On Mars Hill, Paul championed reasonable faith. To be clear, I use the term *reasonable* because Paul's faith was complemented by *reason*—that is, deliberate and judicious thought.[46]

Paul's faith was not small. On the contrary, it was expansive and made an indelible mark on the world. But we would be remiss if we overlooked his commitment to thinking. This is the same apostle who appealed to the credible testimony of living witnesses in defense of the resurrection (1 Cor. 15:6). Such an appeal would not imply blind, speculative belief. Paul surrendered to the Holy Spirit while remaining an intellectual. He was able to do so because faith and reason are compatible—even complimentary.

We cannot know everything; omniscience is an attribute that is unique to God. However, we should never treat intellectual blindness as a higher state of holiness. Pitting knowledge and faith against one another only perpetuates a false dichotomy.[47] If Paul serves as our model, we must concede that aspects of our faith can be known. God's fingerprint on creation has made his existence undeniable (Rom. 1:16–20). Christianity is defensible! I reject the idea that our belief in the risen Christ is an irrational, running leap across the chasm of doubt. It is more like an informed, exerted hop. In many regards, when we advocate for the King, we can appeal to ideas that are knowable and evident to the world.[48] Our faith is not that of a hopeful gambler. It is solid belief in a real God.

THE LAWS OF LOGIC

Philosophy is sometimes treated as subordinate to the other academic disciplines. But philosophy is the overseer that allows all discovered truths to be assessed and properly applied.[49] When scientists evaluate their discoveries, they are philosophizing.[50] For example, a scientist may discover how to split an atom, but evaluating the potential uses of atomic power falls into the philosophical subcategory known as ethics. Should the knowledge be used to power a city with a nuclear reactor? Should it be used to devastate a city using a nuclear bomb? Pondering the differences between these two uses is a philosophical venture. While a scientist can discover what we are able to do, it is the philosopher who determines whether or not we should do it. Philosophy has this role in all fields of study (e.g., history, mathematics, empirical sciences, humanities, etc.).[51] The truths discovered in these diverse disciplines should be examined, interpreted, and implemented under the philosopher's vigilant eye.

In part, philosophy's devaluation derives from our culture's shift toward *scientism*, which is the contention that the hard sciences are the sole means of discovering reality.[52] Treating philosophy as subordinate to science serves only to disregard philosophy's investigative efficacy. Philosophy does not rest upon the scientific method, which is improperly advertised as the sole means of truth discovery.[53] However, philosophers do honor the inviolable confines of logic.[54] The laws of logic serve as a multitool. With them, sound arguments are assembled, and unsound arguments are dismantled. As I noted above, logical coherence is essential to a credible worldview, so an appreciation for the four fundamental principles of logic is indispensable. These principles are authoritative. I cannot improve upon Douglas Groothuis's cautionary summary: "These laws are not descriptive, but normative, as are moral laws. When we violate them, we are guilty of lawless thinking, or illogic. We break ourselves against their authority."[55]

The Law of Identity

The law of identity is essential to all logical laws. It holds "that something is what it is: A = A."[56] Brandon is Brandon. This computer is this computer. Two is two. Blue is blue. Consequently, "*if any statement is true, then it is true*."[57]

This may seem like nitpicky wordsmithing, but it is necessary to avoid confusion while evaluating propositions. Specifically, the law of identity obligates us to be mindful of definitions while trying to understand relevant terms and their corresponding ideas.[58]

I regularly apply the law of identity when I engage in apologetics in my local barbershop. I intentionally chose a barbershop that is patronized and managed by men belonging to an array of pseudo-Islamic sects (e.g., Five-Percent Nation, Nation of Islam, Moorish Science Temple). I am not there under false pretenses—they know I am a pastor in the community.

During my barbershop interactions, I have to vigilantly apply the law of identity to avoid vagueness. I carefully define terms because the pseudo-Islamic sects have incorrectly redefined Christian ideas. They will use the same term as me, but the term has a different meaning. Sometimes the difference is subtle; other times it is immense. For instance, many of them affirm the existence of a historical figure named Jesus. However, the one of whom they speak is not incarnate deity or the messiah. They reject his supremacy and effectual sacrifice. Instead, they recognize him as only one of many prophets. Thus, when we discuss Jesus, we are talking about two fundamentally different people, even though we are using the same name. If I do not carefully define terms, then A = non-A or Jesus = non-Jesus.[59] I don't want them to merely embrace the word "Jesus"; they have already done that. I wish to *introduce them to the historical person named Jesus.* For this to happen, I must first imbue the term "Jesus" with the identity of the person who reigns as God in the flesh, the Messiah.

The Law of Noncontradiction

The second law is known as the law of noncontradiction: "Nothing can be both itself and not itself in the same way, at the same time, and in the same respect. More formally, A cannot be non-A. That is, nothing can possess incompatible properties."[60] In other words, *"no statement can be both true and false."*[61] If a set of propositions contradicts itself, then it is not credible. Irreconcilable incoherencies discredit an argument. For example, during a presidential debate, we should not merely compare each candidate's statements to those of the other candidates. While cross-candidate comparisons are essential, they are insufficient. Ideally, we should examine each candidate's comments in a debate and compare them to their comments in previous debates and press conferences. This approach allows us to evaluate the overall coherence of their political views. The moment we discover an irreparable contradiction between two indispensable aspects of a candidate's political platform, we have reason to doubt their platform.

Another application of the law of noncontradiction derives from religious pluralism, a view that assumes all religious paths lead to the same destination.[62] If that were true, then the religious pluralists would have to uphold that Christianity and Islam worship essentially the same God and that the theological conflicts between these religions are inconsequential.[63] But, considering that Christians and Muslims use the term "God" to describe very different beings, the law of noncontradiction exposes the logical incoherence of religious pluralism. The assumption that Islam and Christianity are the same comes from an oversimplification of similarities and woeful disregard for differences.[64] The similarities are undeniable, but the list of irreconcilable beliefs is extensive.[65]

Consider, for instance, Christianity's beliefs regarding the nature of Christ. For orthodox Christians, Christ is the incarnate *logos*, the eternal Son of God, a coequal member of the Trinity; as such, he is God in the flesh.[66] Yet Islam categorizes such a view of Christ as "Shirk," an act of idolatry or polytheism.[67] According to Islam, identifying Christ as the eternal Son serves only to demote Allah, which is blasphemous.[68] This is noteworthy because the eternal Sonship of Christ is essential to the historic Christian faith.[69] If Christianity deems Christ's Sonship essential, and Islam considers it blasphemy, then the two faiths contradict one another regarding a doctrine that is fundamental to both. Thus, the two religions cannot be philosophically the same.[70]

Religious pluralism may be a well-intended worldview, but it erroneously obligates us to affirm contradicting theological camps. Rejecting this obligation is compulsory because it is absurd to confirm two opposing claims.

The Law of Excluded Middle

The law of excluded middle is similar to the law of noncontradiction. I refer to them as fraternal twins because they are akin but not identical. They both focus on the significance of contradictory statements. In summary, the law of excluded middle recognizes that a proposition and its denial cannot both be true.[71] So, *"every statement is either true or false."*[72] If two propositions are logically contradictory, then either one of them is false, or both of them are false; it is impossible for both of them to be true. If a US coin is flipped and lands flat, then the results will be either heads or tails. It can be only one or the other, and it is impossible for it to be both at the same time. During a coin toss, each side excludes the other. When the referee flips a coin and reports that the result is heads, you automatically know that the answer is *not* tails. It goes without saying; the referee need not mention it. By announcing what it is, he has also published what it is not.

According to the law of excluded middle, if a statement is true, then all statements that oppose it are false. In other words, *truth is, by definition, exclusive*. This is relevant because I am convinced that Christianity is grounded in truth. I am a theologian, Christian apologist, and pastor, so I routinely advocate for the supremacy of Christ. When I do so, my readers can come to numerous logical inferences. For instance, Islam opposes fundamental aspects of Christianity, so the two faiths are mutually exclusive. When I advocate for the trueness of Christianity, by implication, I am making an equally definitive claim regarding Islam—namely, that it is false. Because Christianity and Islam are contradictory, my emphatic affirmation of Christianity is an equally emphatic rejection of Islam.[73]

The Law of Bivalence

According to the law of bivalence, "any unambiguous declarative statement is either true or false."[74] If a statement corresponds to reality, then it is true; if it does not correspond to reality, it is false. Regarding unequivocal propositions, true and false are the only available options, and the proposition must be one or the other.[75]

Unambiguous claims make objective assertions, and the listener must test their veracity. For example, Christian apologists affirm that "Jesus is Lord." This is a candid statement. In other words, it means precisely what it says—Jesus is the sole King and Master of humanity. Those who assess the statement must work within the confines of only two options: it is either true or false. It is impossible for it to be neither, and it is impossible for it to be both. An explicit proposition is not plagued with ambivalence.[76]

When engaging an urban sect, both you and your detractor are making clear-cut declarations regarding Christ's identity—either he is Lord, or he is not. These are the only options you have. Your belief in his lordship should be assessed, but once you have justification for believing it, the law of bivalence lends itself to standing firm. You are to be gracious yet unwavering. If he is truly lord, then we are to shamelessly present him as such (Rom. 1:16–17).

SUMMARY AND APPLICATION

Space does not allow for exhaustive consideration, but I set out to equip you as responsible thinkers. Specifically, I hope you will effectually apply a sound understanding of truth, knowledge, and logic to appraising the sects common to urban contexts. They are merely schemes in need of your philosophical scrutiny. While my colleagues have provided insight into urban identity cults, you are tasked with evaluating their claims. Are their assertions true, coherent, and existentially viable? Only after you have applied these criteria are you able to engage representatives of these various camps in a manner that honors your calling as a Christian apologist. Our King, the prototypical intellectual, has both commissioned and equipped us to be kingdom thinkers. Sitting idly by and allowing ghastly ideas to run roughshod over the urban community is an abdication of our calling.

A few years ago, I had a conversation with a dear friend who has succumbed to the allure of a Black identity cult. (I will call him David to preserve his anonymity.) David and I met over coffee and discussed the details that prompted his decision.

First, he mentioned the "whiteness of Christianity" and argued that Black people embraced the church only because it was forced upon us during North American slavery. I replied by telling him that, during her first millennium, the church was notably influenced by Eastern contexts, and Africans were among the prominent theological voices.[77] Many of the early theologians who codified the church's doctrines were continental Africans. I mentioned Tertullian, Athanasius of Alexandria, and Saint Augustine as a mere sampling of Africans who served as foundational theological voices.[78] I told him of the Black Ethiopic church, which has been influential and predates the transatlantic slave trade by centuries! Its age and influence on the African continent undermines the belief that Black people were sweepingly forced into Christianity during North American slavery.[79] (I would be remiss if I failed to mention that, prior to our conversation, he was entirely unaware of these facts!) Providing a sound church history proves one of his foundational beliefs false and discredits his worldview.

Second, we discussed theology. David identifies god as "totally transcendent and unknowable." He denies the immanence of God. That sounds like deep theological rhetoric, but in the next sentence he said, "the Black man is God." He and his associates use the title "God" when they greet one another. His contentions regarding God's total transcendence are problematic because we were sitting only three feet from one another and having a dialogue regarding God. If David, a Black man, is God, then I was having a conversation *with* God *about* God. Such an experience requires God's immanence! He must be knowable. He is in my immediate presence and having a conversation with me, so he cannot be "totally transcendent." An irreconcilable conflict plagues his ideas regarding a transcendent god and the divinity of the Black man. The two ideas are essential to his theology, but they are contradictory. So his worldview is incoherent.[80]

Third, we discussed the reality that his Black identity cult has no answer for human depravity. They concede the human condition, but they have no solution for it. David espouses teachings that uphold ethnic division, hatred, and conflict. He left the church because there were "too many white people in the congregation." He is affirming depraved segregationist behavior. His cult does not improve the human condition; it only perpetuates the problem. His views are functionally untenable; they have no existential viability.

His worldview is based on ideas that are untrue, incoherent, and unviable. He needs to fail only one of these criteria for his scheme of ideas to be discredited. He failed all three!

I did not dedicate our time only to tearing down his ideas; that would be irresponsible and unloving. Once there is an intellectual void, we are compelled to replace it with a viable alternative. To that end, I shared the gospel. Without reservation, I contended that the doctrines of the historic Christian faith are true, coherent, and the epitome of existential viability. To this day, I pray that God intervenes and brings David into the kingdom. I planted a seed. Prayerfully, someone else will water it, but it is God who gives the growth (1 Cor. 3:5–9).

My encounter with David was a Spirit-led dialogue regarding the supremacy of Christ. Simultaneously, it was an intellectual conversation that philosophically assessed our worldviews. We need not choose between surrendering to God and thinking because surrender lends itself to thinking well. When you engage the world for the kingdom, you are standing on a stable and tested foundation. You are a kingdom agent who is to familiarize yourself with authentic doctrine to missionally engage that which is inauthentic. I pray that what I have written contributes to your conviction and equips you to, by God's grace, contend for the historic Christian faith (Jude 3).

CHAPTER 13

OUTREACH AS APOLOGETICS

Doug Logan

APOLOGETICS TAKES many forms. It can look like sensitive comments defending biblical truth on an online article promoting falsehood. It can look like passionate face-to-face discussions with people promoting an alternative belief system. Or it can look like acting as Jesus's hands and feet, spreading the truth of his love through our actions and service.

My middle son, Aharon, recently purchased a new home with his new wife. On moving day, they asked me to haul a few pieces of unwanted furniture to the curb with the hope that someone from the neighborhood would salvage them. As I set the final piece of furniture down, an older woman with a cane shuffled up to me. She told me that her daughter had recently died, and she was left with the duty of raising her grandchildren alone. My heart was shattered. I hadn't been able to formulate an appropriate and consoling response when she added that a couple months earlier she had suffered from a stroke, which impeded her ability to walk.

She gestured to the cabinet and asked how much I wanted for it. I replied, "If you can afford free, then it's yours!" She laughed in disbelief for a minute, then realized that I was serious. She phoned her nephew, who told her that he would charge ten dollars to transport the furniture to her home, which was less than two blocks down the street. "Ma'am, there's no need for all of that," I told her. I borrowed three gentlemen from my son's moving crew to help me carry a cabinet and bookshelf to her house.

The house was dingy and unkempt. I noticed toys on a filthy rug and realized that her grandchildren played on it. I told her that we would get her a new rug to match her new furniture, free of charge. She responded with dubious enthusiasm. "Y'all jokers must be Christians cause ain't nobody from this area just gonna help nobody for free," she said. We all laughed and in an odd unison responded, "Yes, we're Christians." We told her about our love for the city, and our love for her. Before we left, we prayed with her, and she received our prayer gladly.

In my first book, *On the Block: Developing a Biblical Picture for Missional Engagement*, I discuss the idea of living missionally. Whenever we talk about mission, we are also talking about apologetics to one extent or another. Those two ideas go hand-in-hand. If the mission of the church is to live under Christ's lordship in the world, to demonstrate the truth of the gospel by the power of the Holy Spirit, and to call people to respond in repentance and faith, then apologetics is woven into mission. We can't provide a defense for the faith if we aren't lovingly committed to and invested in the people of our cities.

Helping that woman with the furniture was our apologetic that day. It was the simple act of gifting something with no strings attached. As urban missionaries, we are seeking to minister to the whole person with the whole gospel. The practice of apologetics is essential in reaching our communities with the gospel of Jesus Christ. To see transformation in our cities, in our culture, and in our time, however, we need the power-packed, missional tool of a lifestyle apologetic, which is made up of both our verbal profession and our personal ethic.

LIFESTYLE APOLOGETICS

Traditionally, apologetics is understood to be a method of discourse which seeks to systematically defend, or give reason for, religious faith. Apologetics is still a necessary discipline because the block is loaded with people who are loaded with questions, and other religious sects in the inner city are currently answering those questions with authoritative fervor. The urban apologist's approach must consist of a fully biblical, theologically rich, and developed argument that brings about gospel clarity through the Christ-centered biblical narrative. This systematic approach to apologetics can't just seek to refute falsehood; it has to aim higher. The darkness of this world is not limited to thoughts but includes feelings and action. So our response to this world must be thoughtful, emotional, and active.

I grew up in Paterson, NJ, and I have served in many urban contexts: Burlington City, Kensington (a predominantly Latino neighborhood in Philadelphia), and in various areas throughout North Philadelphia. In 2011 my wife and I planted Epiphany Fellowship Church in Camden, New Jersey, which at the time was America's most dangerous, most violent, and poorest city. I've been a pastor for a little more than two decades now, and I've done outreach in every city I've lived in; however, no time was more challenging, constructive, and edifying than my season in Camden. That's where I learned that in order to penetrate people's hearts with the gospel, we first need to have hearts that are saturated with the gospel and actually live it out. Most people won't listen and receive what we have to say if we aren't living what we preach.

The principle of practicing what we preach appears all over Scripture. Following Jesus's resurrection and ascension, the apostle Peter took the missions baton and ran with it. He primarily targeted Jews with the gospel message. Jewish converts to Christ throughout Asia Minor faced terrible persecution in the early days of the church. In this context, Peter wrote letters to encourage and instruct Christians. In 1 Peter 3:15–16, he writes,

> But in your hearts regard Christ the Lord as holy, ready at any time to give a defense to anyone who asks you for a reason for the hope that is in you. Yet do this with gentleness and reverence, keeping a clear conscience, so that when you are accused, those who disparage your good conduct in Christ will be put to shame. (CSB)

Though written to the early church, the imperative still stands for us today. Christ's followers are charged with preparedness. We are to be ready to give real, helpful, true, and clarifying explanations of our faith. More than that, the passage warns that we are to have the proper posture in our gospel proclamation: a heart of gentleness and respect. The urban apologist must have a heart that can sympathize with the infirmities of people who are separated from God. Simply put, our lives ought to reflect the unfathomable reality that through Christ, God gives love and grace to undeserving recipients. So our tactics and tone matter. To see the transformation of lives and cities will require more than just precision training to win an argument; it will require that we care. Just like the early church Peter writes to encourage, the aim of our apologetics today has to be comprehensive, encapsulating both devotion to Christ and defense of the Christian faith.

Lifestyle Apologetics in the Scriptures

Earlier in that same letter, Peter equips Christians for effective missions in their extremely hostile context. In 1 Peter 2:9–12, he writes,

> But you are a chosen race, a royal priesthood, a holy nation, a people for his own possession, that you may proclaim the excellencies of him who called you out of darkness into his marvelous light. Once you were not a people,

but now you are God's people; once you had not received mercy, but now
you have received mercy. Beloved, I urge you as sojourners and exiles to
abstain from the passions of the flesh, which wage war against your soul.
Keep your conduct among the Gentiles honorable, so that when they speak
against you as evildoers, they may see your good deeds and glorify God
on the day of visitation. (ESV)

First, Peter reinforces the new identity of the Christians who are living
under terrible persecution, division, and violence. They are God's chosen
race, set apart to declare his excellencies. Peter reminds them that despite
their circumstances (being rejected, persecuted, and challenged because of
the gospel and their Savior), they are of precious value to God. Peter then
transitions, exhorting them to live out their faith so the Gentiles could witness
the difference in their lifestyle. As a group united by common faith amid a dark
cultural context, their Christlike conduct should stand out and cause people to
ask questions. Simply put, they are to understand that their lifestyle apologetic
would create opportunity for their verbal apologetic.

Ultimately the glory of God displayed through Christ's church is the
evangelism plan. On the block, loving people who hate us, helping people we
don't really know, and being generous with our lives and resources does not
make sense to people. God uses the countercultural posture of the Christian
community to display a love that will break down barriers between the church
and people on the block. The church's Christ-centered love, counterintuitive
generosity, and countercultural relational living brings about a neighborhood
credibility that opens up opportunities for our gospel message.

While Peter emphasizes the identity of believers united together as the
church, Paul brings into focus the sovereign work of God in giving the church
opportunities to share the gospel message. In Colossians 4:2–6, Paul encourages the church,

Devote yourselves to prayer; stay alert in it with thanksgiving. At the same
time, pray also for us that God may open a door to us for the word, to speak
the mystery of Christ, for which I am in chains, so that I may make it known
as I should. Act wisely toward outsiders, making the most of the time. Let
your speech always be gracious, seasoned with salt, so that you may know
how you should answer each person. (CSB)

Paul is asking the church to pray that the Holy Spirit would create opportunities for him to invade the darkness of unbelievers' lives. He recognizes that

it takes a sovereign God to heal people's blind eyes so they can see the glory of God in the face of Jesus Christ.

Likewise, the church's mission today must be built on the same twofold biblical foundation of Peter's identity theology and Paul's sovereignty theology. When we integrate these two realities, we operate with a biblically rooted, Christ-centered, and contextually focused lifestyle apologetic that allows us to bring the life-changing gospel to the people of our city, our neighborhood, and our block.

The goal of lifestyle apologetics is that the love of God will become the missional foundation of life, love, and labor as God sovereignly creates opportunities for the church to call people to repentance and faith. As we live on the block, God creates opportunities for the gospel to invade our communities through ordinary life. As we love on the block, God ordains divine appointments for us to love others as Christ has first loved us. As we labor on the block, God uses us as his instruments to make known his offer of rest and peace in Christ to all those "who are weary and burdened" (Matt. 11:28).

As God sovereignly works through his chosen people, his royal priesthood, our unbelieving neighbors will fall on their faces, worship God, and declare that God is really present with and working through his church.

Lifestyle Apologetics in Church History

The New Testament is not alone in demonstrating the lifestyle apologetic of the church; the church's enemies also saw the power of the church's witness in word and deed. By the time Julian, later known as "the Apostate," became the undisputed emperor in AD 361, about fifty years had passed since the emperor Constantine had converted to Christianity. Although Julian was educated and raised as a Christian, when he became emperor he committed himself to the restoration of Hellenistic pagan religion. Julian was no friend to the church, but he could clearly see the power of the church's witness. This is what he wrote to a pagan high priest in Galatia:

> The Hellenic religion does not yet prosper as I desire, and it is the fault of those who profess it . . . why do we not observe that it is their benevolence to strangers, their care for the graves of the dead and the pretended holiness of their lives that have done most to increase atheism [Christianity]? I believe that we ought really and truly to practise every one of these virtues. . . . For it is disgraceful that, when no Jew ever has to beg, and the impious Galileans [Christians] support not only their own poor but ours as well, all men see that our people lack aid from us.[1]

Despite the emperor's best attempts to reestablish pagan religion, Christians' love for their neighbors was a testimony to the truth of the gospel.

The church's mission in the first century was to invite people to receive Christ as Savior and call them, after their conversion, to live a life in community with the church and to carry out the mission to the world. This calling required the early church to incarnate—be local and present—all throughout the world. They were to be family to families, always seeking to serve the people of the city, compelled by the hope that Christ would save the lost, heal the sick, transform lives, and build his church. Missionary journey after missionary journey, Paul sought to reach the known world with the gospel of Christ in both proclamation and practice. Jesus also sought to get the gospel to the lost sheep of Israel during his three-year ministry, while ultimately launching a worldwide rescue mission for lost humanity.

Lifestyle Apologetics in Everyday Ministry

Though our objective is the same as the first-century Christians, the culture and context in which we do lifestyle apologetics has changed today. Let's keep it all the way real here: the people in our cities and on our blocks have an established perspective of Jesus and his church—whether positive, negative, true, or false. Often one's perspective about Christ's church is developed from culture and experience, not the biblical text.

People in the city often establish their theological understanding of the role and function of the church in the world on negative, false, and unbiblical ideas propagated through memes, television shows, social media, inaccurate depictions in movies, and some false teachers on "Christian" television broadcasts. These negative depictions of the local church have the church in a credibility deficit in the eyes of our neighbors from the start. People on the block are suspicious of Christians, especially pastors. They suspect believers have ulterior motives in gospel interaction on the streets.

Because of these negative assumptions and suspicions, mere intellectual apologetics arguments won't cut it. The church must seek to demythologize false ideas about Christ and his church through the process of knowing the culture, identifying with people, and finding common ground to get into people's lives on the block. These new and growing relationships are cultural connection points with our neighbors; God often uses them to create opportunities to enter into our lost neighbors' lives both relationally and missionally.

While I served as lead pastor of Epiphany Fellowship Church in Camden, I noticed that a certain park created an environment for violence and murder to thrive, and it brought disarray to the community. My staff and I saw this as another opportunity to invest in our city and practically demonstrate our lifestyle apologetic. So we took action. Epiphany Church raised 30,000 dollars and rallied nearly one hundred volunteers to revitalize the park. After hours of hard work and dedication, we stood before a totally transformed area, which became a safe place for our community.

As we were laboring, the people of Camden took notice. They came out to ask us why we were giving and what we expected to gain. Our testimony was that God loves beauty, joy, hope, and people. Our lifestyle apologetic made room for our verbal apologetic to have street credibility, and we had the chance to give the reason for the hope we profess.

You see, people have to see something in you before they will be open to receive a message from you. This is especially true in the urban context. Credibility is attributed to those who demonstrate commitment. To win people to Christ and have any actual impact on a city, communities investing in a lifestyle apologetic is critical. Many people in Camden recognized that our commitment wasn't just to a city, but to *our* city—and that distinction made all the difference.

ESSENTIAL ELEMENTS OF LIFESTYLE APOLOGETICS

How do we begin to practice lifestyle apologetics in our everyday ministry? What are the essential elements we must keep in mind when seeking to live on mission and do apologetics? As we aim to do mission and apologetics in any context, I believe that we must have a robust understanding of both the Bible and of the cultural context we are seeking to reach. As urban missiologist and seminary professor Harvie Conn says, "Our theologies of the city must be constructed with one eye on the Bible and one eye on the place where we put up our church signs."[2]

I like to call these dual-nature missional apologists "Berizacharrian." In Acts 17, Luke describes the Bereans as a group of people who are noble in character and avid in the study and examination of God's Word for greater depth and understanding. Like the Bereans, all of Christ's followers are called to eagerly learn from God's Word and to investigate new teachings in comparison with Scripture. The practice and posture of the Bereans is a model for all who desire to grow spiritually today as Christians and, particularly, as apologists.

Along with knowing the Scriptures (which is huge, necessary, and commanded), the apologist must understand the cultural context into which Christ has placed the church and to which they are committed. First Chronicles 12:32 speaks of the soldiers of the tribe of Issachar who come to David's aid as those "who understood the times and knew what Israel should do" (CSB). These men of Issachar have a proper understanding of the socio-political direction that God's people, the Israelites, should follow. They have a contextually accurate take on the world and the community of which they are a part. Clearly their understanding of God's Word, God's people, and the cultural context in which they dwell brings about a comprehensive understanding for applying God's Word in season. They have cultural intelligence and leadership wisdom. They know what timely moves the people of God ought to make in light of God's Word.

Know the Gospel: Berean

In Acts 17 the Apostle Paul spends time engaging with the Jews and Greeks of Thessalonica about the things of Scripture, arguing that Jesus is the Christ. While there are some who receive the message, a force of opposition arose that "set the city in an uproar" (17:5 ESV). Some of the brothers stand before the leaders and are penalized for being associated with the message, but others work an escape strategy for Paul and Silas: they travel to Berea. Undeterred by what had just unfolded in Thessalonica, the guys get right back to proclaiming the same message—but the Bereans receive them completely differently. The Jews of Berea "received the word with all eagerness, examining the Scriptures daily to see if these things were so. Many of them therefore believed, with not a few Greek women of high standing as well as men" (17:11–12 ESV). Note that contrast: the Bereans are eager to hear the message and study for themselves. They dig into the Scriptures and search out the truth.

This type of diligence is too often lacking in Christian ministry today. Christian ministers on the streets will come face-to-face with false gods, false religion, heresy, and spooky, made-up mystery occult ideologies, all of which crumble under the weight of truth. The Bible can stand up against any false claim, and it is loaded with answers that bring the freedom of truth. Without this type of personal theological knowledge and application, however, it will be impossible for the urban apologist to be prepared to engage the culture effectively and glorify God on the day of visitation (1 Peter 2:12). To be postured for impact, urban missionaries practicing apologetics must be Berean in that they eagerly seek an ever-deepening understanding of Christ's gospel.

Know the Context: Issachar

As we saw in 1 Chronicles 12:32, we must know the cultural contours and crevices to be effective missionaries with effective apologetic methods. We must study the culture so that we can have an active, informed, working knowledge of the neighborhood and region so that our missional strategies bear fruit. This means that mission strategies cannot be one-size-fits-all. Wherever you live and serve, that community has a *Zeitgeist*—a spirit of the age—that is unique to it. Often we refer to that as the "culture" of a place. As an urban missionary, connecting to it and allowing it to flavor missional interaction is a key contributor to gaining influence with people and, ultimately, winning souls to Christ.

We need to read both Christian and non-Christian magazines. We need to watch iconic movies and understand secular music and up-and-coming artists from all spheres of culture. We must know the block well. We must be diligent in gathering cultural data while building relational equity and trust from the residents of our neighborhood. This information will directly affect our understanding of the times and context, to the end that we might raise up people for culturally relevant, biblically committed gospel engagement. From the mayor and the city council to the happenings around the bodega on the corner, we must intimately know our block. Much like Paul in Acts 17 was able to quote from the popular authors and poets of Greco-Roman culture and preach the gospel using cultural references, you must be Issacharian.

Pastor and theologian Elmer Towns sums up beautifully why today's leaders and the next generation of urban leadership must know both the Bible and the block:

1. [The sons of Issachar] understood the times in which they lived. If we don't understand our culture and its pressures, we will be a slave to it.
2. They knew what the Scriptures wanted for Israel. If we don't know the Bible, we can't focus our lives on God's will.
3. They knew how Israel should live for God. If we don't know how God wants us to live, we will live for selfish reasons in our culture.
4. They knew the Person of God. If we don't know God by doctrine and experience, we will never do right.[3]

Know the Mission: Soul Winning

My friend Jonathan Leeman recently wrote an article about lifestyle apologetics, "The most powerful apologetic for the gospel, the thing that gives credit to the evangelistic message once it's spoken, will generally not be a philosophical argument, whether evidentialist or presuppositionalist. It will be the loving and holy life of a people in community, a church."[4]

Unfortunately, there's a lot of argumentative apologetics in our day. Whether online or face to face, many well-meaning apologists have become so focused on argument winning that they've lost sight of the goal of our overall mission: soul winning. While God certainly calls believers to contend for the truth of the gospel (Jude 3), the way we interact with unbelievers matters as much as the way we reason with them. Believers need to "be prepared to give an answer to everyone who asks you to give the reason for the hope that you have . . . with gentleness and respect" (1 Peter 3:15). Jesus told his disciples, "By this all people will know that you are my disciples, if you have love for one another" (John 13:35 ESV). Additionally, Jesus taught his disciples to be "wise as serpents and innocent as doves" when he sent them out into the world (Matt. 10:16 ESV). Being strategic and gentle in our interactions with those in our community is an essential part of effective apologetics.

Know the Mechanisms for Mission: Building Bridges

As noted earlier, we need to know the culture in which we live on mission and do apologetics. Understanding the heart of the neighborhood helps the church to *communicate* with our neighbors effectively. However, we must also live in our culture so that we might *bond* with our neighbors. It's not enough to know the Bible or the culture; we must also build bridges into the lives of our neighbors by finding common ground—what I like to call "mechanisms for mission."

When my wife and I began our time in Camden, we understood the value of understanding the culture to establish mechanisms for mission, so we found a house on the corner of the block just down from the weed spot (a place to purchase marijuana illegally). It was the heart of the neighborhood, with a constant flow of people headed to the bodega (Puerto-Rican owned corner store), the Chinese food store, the bus stop, and the fried chicken place. As is the custom for most urban dwellers, we would sit on the stoop during the evenings and take in the sights of the neighborhood—basketball games, pedestrians, and people on their way to buy weed. Our positioning there was strategic, affording us the opportunity to interact with and even pray over the people of our community. We got to know the flow, the culture, and the people on the block.

After a while, I realized how many people were passing by on the way to buy breakfast sandwiches, and I saw an opportunity to deepen my connections with them. So I started serving up breakfast sandwiches and coffee three mornings a week. That's not all I did to connect with people and build bridges into their lives in my neighborhood. In my inner-city neighborhood, I bred American Bully puppies to help people feel safe. I picked up people from the block for church on Sundays because they had no transportation. I held cookouts when I noticed people were hungry. I saw a need for a basketball court, so we built one.

I offered men who were trying to stop dealing drugs simple jobs like cleaning our church building and painting my home. I hired teenagers to cut my grass weekly, building in them a work ethic and entrepreneurial vigor that would help develop them into providers for their families. When my neighbor Miss Jannie sold soul food on Fridays, I was the first to buy five plates for my whole family and take a selfie with her so she could post my support on social media. I met and talked to hundreds of people about Christ, I prayed over homes, I broke up knife fights, and I mediated a truce between two rival gangs—all by being connected to the culture of Camden and by positioning myself in the heart of the block to establish mechanisms for mission.

We knew the gospel, we learned the culture, and we put ourselves in a place to have relational interaction for the sake of stirring up spiritual conversations. We did these common-ground, connection-point relationship builders to establish lasting friendships with our neighbors. We prayed that God would provide opportunities for sharing the gospel and seeing some of our neighbors transformed and converted to life in Christ as believers. We were there, the gospel incarnate, and so the people walking the block in Camden walked right into Jesus. What are you doing in your neighborhood? How are you bonding with your neighbors? Do you not only understand how to communicate with them but also how to bond with them?

PERSEVERING AGAINST OPPOSITION TO LIFESTYLE APOLOGETICS

As you put Scripture savviness, cultural awareness, soul willing, and bridge building into practice, you're going to face opposition. You're going to see many people trust in Christ by God's grace and the power of the gospel, but the devil is also going to try to punch you in the mouth. Satan will use many different tactics to deter you, but you must persevere in doing lifestyle apologetics, no matter the opposition you face.

Just like the early Christian converts Peter wrote to encourage, responses to our lifestyle apologetic in Camden were mixed. That's always going to be the case. While some people were compelled toward conversations of faith, many others opposed us to our faces. Modern day apologists should expect nothing different. In many instances over the years, in fact, our mission was met with violence, slander, and hatred.

While we were doing community outreach one day, a man selling drugs on the street accused me of messing with his business by having Christians on the block cleaning up and giving out food and drinks. He asked me theological questions and told me he was a Muslim. He said, "Christianity was the white man's lie and anybody who follows Jesus is as dumb as the Jesus of their Bible." He went on to say, "The Bible was made up by the white man to lead Black folk away from the truth of the Qur'an."

We went back and forth about those points for several minutes until he said to me, "Look, Bro!" revealing to me a gun on his waist. He stepped into me aggressively and said, "Let's see if you believe it with this gun on you: Do you believe it? Do you, huh?" I answered him, "Yep, I do." He stepped back and said, "This crazy joker really does believe the Bible." He went on to say, "I like you, joker, you really out here helping the people because you believe in Jesus. I ain't never seen that." When it all ended, I thanked the living God for his protecting grace, and our outreach team continued to share the gospel, pray over, and serve people. This incident was one of many hostile encounters I experienced.

Hostile times like this one provide daily missional drive as I am always reminded that Jesus came to seek and save the lost, and he has charged us with that same mission. While many received his message, many others rejected him and showed contempt for his mission. The same will be true for us, his followers. Yet even in the face of hostility, opposition, and violence, we must be unwavering in authenticating the gospel of Christ to the souls of men and women far from him. It's love that emboldens us—love for God and love for people who don't know him.

I am still praying for that young angry man, but I have confidence that the glory of God is the best evangelism to the block. The apostle Peter speaks of giving a persevering defense of the faith: "Dear friends, I urge you as strangers and exiles to abstain from sinful desires that wage war against the soul. Conduct yourselves honorably among the Gentiles, so that when they slander you as evildoers, they will observe your good works and will glorify God on the day he visits" (1 Peter 2:11–12 CSB). Peter calls us to patience in our evangelism and apologetics.

When we seek to reach people, we will face rejection and hostility on the block. Yet our constant hope is that one day, the conversation we had with a person will bring about real conviction and prompt their conversion to Christ. May our Christ-glorifying lifestyles be used by God to reach those who were formerly hostile to the gospel, that they would begin to trust Christ.

CONCLUSION

The apostle Paul sets the missional target for Timothy when he writes, "The aim of our charge is love that issues from a pure heart and a good conscience and a sincere faith" (1 Tim. 1:5 ESV). We have to keep our focus right there. Apologetics plays an important role in our mission, yes; but to have real, lasting, soul-winning impact, apologists today must do more than argue to defend the faith, proclaim right facts about God, and correct falsehood. To lead others from spiritual death to life in Christ, we must actually invest *ourselves*, committing to our cities by living consistent, generous, gospel-centric lives. When our verbal apologetic and our lifestyle apologetic join forces on mission from a heart emboldened by love, we'll see the power of God open the eyes of the blind, free the captives of sin, and give sinners new life in Christ.

CHAPTER 14

KNOWING YOUR BIBLE

Blake Wilson

IT'S DIFFICULT to defend something that you don't understand. It's even harder if it seems like your opponent has a better understanding of Scripture than you do, but you can't explain why. Embracing biblical literacy isn't an option for the urban apologist. Knowing the Bible intimately is essential for contending for the faith.

Peyton Manning and Michael Vick's NFL careers overlapped from 2001 to 2015. Both men were known as gifted and talented quarterbacks, but for different reasons. Manning was known as a mastermind of his team's offensive playbook. He had the unique ability to situationally assess his opponent's defensive strategy and then call an audible that set his career and team up for success. Vick, on the other hand, was known as the most athletically gifted, dynamic, and electrifying quarterback to ever play football. It was Vick's cannon of an arm, which could throw the football seventy to eighty yards, and the quickest legs ever given to a quarterback that marked his career.

While both men had a Hall of Fame–ability to produce the numbers necessary to be inducted among the elite, only Manning will receive that award. What set Manning apart from Vick? It is clear that Vick was far more talented as an athlete. But Manning was far more dedicated to playbook "literacy." Manning became so "literate" as it relates to the offensive and defensive strategies that he could approach each individual situation and prepare his team for success.

When it comes to biblical literacy, every believer should strive to be like Peyton Manning. Each of us should strive to become masterminds of God's heart and mind as expressed in the Scriptures to the degree that we are prepared at any moment offensively to address a brother or sister on the other side with care, concern, and compassion that may persuade them to place their faith in Christ.

WHAT IS BIBLICAL LITERACY?

Literacy has been defined by the United Nations Educational, Scientific and Cultural Organization (UNESCO) as "the ability to identify, understand, interpret, create, communicate and compute using printed and written materials associated with varying contexts." UNESCO further writes, "Literacy involves a continuum of learning in enabling individuals to achieve their goals, to develop their knowledge and potential, and to participate fully in their community and wider society."[1]

Biblical literacy, in like manner, is the believer's ability to know God's heart and mind, having been opened up by Jesus upon salvation to know the Scriptures—how to use them to experience his transforming power personally and how to share them with others so they may experience him as well (Luke 24:44–49). Biblical literacy is not the ability to study and know key doctrines to the degree that one is able to divide themselves from other believers based on a disagreement in theology or to win a debate against another group in a contrary belief system. The goal of biblical literacy is not to win a debate, but to win souls from all nations.

In this chapter, we'll see that those who are biblically literate in the New Testament use their knowledge of God's heart and mind to build up those in the body or evangelize those outside the body. The intent of biblical literacy then and now is to impact those without the light of Christ, drawing them to trust him for the forgiveness of sins and to become members of the body of Christ. Whether facing the Epicurean and Stoic philosophers at Mars Hill back then or an atheist, Muslim, or Black Hebrew Israelite now, the goal of the biblically literate believer should be to share the gospel and answer questions about the hope of Christ with "gentleness and reverence" (1 Peter 3:15 NASB).

GOALS OF FOUNDATIONAL BIBLICAL LITERACY

Biblical literacy is as essential in the life of the new believer as a mother's milk is to a newborn baby, offering the best nutrients to help them grow and develop properly. The apostle Peter informs us in 1 Peter 2:1–3 that, as a result of being born again, the newborn believer should have a supernatural appetite for the Word of God. This is what we will refer to as "foundational biblical literacy."

The first goal of foundational biblical literacy in the life of the newborn believer is to help remove the remnants of fleshly attitudes and actions that reigned and ruled in our hearts and minds as nonbelievers (Rom. 6:12–14; Eph. 2:1–3). The newborn believer now has Holy Spirit access to learn the Word of

God and be personally transformed by its power to live a life pleasing to the Lord, loving him and our neighbors. The apostle Paul says in 1 Corinthians 2:16 that "we have the mind of Christ." This is a critical principle as it relates to biblical literacy for all believers; we now have the God-given ability to read with insight and understand not only *what* God wants us to do but also *how* God wants us to do it. James, like Peter, teaches that the first and foremost priority of biblical literacy is personal transformation (James 1:19–21). A transformed life lived by the power of the Spirit serves as an observational witness to those who knew us prior to being born again (1 Peter 4:1–6).

The second goal of biblical literacy in the life of the newborn believer is spiritual maturity (1 Peter 2:1–3; James 1:22–25). It is important for those both in the body and outside the body to recognize the gospel's power to transform a person's life for God's renewed purposes. A primary example of this great transformation is seen in the life of Saul, who was a fierce persecutor of the church of God; but upon being born again, he became the lead promoter of the church (Acts 9:20–22, Gal. 1:22–24). Like the apostle Paul, each of us who has the Holy Spirit residing in us has the opportunity to experience a 180-degree transformation of our life passions, pursuits, and purpose.

A believer's spiritual maturity comes from not just knowing information about the Bible, but applying that information and allowing it to transform us. Biblical literacy is designed to confront the old self, leading to the replacement of old ways with the transformed life found in the power of the gospel (Gal. 5:16–24). Notice that biblical literacy begins by working on us, not working on others. The power of the Word of God must continually transform us into his image so that our transformation can validate the good news we have to share with those outside the body of believers (2 Cor. 3:18). The biblical writers often mention that the way we behave among nonbelievers is critical to their ability to receive our verbal witness because they have first seen our lifestyle witness (Col. 4:2–6; 1 Peter 2:11–12).

However, just because a believer is exposed to solid doctrine and sound theology does not mean that the believer will become biblically literate. The Corinthian church was exposed to some of the best Bible teachers of their day— Paul, Peter, and Apollos—but they were still carnal and struggled with becoming truly biblically literate. Their failure to understand God's Word and will led to moral failure, which led to the failure of their witness. We must be careful that, in like manner, we to do not fall short of biblical literacy while being exposed to the best preachers and teachers of our time. Real biblical literacy is only achievable for believers who are confronted by remnants of fleshly ways and surrender to the change that comes about through the application of God's Word in our lives.

RECOGNIZING THE BARRIER

No believer should take biblical literacy for granted because not everyone can be biblically literate. A nonbeliever can never achieve biblical literacy, unless they are born again by trusting Christ's finished work on the cross on their behalf. Biblical literacy is a unique privilege given to believers from God. At the moment a person is born again, they receive the indwelling presence of the Holy Spirit (Eph. 1:13) and the mind of Christ (1 Cor. 2:16), which allow us to understand the Scriptures. Understanding this privilege, the urban apologist should be spiritually sensitive in dealing with those outside the faith.

Jesus and the apostles agree that all nonbelievers are biblically illiterate and unable to understand the Word of God without the Spirit of God (John 8:43–47; 18:33–38; 1 Cor. 2:14). As we encounter those outside the faith, if our short-sighted goal is simply to win a debate and not win a soul, we will lose every time. The reason for our loss will not be the inaccuracy of the Scripture we presented or the argument we used. The loss will result because we forgot that unless the Holy Spirit attaches his power to the presentation of the gospel, the nonbeliever will not understand and will remain a nonbeliever (Titus 3:3–8).

The Holy Spirit and our motives play a significant role in our success or lack of success in urban apologetics. For example, Jesus, the greatest preacher and apologist of all time, indicates in his conversation with Nicodemus that outside of the power of God, a nonbeliever will not and cannot believe the Word of God (John 3:1–15). Nicodemus can only interpret Jesus's message through the lens of the physical realm: As Jesus speaks of being born again, Nicodemus speaks of going back into a mother's womb. He simply does not understand that Jesus is speaking about being born from above (3:4, 9). In like manner, we need to realize that those outside the faith cannot and will not understand what we say unless the Holy Spirit moves and influences them to trust Christ. It is our responsibility to solicit the work of the Spirit in our apologetics, praying that outsiders would come to the knowledge of the truth and not just the facts of our argument.

Jesus recognizes a major communication barrier between himself and the Pharisees and Jews in their discussion in John 8:43–47. Jesus states that they are unable to understand the implications of the Word he is sharing with them because they are not of God. This is a gruesome reality that should infuse our apologetics with care, concern, and compassion. The people we are talking to are still disconnected from God and remain in the domain of darkness, like we once were as well (Eph. 2:1–3; Col. 1:13).

The Jewish people and their leaders aren't the only ones with a literacy barrier between themselves and the truth; Pilate experienced this barrier, as we see in his one-on-one conversation with Jesus at Jesus's trial. As Jesus spoke to Pilate directly about the truth of his identity and his kingdom, Pilate asked a simple but profound question: "What is truth?" (John 18:38). Pilate finds no fault in Jesus, but he still sends him to his death and lets Barabbas free. The irony is that Barabbas is a surname that means "the Son of the Father," and Pilate let the guilty man go so that the innocent man, the true Son of the Father, could die in our place. If the people of Jesus's time rejected him even after they heard his words and saw his works, we should recognize that the work of persuasion is not about mere debating skill. The work of persuasion must be motivated by a desire to win souls to Christ. Even though that doesn't guarantee that people will embrace Christ as Lord and Savior, as we see in the ministry of Jesus, it will give us optimal impact and create better natural conditions for people to experience spiritual conversions.

In light of the reality that those outside the faith have no opportunity to become biblically literate, let us now turn our attention to some people in the New Testament who used their biblical literacy to either edify those in the body or to win those outside the body to faith in Christ.

JESUS'S EXAMPLE OF BIBLICAL LITERACY FOR SOUL WINNING

Jesus is the chief example of one who is biblically literate. Jesus regularly uses his biblical literacy to comfort those who are downcast and encourage them to share the truth with others. He appears to and commissions those who receive the truth, having opened their minds to understand the Scriptures and announce the gospel to the nations.

The story of Jesus's encounter with two men on the Emmaus road in Luke 24:13–49 illustrates this well. The most powerful event in human history has just occurred—Christ has been crucified. Two men are journeying on the Emmaus road, and suddenly they are interrupted by another man, whom they fail to recognize as Christ himself. As they contemplate the reality of Christ's crucifixion and his messianic claims, they have lost hope, realizing that it is the third day. It is at this point that Christ engages these men about their concerns and their lost hope.

He begins by calling them "foolish men and slow of heart to believe in all that the prophets have spoken" (24:25 NASB). Jesus is calling out these men for their biblical illiteracy; they fail to trust the truth of Scripture even when the facts don't seem to add up. It is at this critical point that Jesus centralizes their discussion on the sufferings of Christ. Their question and loss of hope centers on the person of Christ, and Jesus centers his apologetic on the person and finished work of Christ. As urban apologists, if we are going to be centered on God's heart and mind as we contend for the faith, it is extremely important that we also center the discussion on the finished work of Christ.

As Christ concludes his discussion with them, they invite him into their home, where he breaks bread and reveals himself to them. This is the moment they go from being "foolish" and "slow of heart to believe" to having "hearts burning" over Jesus's explanation of the Scriptures (24:25, 32 NASB).

The immediate response of these two men after having been impacted and influenced by Jesus's biblical literacy is to go and share with others that Christ has truly risen. They have not remained hopeless; they are bursting, eager to go and tell of the good news of the resurrected Savior. Jesus appears when they share their experience of him with the apostles, and he opens "their minds to understand the Scriptures" (Luke 24:45 NASB). After teaching them biblical literacy, he gives them the greatest assignment of all time: to proclaim forgiveness of sins in his name upon receiving the promised Holy Spirit (Luke 24:46–49).

BIBLICAL LITERACY IN THE EARLY CHURCH

For all of us seeking to be used by God through urban apologetics, it is important that each of us go back to the Bible to recognize that the goal of biblical literacy is moral purity, spiritual maturity, and salvation of souls. As the New Testament progresses and the era of the church is inaugurated, we continue to see this pattern of the biblically literate believer using this God-given privilege to edify and share Christ with others.

Peter

In the book of Acts, the church age is inaugurated at Peter's preaching of the gospel at Pentecost. The presence and power of the Holy Spirit comes upon them as they gather together, and then Peter preaches. Interestingly enough, his first sermon is not to an audience of supporters, but to Jews who had traveled to a feast. These are the same Jews who, fifty days before, would have witnessed and supported the brutal crucifixion of Christ, so they are probably hostile toward Jesus sympathizers. But the Holy Spirit moves them to engage the apostles, which then leads to a gospel presentation of immense magnitude—urban apologetics at its finest.

When the apostle Peter reaches back to the book of Joel and then Psalm 16:9–10 to provide an understanding of current events, God draws to himself three thousand souls. God uses Peter's biblical literacy, empowered by the Holy

Spirit, to turn an audience of hostile nonbelievers into the first converts of the church of the living God.

How does this relate to urban apologetics today and throughout history? In this story, we see people who were originally adverse or neutral toward Christ coming from diverse nations to a centralized urban center to become believers in Christ. If there was ever a reason to be encouraged in urban apologetics, it is the knowledge that even the most hostile audiences can be won over to become devoted followers of Christ. No city—no soul—is outside God's grasp.

To be effective, biblically literate urban apologists, we, like the Apostle Peter, must keep the focus on winning souls and not winning debates. Compassionate motives and the power of the Holy Spirit in our presentation of the truth of Christ have more power than facts to transform once hostile agents into God's ambassadors.

Philip

God moves one of these 3,000 converts to share the gospel with an Ethiopian, who then impacts the continent of Africa. The early believers, who were known for being devoted to the "apostles' teaching" (Acts 2:42), shared the gospel daily. By Acts 4:4, there are 5,000 males in the church. Many of them become biblically literate, including a man named Philip. Philip was one of the original seven men chosen to serve the Hellenistic Jewish widows in Acts 6. As he grew in the faith, he eventually grew from sitting under the apostles' teaching to serving the widows to sharing the gospel. Philip shares the gospel with those in Samaria in Acts 8 and witnesses the salvation of many.

Philip is largely known for his engagement with an Ethiopian eunuch in Acts 8:26–40. The eunuch is returning from Jerusalem and reading the Scriptures, but he does not understand them. At that moment, the Holy Spirit leads Philip to the caravan to share with the Ethiopian. Philip begins by asking the eunuch a question: "Do you understand what you are reading?" (8:30 NASB). The eunuch responds, "How could I, unless someone guides me?" (8:31 NASB). The story continues: "then Philip opened his mouth, and beginning from this Scripture he preached Jesus to him" (8:35 NASB).

Philip, because of his previous devotion to the Word under the apostles' teaching, is now situationally, spiritually, and scripturally ready to address the eunuch's questions. The phrase "beginning with that Scripture" implies that they begin their discussion with the Scripture the eunuch was reading, but that is not where their discussion ends. When Philip and the eunuch finish their discussion, the eunuch expresses his desire to be baptized because he now trusts Christ.

Urban apologists should take notes, especially in light of the fact that Philip becomes the only person in all of Scripture to be called an evangelist (Acts 21:8). Philip keeps the discussion biblical and Christocentric, leveraging his own knowledge of Scripture to meet the eunuch in his need and persuade him that Christ is the answer. As we engage in urban apologetics, we must be able to address various issues that serve as barriers to effective communication with others, never losing focus on Christ and winning souls.

Paul

Our journey through New Testament students of the Scriptures brings us to a giant of apologetics: the apostle Paul. The dynamic conversion of Saul from great persecutor of the church to great preacher in the church is an amazing example of a 180-degree shift in passions, pursuits, and purpose. Saul, as a Pharisee, would have been intimately acquainted with the Old Testament Scriptures. But, as we saw with Nicodemus, being familiar with Scripture is not the same as personally knowing and seeing Christ in the Scriptures (John 3:1–15; 5:39–44).

It was during his journey to Damascus that Saul is personally transformed by his encounter with Jesus and the gospel. We see in the book of Acts that from that moment on, Paul is overcome with the burden to share the gospel and to persuade mankind to trust Christ. Paul potentially deals with more people of various backgrounds than all of the other apostles. As urban apologists, we also will deal with people of diverse backgrounds.

Acts 17 is an example of Paul's biblical literacy providing the foundation for his apologetics. Paul moves throughout the Macedonian region, having had a dream in which a Macedonian calls for his help (Acts 16:6–10). He shares the gospel of Christ, "reason[ing] with them from the Scriptures," and both Jews and Greeks come to faith in Christ (Acts 17:1–4). As he journeys to Athens, he has a famous experience at Mars Hill. There, he draws common ground with the Epicureans, Stoic philosophers, and Athenians, preaching Christ by beginning with the "unknown god." As a result of this encounter, both Jews and Greeks become believers in Christ (Acts 17:16–34). Urban apologists likewise must recognize the common ground we share with those to whom we speak, not just our differences.

The book of Acts puts biblical literacy on display as the apostles follow the model of Jesus as outlined in Luke 24:44–49. The apostles not only rely heavily on the Scriptures for their urban apologetics; they relayed their faith in the power of the Scriptures to their disciples so that the Bible would be the foundation of apologetics for generations to come. If one as greatly opposed to the church as Saul could be saved and turned by Christ, we must know that any atheist, Muslim, Black Hebrew Israelite, or agnostic brother or sister can likewise be overtaken by the transforming power of the true gospel of Jesus Christ.

BIBLICAL LITERACY FOR ALL

In our church culture today, we act as if there are certain specialists who engage this great task of urban apologetics, but the Bible teaches quite the opposite. In the early church, being biblically literate was the expectation, not the exception. Those in the church of Jerusalem knew the Scriptures because they devoted themselves to study under the apostles. But they did not just witness them teach; they also witnessed them actively share the gospel with others and were involved in that process. This was a daily lifestyle for the early church.

The apostles taught and expected all members of the body to care about, be concerned for, and show compassion to those outside of the faith through gospel witness. This expectation can be clearly seen when the church is scattered due to the persecution Saul led against them (Acts 8:1–5; 11:19–24). All of the members of the church of Jerusalem are scattered except the apostles, and as they travel back to the nations from which they had come, they share the gospel and start churches, just as Jesus commands.

We see another example of the expectation for all believers to be biblically literate in tentmakers Aquila and Priscilla. In Acts 18, we meet Apollos, an Alexandrian who is known for being mighty in the Scriptures and actively sharing with others, but he was only acquainted with John's baptism. The common tentmakers Aquila and Priscilla hear him and, because of knowledge of the apostles' teaching, have the courage to take him aside and explain the way of Christ to him more accurately. This husband and wife instruct Apollos, who is obviously gifted, and give him greater insight into the truth of Christ. Apollos's humility allows him to receive this instruction and strengthen his ministry (Acts 18:24–28). As a result, he builds up the believers and refutes the Jews effectively so they can see Christ properly.

In order to comprehensively address those bound in the culture to experience freedom in Christ, we must also use our biblical literacy to share the gospel. It is not just professional apologists and pastors who must be biblically literate; even "common" Christians must know their Bibles intimately. Such knowledge should be the norm, not the exception. When believers are equipped in the Scriptures and empowered by the Holy Spirit, we are able to focus on what the Lord wants most: souls being saved. Biblical literacy must be rooted in its original intention, or urban apologetics will lose the impact that it could have.

BIBLICAL LITERACY IN URBAN APOLOGETICS

Many of us recognize that today we are experiencing an onslaught against the Christian faith. Let me remind you that, though the arguments we face today may differ from those faced by the early apologists in the book of Acts, the gospel of Jesus Christ is unchanging. We must stop to check our motives by considering these questions:

- Have we actually embraced God's heart and mind, agreeing that the Lord's intent for biblical literacy is saving souls?
- Are we positioning ourselves under the instruction of solid, sound Bible teaching and serving in ministries that will invest in and equip us?
- Are we growing daily in our relationship with Christ and becoming both a visual and verbal witness for Christ to those currently opposed to him and the Christian faith?
- Are we actively engaging the culture, aware of the issues and concerns they have with the Christian faith so that we might recenter them on Christ?
- Are we truly relying on the Holy Spirit through prayer to be with us, softening even those most aggressively opposed to Christ?
- Are we maintaining a loving and prayerful posture toward Christ's enemies, for whom he died to save? (Matt. 5:44-48; Rom. 5:8–10).

We must use biblical literacy in urban apologetics both offensively and defensively, as did the apologists we see in the Bible (Acts 18:24–28; Gal. 6:17; Titus 1:9). Offensively, we use it to build up those in the body and win souls to join the body. Defensively, we use it to protect the body from being infiltrated with false doctrine. I pray that this generation and those that follow will take marching orders from the Lord Jesus Christ, embracing his heart and mind, pursuing biblical literacy, engaging in urban apologetics to win souls, and witnessing the power of the gospel turn God's enemies into our gospel partners.

CHAPTER 15

APOLOGETICS AS SPIRITUAL WARFARE

Eric Mason

Lately I have been into vintage things—shoes, cloths, homes, and even cars. I like vintage products because, compared to the cheap quality of so many things made today, the products of the past were built to last. I saw a classic car I really liked, but it had been updated with some recent additions that lowered its value. It was so decked out that you couldn't recognize the original any longer; all of the recent updates had masked its identity. The further it got away from the original car, the lower its value.

The Black community faces the same threat to its identity as this vintage car. Over several decades of gospel engagement, I've found that the question of Black identity is an ongoing issue that the church needs to address. The Black conscious community offers cheap costumes for us to wear in an attempt to give us that vintage feel, clothing us in inauthentic garb to "enhance" us. There isn't anything wrong with celebrating African American identity, but we can't at the same time deny who God has made us to be in our innermost being. In Christ, God restores us through the gospel to our God-ordained identity, stripping away inauthentic imitations and restoring *both* our ethnic life and our eternal life (Rev. 7).

UNION WITH CHRIST VS. UNION WITH SATAN

The question of Black identity is not just a matter of religious labels; it is a battle for ultimate allegiance. In John 8, Jesus tells the Pharisees that they belong to their father Satan (8:39–47). This seems harsh, but it reflects the reality that since the beginning, there have been two spiritual bloodlines at war with one another: Eve's seed and the serpent's seed. Eve's seed represents the godly line, and the serpent's seed represents the godless line. In Ephesians 2:1–3, Paul makes it clear that until we are regenerated or made new by God's Spirit, all humans are Satan's spawn:

And you were dead in your trespasses and sins in which you previously walked according to the ways of this world, according to the ruler of the power of the air, the spirit now working in the disobedient. We too all previously lived among them in our fleshly desires, carrying out the inclinations of our flesh and thoughts, and we were by nature children under wrath as the others were also. (CSB)

When a person comes to know Christ, they are now in a different family—under a different father with new brothers and sisters. They are now "in Christ." That short phrase "in Christ" has massive identity implications, both for who we are in Jesus and also for what Jesus has empowered us in the gospel to do.

"In Christ" is a shorthand reference to the doctrine many call "union with Christ." This is the inauguration of our full, imputed, new life in Jesus. According to Bruce A. Demarest, union with Christ constitutes:

A union of life, in which the human spirit, while then most truly possessing its own individuality and personal distinctness, is interpenetrated and energized by the Spirit of Christ, is made inscrutably but indissolubly one with him, and so becomes a member and partaker of that regenerated, believing, and justified humanity of which he is the head.[1]

The first thing we can say about union with Christ is that it *originates* with God's elective decision, made before the creation of the world, to save his people in and through Jesus Christ (Eph. 1:3–4). "Union with Christ is not something 'tacked on' to our salvation; it is there from the outset, even in the plan of God."[2]

This means, secondly, that union with Christ is *grounded* in the Savior's redemptive work on the cross in history. Christ performed his saving work not on behalf of the world as a whole but for a distinct group of people—those in union with him (Eph. 5:25; Titus 2:14).

Third, as Anthony Hoekema reminds us, union with Christ is *established* with the elect once we place our faith in Christ throughout the course of our lives. The elect (1) are initially united with Christ in regeneration (Eph. 2:4–5, 10); (2) live out this union by faith (Gal. 2:20; Eph. 3:16–17); (3) attain righteousness or justification through this union (2 Cor. 5:21); (4) are sanctified through union with Christ (John 15:4–5; Rom. 6:4, 11); and (5) persevere to the end in union with him (Rom. 8:38–39).

Fourth, and finally, union with Christ is *consummated* following death in the life to come. Thus, when Christ returns and initiates the end-time judgment and redemption, believers will be raised with Christ and glorified with him forever (1 Cor. 15:22–23; 1 Thess 4:16–17). In sum, "union with Christ was planned from eternity, and is destined to continue eternally."[3]

Why is this doctrine so important for our discussion of urban apologetics and Black identity? First, it assures us victory in spiritual warfare, and second, it makes us who we are in Jesus. Some see their identity in Christ not in the reality of adoption and union, but through the lens of "identity theory," which is individualistic and based in nurture and self-actualization. But union with Christ defines our identity, heals our ethnic brokenness, and provides power for the spiritual battle. As we are driven by our union with Jesus, how we communicate the gospel in dark urban spaces becomes more redemptive and supreme.

THE FIGHT FOR THE BLACK SOUL

Scripture's identification of individuals as either united with Christ or submitting to Satan highlights that this attack on the Black community from without and within is ultimately spiritual warfare. Spiritual warfare is the unseen fight in the unseen realm between the powers of God's kingdom and Satan's kingdom. This epic battle for dominion affects the natural realm. In light of this, God's people must understand that our ultimate fight isn't physical, intellectual, psychological, sociological, economical, or political—it's spiritual. As Paul writes, "Our struggle is not against flesh and blood, but against the rulers, against the authorities, against the cosmic powers of this darkness, against evil, spiritual forces in the heavens" (Eph. 6:12 CSB).

The spiritual fight shows its face in many facets of our natural life and world. The fall in Genesis 3, the plagues in Exodus, David's pride in Chronicles, the Israelites' rejection of Jesus, and Paul being hindered in his missionary journeys are just a few examples that demonstrate that spiritual warfare is found throughout the Bible. Not only is it a major theme in Scripture, but it is a major challenge in our lives, families, and ministries today.

Unseen rulers, authorities, cosmic powers, evil, and spiritual forces are still at work today. Scholars have in the past denied a cosmic order in Satan's kingdom, but a closer look at the Scriptures makes a pretty strong case for it. After Jesus died and was raised from the grave, he passed through the heavens (Heb. 4:14). Jesus surpassed all of the authorities that were between earth and the highest heaven. God exercised power in Christ by raising him from the dead and seating him at his right hand in the heavens, "far above every ruler and authority, power and dominion, and every title given, not only in this age but also in the one to come" (Eph. 1:20–21 CSB). At his ascension, Jesus rode a cloud to his throne at the right hand of the father (Acts 1).

These unseen rulers are who we are fighting—the fallen angels, demons, Satan himself, and all fallen entities that war against God's kingdom. Satan isn't the only being who fell from heaven—others fell as well. Psalm 82:6–7 states, speaking of these angelic beings, "You are gods; you are all sons of the Most High. However, you will die like humans and fall like any other ruler" (CSB). As Michael Heiser and Clinton Arnold argue, the sons of God referenced here aren't human beings, but rather eternal beings who are or were a part of the heavenly council of God.[4] In Psalm 82 Yahweh calls a meeting of the divine council because they have overstepped their role and will be judged. Deuteronomy 32:8–9 lets us know that these sons of God were given different territories: "When the Most High gave the nations their inheritance and divided the human race, he set the boundaries of the peoples according to the number of the people of Israel. But the LORD's portion is his people, Jacob, his own inheritance" (CSB). They weren't to be worshiped or to sinfully interfere with humanity, but were to monitor and have holy, God-appointed dealings with humanity. Instead, they fell headlong into the fallen world, as we read in Genesis 6.

Fallen sons of God and demons are sometimes also called territorial spirits. Again, Michael Heiser writes, referring to the different types of spiritual beings:

> The unseen world has a hierarchy, something reflected in such terms as archangel versus angel. That hierarchy is sometimes difficult for us to discern in the Old Testament, since we aren't accustomed to viewing the unseen world like a dynastic household (more on that following), as an Israelite would have processed certain terms used to describe the hierarchy. In the ancient Semitic world, sons of God (Hebrew: *beney elohim*) is a phrase used to identify divine beings with higher-level responsibilities or jurisdictions. The term angel (Hebrew: *mal'ak*) describes an important but still lesser task: delivering messages.[5]

We see in the book of Daniel that "the kings" and the "Prince of Persia" were spirit beings who warred with the hosts of heaven. Persia was their territory of rule. And as we better understand these divine dynamics, we see that globally there are spirits in cities and regions resisting the work of the kingdom of God. Moreover, they are intertwined with everything from political conflict to spirituality and false doctrine. Clinton Arnold writes that today,

Numerous stories of Christians effectively battling principalities and powers are surfacing from all over the world, including Korea, Argentina, Canada, and elsewhere. A few Christian leaders are now culling insights from these accounts and advocating new and specific strategies for battling higher-ranking spirits that wield influence over neighborhoods, cities, geographical territories, and even whole countries. Using the references in Daniel 10 to the evil angelic princes over Persia and Greece as a starting point, these leaders are contending that Christians need to begin doing battle against the territorial spirits in order for successful and effective Christian ministry to occur.[6]

According to 1 Timothy 4:1, "the Spirit explicitly says that in later times some will depart from the faith, paying attention to deceitful spirits and the teachings of demons" (CSB). Demons are the lower-level evil spirits in the Bible who work directly with regular people (as narrated in the Gospels). Just as angels are at times means of divine revelation of God's Word (e.g. in the book of Revelation), demons are agents at times of false doctrine.

URBAN APOLOGETICS AS SPIRITUAL WARFARE

Every group we have examined in this book—the Black conscious community in general, the Nation of Islam, Hebrew Israelism, West African religions, Kemetic/Egyptian spirituality, Black atheism, and feminist ideologies—has demonic forces at their roots. These movements and belief systems attempt to restore our destroyed human value in the Black community by offering a pseudo-identity, but this identity keeps people on a never-ending search. This is because *only* the gospel can connect us to our true ancestor, Jesus—to the true and original spirituality, to being the true chosen people of God. Only the gospel can restore the lost value of Blackness that has been destroyed by white Western culture.

These promoters of false doctrine used to be somewhat limited, operating only in a few geographical locations. The northeastern United States has been and still is the primary headquarters for most of these groups, and I believe there is a concentration of demonic power from Washington, DC, to New York City. Most of the media outlets, camps, and authors of these heresies live in the New York and Philadelphia area. However, because many Black people are moving south and most have access to these doctrines through the internet, these false doctrines are now spreading like wildfire across the country. This brings a fresh urgency to our work of resisting these false doctrines and teachings.

If we are going to take back these strongholds, we must know our enemy:

a dark, evil, unseen, spiritual opponent. You may think I'm overspiritualizing this, but the Bible makes it clear that the war rages far deeper than we typically think. Genesis 3 demonstrates that the goal of the serpent and the fallen sons of God is to undermine and deceive those made in God's image in order to reproduce their own image, usurping God. Jesus, the true seed of Eve, is the one who will deal the death blow in the battle and crush Satan's works (Gen. 3:15).

Black religious identity cults have established themselves as opponents of Christ, and their false teaching is just as deceptive and damaging as the serpent's. Paul refers to twisted teaching like theirs as witchcraft in Galatians 3:1. Similarly, 2 Corinthians 4:3–5 says,

> But if our gospel is veiled, it is veiled to those who are perishing. In their case, the god of this age has blinded the minds of the unbelievers to keep them from seeing the light of the gospel of the glory of Christ, who is the image of God. For we are not proclaiming ourselves but Jesus Christ as Lord, and ourselves as your servants for Jesus's sake. (CSB)

All the ideologies and identity cults we have looked at in this volume are, at their core, demonically influenced doctrines that seek to throw Black people into a tailspin and keep us away from the glorious gospel.

CHRISTIANITY IS A WHITE MAN'S RELIGION

Satan has used Black identity issues to fool Black people into believing that the gospel is insufficient. Satan wants us to believe that the gospel cannot restore our lives. His lies underly the popular adage, "Christianity is the white man's religion." The truth is that Christianity and the gospel at the heart of it is not the possession of any one people group or continent, let alone white people. It is global, for all people! In fact, Jesus says that he won't return until his gospel has been preached in all the nations (Matt. 24:14). Vince Bantu states:

> Christianity is and always has been a global religion. For this reason, it is important never to think of Christianity as becoming global. . . . Too many people, both Christian and non-Christian, still perceive Christianity as the white man's religion. . . . Many contemporary missiologists and church historians would have us believe that Christianity came into Africa and Asia from Europe when the reality is quite the opposite in several significant respects. Christianity is not *becoming* a global religion; it has always been a global religion.[7]

The current popular forms of conscious Black ideology and other Black identity movements are themselves based in white mystic movements of the 1800s. Originating with white mystics like Gerald Massey, Alvin Boyd Kuhn, Helena Blavatzky, and building on the adoption of Masonic cultic practices, all of what these "Black" movements teach is rooted in the theosophical, new thought, and new age ideologies from the 1800's—all propagated by white men. Afrocentric scholars coopted the teachings of these men and painted them with blackface to continue their onslaught against Christianity. One of the leading mystics, Helena Claimed, hoped that theosophical philosophy would merge science, religion, and philosophy. Kemetic spirituality seeks to do the same thing today, again with a blackface. My point is that all of these conscious ideologies and identity movements are just recycled forms of failed spiritualities of the past. In the Black community we don't always realize that the (fake) historical discoveries of our heritage are many times simply recycled and substandard forms of spirituality.

For example, there is a movement now in the Black community to get back to our ancestral spiritualities. This requires viewing spirituality through an ethnic lens, and the thinking is that because it's not white in origin, but rooted in African history and culture, we should engage it, that it is good for Black men and women. Some people are so thirsty for identity that we will allow any inkling of "positive Blackness" influence us without vetting its validity. We must hear Paul clearly when he says, "Then we will no longer be little children, tossed by the waves and blown around by every wind of teaching, by human cunning with cleverness in the techniques of deceit" (Eph. 4:14 CSB). In other words, while it is good to affirm Black dignity we must also be careful of human cunning.

Another new practice among some African Americans is burning sage.[8] Burning sage in general isn't a problem, however, when it is connected to evoking certain spiritual "vibes" it changes from being something environmental to something spiritual. Some people use it to clear their home of negative energy. I appreciate what Damon Richardson has to say about this in a post he had on Facebook:

> I really don't understand how Christians are actually debating about use of sage. Clearly medicinal and or aromatherapy usage is fine, we often burn candles and incense for the same reason. HOWEVER . . . no Bible believing Christian should be burning sage to emit or drive out evil spirits and bad energy. That is nothing short of witchcraft and is definitely occultic as it seeks to address or remove spiritual problems by illegally accessing

and soliciting the spiritual realm for spiritual solutions. Such recourse is demonic and is tantamount to seeking demonic assistance for removal of demonic presence and problems. In short, it's trying to get the devil to cast out the devil. It doesn't matter whether one knows this or has this motive in mind, spiritual use of sage is witchcraft and that's not an opinion! If people would get out of these gospel free and doctrine lite churches and get somewhere they'd know these things!

I realize this isn't just something being done among Blacks, and it is prevalent in many ancient cultures. But we need to be aware that syncretism—the mixing of various belief systems together, including Christianity—has been on the rise among Black Christians lately. Adopting practices from other religions or belief systems makes gospel engagement a challenge because people who see this will tend to view Jesus as just another notch on their spiritual belt, as one option among many options.

THE GOSPEL EQUIPS CHRISTIANS FOR BATTLE

The false teachings of Black religious identity groups will fail to deliver on their promises in the end because the *gospel* is the power of God unto salvation. Trusting Jesus Christ as Savior is the only way a person can experience freedom from these false, demonically driven ideologies and cults.

In a powerful story on his YouTube channel, Dr. Michael Heiser interviews a young man named Steven who was into New Age philosophy. Steven got into all sorts of theosophical ideologies. As he was engaging in chat rooms and reading everything he could on the subject of opening his *chakras* and third eye, he didn't realize he was being lured in by evil spirits. He viewed what he was doing as self-exploration and spiritual improvement. He began seeing a teacher who was mentoring him in opening his third eye, practicing astral projection, and controlling things through lucid dreams. Once, in what he thought was a lucid dream, he met an unknown being. He had seen other beings, but this one had an eye on his forehead. The person seemed powerful, so Steven approached him in his dream, thinking that he could interact with him and that he was more powerful than the being. As Steven got closer, the being was levitating, and instead of controlling the being, Steven found that he was being controlled. The man drew Steven into his eye and took him on a journey he couldn't control. Over and over Steven would have this experience, and it greatly scared him. Eventually, he heard the gospel message and gave his life to Jesus. At that point, the dreams ended.[9]

Paul states, "For I passed on to you as most important what I also received: that Christ died for our sins according to the Scriptures, that he was buried, that he was raised on the third day according to the Scriptures" (1 Co 15:3–4 CSB). Apologists of all kinds must make the gospel the reason for their apologetics—the reason cannot merely be arguing or being right. Whenever we engage in apologetics, we must ask ourselves: "How does my communication lead to Jesus and the cross?"

In October 2019, my church partnered with the KING movement, led by Chris Broussard. We organized a debate between Bro. Jabari Osaze, a Kemetic priest, and Dr. Vince Bantu, a patristics scholar. Their topic was: "Is Christianity the white man's religion? Is Christianity a copy of Kemetic Spirituality? Who has the answer for the Black community: the church or the conscious community?" It was an interesting debate, but what was most striking to me was how Dr. Bantu kept communicating the content and scope of the gospel in every portion he had available to him.

During question and answer time, a member of the conscious community who was fully garbed in African regalia asked a question in a pretty aggressive way. At the end of the debate, he made a beeline toward me and asked me a number of questions, and I engaged him in love. At the end of the mild exchange, he asked me to pray for him. I was floored! As I began to pray, I held one of his hands and put my other hand on his shoulder. I started calling out for his soul and praying for his circumstances in Jesus's name, and he began to crumble, holding one hand up. He didn't make a profession of faith that day, but something profound happened to him.

We must remember the core of what we do in urban apologetics is waging war in a spiritual battle. Paul says, "For although we live in the flesh, we do not wage war according to the flesh, since the weapons of our warfare are not of the flesh, but are powerful through God for the demolition of strongholds. We demolish arguments and every proud thing that is raised up against the knowledge of God, and we take every thought captive to obey Christ" (2 Cor. 10:3–5 CSB).

We are fighting strongholds: false arguments that are planted in people's minds to blind them to the glory of the gospel. The New Testament authors use the term "stronghold" to represent a system of philosophy and reasoned arguments opposed to the true knowledge of God.[10]

In its original context, demolishing strongholds refers to changing wrong ideas about Christ in the minds of believers who have been influenced by demonically inspired teaching. . . . The demonic strongholds that had settled into their minds needed to be demolished by spiritual weapons, which include confrontation with the truth and fervent prayer. . . . These demonic strongholds need to be discerned, rooted out, and replaced by the truth.[11]

The stronghold isn't the particular outward sin but the sinful mindset that creates an environment for sin. A stronghold is a mindset, value system, or thought process that hinders your growth, the growth of others, and your willingness to exalt Jesus and maximize fruitfulness that brings glory to God.

In the gospel, God has equipped us with a complete set of armor for the battle (Eph. 6:10–20). When dealing with all the complexities of false ideas, we must utilize all of the tools we are given to engage in the work of urban apologetics, including:

- The *belt of truth*, which holds the armor together (6:14)
- The *breastplate of righteousness*, which protects the heart, including values, emotions, and volition (6:14)
- The *shoes of the gospel of peace*, which stabilize movement in hard terrain and gives solid grounding (6:15)
- The *shield of faith*, which covers all pieces of armor for broad defense and neutralizes the enemy's attack (6:16)
- The *helmet of salvation*, which protects the mind, a key battle front (6:17)
- The *sword of the Spirit*, a strategic tool for defense and offense (6:17)
- *Prayer*, the soldier's battle strategy and source of power and dependence (6:18–20)

No matter how strong or smart we might think we are, we need to regularly suit up as we enter battle. Remember that as we engage in the battle, we do so in constant need of the Lord. We have the best arguments, but we must also trust in the Lord. We fight "not by strength or by might, but by [the LORD's] Spirit" (Zech. 4:6 CSB). The Holy Spirit works through us as we use these spiritual weapons.

May the Lord grace us to honor him in the battle for souls among all nations, in urban apologetics, for African Americans, to the praise of the glory of his grace.

NOTES

Introduction

1. George G. M. James, *Stolen Legacy: The Egyptian Origins of Western Philosophy*, rev. ed. (Brattleboro, VT: Echo Point, 2016).
2. Chancellor Williams, *Destruction of Black Civilization: Great Issues of a Race from 4500 BC to 2000 AD*, 3rd ed. (Chicago: Third World, 1987).
3. Kersey Graves, *The World's Sixteen Crucified Saviors: Christianity before Christ* (1875; New York: Cosimo Classics, 2007).
4. Llaila O. Afrika, *African Holistic Health*, rev. ed. (A&B, 2012).
5. Elijah Muhammad, *Message to the Blackman in America* (Phoenix: Secretarius MEMPS, 1973).
6. Haki R. Madhubuti, *Black Men, Obsolete, Single, Dangerous? The Afrikan American Family in Transition* (1900; Chicago: Third World, 1991).

Chapter 1: Restoring Black Dignity

1. Exodus 21:16 says, "Whoever kidnaps a person must be put to death, whether he sells him or the person is found in his possession" (CSB). This theme is picked back up in 1 Timothy 1:10.
2. Justo L. Gonzalez, *The Story of Christianity: The Early Church to the Dawn of the Reformation*, vol. 1, 2nd ed. (New York: HarperCollins, 2010), 200. In the original work, Gonzalez dubbed Athanasius "the black dwarf," but when questions about the source came up later, this nickname was omitted from the later editions. See also Simonetta Carr, "More on the Black Dwarf," Simonetta Carr and Her Books, June 16, 2011, https://simonetta-carr.blogspot.com/search?q=black+dwarf.
3. Thomas C. Oden, *How Africa Shaped the Christian Mind: Rediscovering the African Seedbed of Western Christianity* (Downers Grove, IL: IVP Academic, 2009), chap. 3, Kindle.
4. Oden writes, "Where was this prejudice against Africa manufactured? How could these distortions have happened? How could such widespread developments be overlooked?

   "The most distracting voice was that of Adolf von Harnack, the leading liberal German historian in the 1890s and early 1900s. He argued that ancient Christianity's decisive failure was its accommodation to Greek philosophical language and assumptions. Along with Harnack, the core of the nineteenth-century German liberal tradition—Friedrich Schleiermacher, Albrecht Ritschl, and Ernst

Troeltsch—battled what they regarded as Christianity's regression into Hellenistic abstractions and dualisms.

"This is a prejudicial argument that, regrettably, both Catholics and evangelicals have continued to buy into for several decades. Major participants in Euro-American theology seem to have thus missed entirely the literary richness of the distinctive African Christian imprint on proto-Europe and the formation of the Christian mind. These mistakes have been subliminally passed on through the graduate studies programs that have formed scholars of all continents. Sadly, this dubious legacy still lives on in Africa." Oden, *How Africa Shaped the Christian Mind*, chap. 2, Kindle.

5. Oden, *How Africa Shaped the Christian Mind*, chap. 2, Kindle.
6. Bishop Ithiel C. Clemmons, *Bishop C. H. Mason and the Roots of the Church of God in Christ* (Lanham, MD: Christian Living, 2012), chap. 2, Kindle.
7. Judith Weisenfeld, *New World A-Coming: Black Religion and Racial Identity during the Great Migration* (New York: New York University Press, 2017), Kindle, loc. 151–54.
8. Eric Mason, *Manhood Restored: How the Gospel Makes Men Whole* (Nashville: B&H, 2013), 7.
9. "Dr Umar Abdullah Johnson 'White Jesus Money,'" video, uploaded by Know the Truth News, hosted on YouTube, January 25, 2015, https://www.youtube.com/watch?v=FoT9dIsWqcs.
10. Edward J. Blum and Paul Harvey, *The Color of Christ: The Son of God and the Saga of Race in America* (Chapel Hill: University of North Carolina Press, 2014), 8.
11. J. Daniel Hays, "Racial Bias in the Academy . . . Still?," *Perspectives in Religious Studies* 34, no. 3 (Spring 2007): 315–29.
12. Craig S. Keener, *Acts: An Exegetical Commentary; Introduction and 1:1–2:47*, vol. 1 (Grand Rapids: Baker Academic, 2012), 1550–51.
13. Keener, *Acts*, 1551.
14. "The Significance of the Doll Test," LDF, accessed December 2019, http://www.naacpldf.org/brown-at-60-the-doll-test.
15. "The Significance of the Doll Test."
16. Tony Evans, *Oneness Embraced: Reconciliation, the Kingdom, and How We are Stronger Together* (Chicago: Moody Publishers, 2015), 184.

Chapter 2: All White Everything

1. "Whitewashing," Cambridge Dictionary, https://dictionary.cambridge.org/us/dictionary/english/whitewashing.
2. Ernest Cleo Grant II, "Whitewashed Christianity," The Witness, October 25, 2016, https://thewitnessbcc.com/whitewashed-christianity/.
3. Skot Welch, Rick Wilson, and Andi Cumbo-Floyd, *Plantation Jesus: Race, Faith, and a New Way Forward* (Independence, MO: Herald, 2018), 57.
4. Vince Bantu, "Early African Christianity: Egypt," Jude 3 Project, August 20, 2016, http://www.jude3project.com/blog/2016/8/20/early-african-christianity-egypt?rq=vince%20bantu.
5. Bantu, "Early African Christianity."

6. Eric Mason, *Woke Church: An Urgent Call for Christians in America to Confront Racism and Injustice* (Chicago: Moody Publishers, 2018), 145.

7. Thomas C. Oden, *How Africa Shaped the Christian Mind: Rediscovering the African Seedbed of Western Christianity* (Downers Grove, IL: IVP Academic, 2010), 38–39.

8. J. Daniel Hays, "Racial Bias in the Academy . . . Still?," *Perspectives in Religious Studies* 34, no. 3 (Spring 2007): 316.

9. E. B. Lane, *The African American Christian Man: Reclaiming the Village* (Dallas: Black Family, 1997), 156.

10. Justo Gonzalez, *The Story of Christianity*, vol. 1 (San Francisco: Harper San Francisco, 1984), 173.

11. Hays, "Racial Bias," 316.

12. Kelly Brown Douglas, *Stand Your Ground: Black Bodies and the Justice of God* (Maryknoll, NY: Orbis, 2015), 4.

13. Douglas, *Stand Your Ground*, 6.

14. See the notes on "Jefferson's Proposal, 20 August 1776," Founders Online, https://founders.archives.gov/documents/Jefferson/01-01-02-0206-0002.

15. Thomas Jefferson, Harry R. Rubenstein, Barbara Clark Smith, and Janice Stagnitto Ellis, *The Jefferson Bible: The Life and Morals of Jesus of Nazareth*, Smithsonian ed. (Washington, DC: Smithsonian Books, 2011).

16. Thomas Oden, *The African Memory of Mark: Reassessing Early Church Tradition* (Downers Grove, IL: IVP Academic, 2011), 22

17. Oden, *The African Memory of Mark*, 18.

18. "Was Jesus a Jew?," Got Questions, https://www.gotquestions.org/was-Jesus-a-Jew.html, accessed August 2018.

19. Constantine's legalization of Christianity means that it was already in existence, so he didn't create Christianity at the Council of Nicaea (as some opponents to the Christian faith purport).

20. David R. Cartlidge and James Keith Elliott, *Art and the Christian Apocrypha* (East Sussex, UK: Psychology, 2001), 53–55. See also Robin M. Jensen, "The Two Faces of Jesus: How the Early Church Pictured the Divine," *Bible Review* 18, no. 5 (October 2002); and Robin M. Jensen, *Understanding Early Christian Art* (Philadelphia: Routledge, 2000).

21. Sir Anthony Blunt, *Artistic Theory in Italy, 1450–1600* (Oxford: Oxford University Press, 1962), 112–14, 118–19.

22. Edward J. Blum and Paul Harvey, *The Color of Christ: The Son of God and the Saga of Race in America* (Chapel Hill: The University of North Carolina Press, 2014), 29.

Chapter 3: What Is Urban Apologetics?

1. "Dr. John Henrik Clarke vs Mary Lefkowitz: The Great Debate (1996)," reelblack, hosted on YouTube, posted January 27, 2019, https://www.youtube.com/watch?v=fmei-hUQUWY.

2. Elijah Muhammad, *Message to the Blackman in America* (Phoenix: Secretarius MEMPS, 1973), 293.

3. Ronald Dalton Jr., *Hebrews to Negroes: Wake Up Black America* (Detroit: G Publishing, 2014), Kindle, loc. 971–75.

4. Jabari Osaze, *7 Little White Lies: The Conspiracy to Destroy the Black Self-Image* (Philadelphia: African Genesis Institute, 2016), 66.

5. Timothy Friberg, Barbara Friberg, and Neva F. Miller, *Analytical Lexicon of the Greek New Testament*, Baker's Greek New Testament Library (Grand Rapids: Baker, 2000), 69.

6. Definition provided by *Bible Sense Lexicon*, Logos Bible Software.

7. See also Col. 1:29; 1 Tim. 4:10; 6:12; 2 Tim. 4:7.

8. Clinton E. Arnold, *Zondervan Illustrated Bible Backgrounds Commentary: Hebrews to Revelation*, vol. 4 (Grand Rapids: Zondervan, 2002), 233.

9. Norman L. Geisler, *The Big Book of Christian Apologetics: An A to Z Guide* (Grand Rapids: Baker, 2012), 29.

10. Geisler, *Big Book of Christian Apologetics*, 30.

11. Geisler, *Big Book of Christian Apologetics*, 31.

12. Geisler, *Big Book of Christian Apologetics*, 31.

13. Geisler, *Big Book of Christian Apologetics*, 31–32.

14. As a matter of fact, no scholar in the field—believer or nonbeliever—holds that Christianity is a copy of Egyptian religion. By "copyist theory," I mean the assertion that Christianity is a copy of Egyptian mystery religions, akin to the theory that the Jesus story is a copy of the Horus Mythology (from virgin birth, baptism, twelve disciples, to resurrection from the dead). However, you'll be hard pressed to find an actual primary Egyptian text that affirms this. See chapter 8, "African Spirituality and Kemetics," for more on this topic.

15. Thomas C. Oden, *How Africa Shaped the Christian Mind: Rediscovering the African Seedbed of Western Christianity* (Downers Grove, IL: IVP Academic, 2009), chap. 2, Kindle.

Chapter 4: Black Church History and Urban Apologetics

1. For firsthand accounts of the terror of life under segregation, see William H. Chafe, Raymond Gavins, and Robert Korstad, eds., *Remembering Jim Crow: African Americans Tell About Life in the Segregated South* (New York: New Press, 2014).

2. Carter G. Woodson, "Negro History Week," *The Journal of Negro History* 11, no. 2 (1926): 239.

3. See Eric Mason, "Restoring Black Dignity" (chapter 1), and Jerome Gay, "All White Everything" (chapter 2).

4. Albert J. Raboteau, *Canaan Land: A Religious History of African Americans* (New York: Oxford University Press, 2001), 7–8.

5. Reverend John Bragg quoted in Albert J. Raboteau, *Slave Religion: The "Invisible Institution" in the Antebellum South*, rev. ed. (1978; New York: Oxford University Press, 2004), 103.

6. According to historian Albert J. Raboteau, "English bishops challenged the Protestant colonists to live up to the example of the Catholic missions in evangelizing the Indian and the African slaves." Raboteau, *Slave Religion*, 111.

7. Andrew Bryan quoted in Joseph Early Jr., *Readings in Baptist History: Four Centuries of Selected Documents* (Nashville: B&H Academic, 2008), 59.

8. My personal history and spiritual heritage is indebted to First African Baptist

Church. Over a century after its establishment, my maternal grandparents were married in this church and built their first home around the corner, and the funerals of many of my ancestors took place in this historic church.

9. Albert J. Raboteau, "The Secret Religion of the Slaves," *Christianity Today*, 1992, https://www.christianitytoday.com/history/issues/issue-33/secret-religion-of-slaves.html.

10. Enslaved African Americans were adamant about having control over their own churches so that they could refute the doctrine of the white slaveholding class. For example, in 1818, black worshipers in Charleston petitioned the South Carolina House of Representatives for permission to maintain a separate place of worship. This group of believers were considered radical for preaching that God was on the side of the oppressed. See Juan Williams and Quinton Dixie, *This Far by Faith: Stories from the African American Religious Experience* (New York: Amistad, 2003), 22–23.

11. Richard Allen, "The Founding of the African Methodist Episcopal Church" (1816), in *Let Nobody Turn Us Around: Voices of Resistance, Reform, and Renewal; An African American Anthology*, ed. Manning Marable and Leith Mullings (New York: Rowan and Littlefield, 2000), 20.

12. Frederick Douglass, "What to the Slave Is the Fourth of July?" (July 5, 1852), Teaching American History, https://teachingamericanhistory.org/library/document/what-to-the-slave-is-the-fourth-of-july/.

13. Maria Stewart, "Religion and the Pure Principles of Morality: The Sure Foundation on Which We Must Build" (October 1831), Teaching American History, https://teachingamericanhistory.org/library/document/religion-and-the-pure-principles-of-morality-the-sure-foundation-on-which-we-must-build/.

14. For more on the Christian roots of HBCUs, see B. Denise Hawkins, "Echoes of Faith: Church Roots Run Deep among HBCUs," Diverse Issues in Higher Education, July 31, 2012, https://diverseeducation.com/article/17259/.

15. Carter G. Woodson, *The History of the Negro Church* (Washington, DC: Associated Publishers, 1921; repr., 1990), 304.

16. Woodson, *The History of the Negro Church*, 287.

17. Raboteau, *Canaan Land*, 82.

18. Lacy Kirk Williams, "Effects of Urbanization on Religious Life," in *African American Religious History: A Documentary Witness*, ed. Milton C. Sernett, 2nd ed. (Durham, NC: Duke University Press, 1999), 374–75.

19. S. Mattie Fisher and Mrs. Jessie Mapp, "Social Work at Olivet Baptist Church," in *African American Religious History: A Documentary Witness*, ed. Milton C. Sernett, 2nd ed. (Durham, NC: Duke University Press, 1999), 369.

20. For more on "New Negro Identity," see Alain Locke, *The New Negro: Voices of the Harlem Renaissance* (repr., New York: Touchstone, 1999).

21. Judith Weisenfeld, *New World A-Coming: Black Religion and Racial Identity during the Great Migration* (New York: New York University Press, 2016), 2.

22. For more on the divide among African American Baptists over the issue of Civil Rights see, Joseph H. Jackson, "National Baptist Philosophy of Civil Rights," in *African American Religious History*, 511–18.

23. Jeanne Theoharis, *A More Beautiful and Terrible History: The Uses and Misuses of Civil Rights History* (Boston: Beacon, 2018), xiv.

24. Matt Pearce, "Ferguson October Rally Shows Divide over Civil Rights," *Detroit Free Press*, October 13, 2014, https://www.freep.com/story/news/nation/2014/10/13/ferguson-october-rally-shows-divide-civil-rights/17196139/.

25. Rahiel Tesfamariam, "Why the Modern Civil Rights Movement Keeps Religious Leaders at Arm's Length," *The Washington Post*, September 18, 2015, https://www.washingtonpost.com/opinions/how-black-activism-lost-its-religion/2015/09/18/2f56fc00-5d6b-11e5-8e9e-dce8a2a2a679_story.html.

26. For more on the impact of gentrification on Black churches, see Kristin Holmes, "As Areas Gentrify, Black Churches Lose Their Base, Depart," *Philadelphia Inquirer*, July 14, 2018, https://apnews.com/9254f2a17b774f8c86ff28a41ddeb571/As-areas-gentrify,-black-churches-lose-their-base,-depart; Alessandra Ram, "In Changing Neighborhoods, Black Churches Face an Identity Crisis," *The Atlantic*, October 12, 2012, https://www.theatlantic.com/national/archive/2012/10/in-changing-neighborhoods-black-churches-face-an-identity-crisis/263305/.

27. Check out appendix B, which is available as a digital download, for recommended reading on the history of the Black church.

Chapter 5: Why the Black Church Must Be Relevant

1. Cornel West, "Black Identity," in *Encyclopedia of African-American Culture and History*, ed. Jack Salzman, David Lionel Smith, and Cornel West, vol. 1 (New York: Macmillan, 1996), 353.

2. By now you've noticed my use of the term "African American" when referring to the church within our present context. As they are so often used, I will be interchangeably employing both terms, "African American" and "Black," when referencing the church. Understanding that the Black church is no more monolithic than the diverse people of the African diaspora who call it home, when used, I am speaking with regards to those whose immediate ancestry is derived from former slaves within the contiguous United States.

3. Samuel D. Proctor and Gardner C. Taylor, *We Have This Ministry: The Heart of the Pastor's Vocation* (Valley Forge: Judson, 1996), x.

4. The conscious (or "konscious") community is the self-described label of an anti-/non-Christian collective of religious and philosophical perspectives within the African American community, united first and foremost by their Negroid and ethnocentric identity, otherwise regarded as blackness. This community includes, but is not limited to, a variety of Black Hebrew Israelite camps, practitioners of African Spirituality/Kemetic Science, various denominations of Islam, and proponents of agnosticism and atheism/humanism.

5. Christopher W. Brooks, *Urban Apologetics: Why the Gospel Is Good News for the City* (Grand Rapids: Kregel, 2014), 29.

6. Cardinal William Levada, "The Urgency of a New Apologetics for the Church in the 21st Century," *The Vatican*, April 29, 2010, accessed December 12, 2019, http://www.vatican.va/roman_curia/congregations/cfaith/documents/rc_con_cfaith_doc_20100429_levada-new-apologetics_en.html.

7. Hans A. Baer and Merrill Singer, *African American Religion in the Twentieth Century: Varieties of Protest and Accommodation* (Knoxville: University of Tennessee Press, 1992), 28.

8. Brooks, *Urban Apologetics*, 27.

9. Thomas E. Carney, "Black Church," in *Encyclopedia of African American History: 1896 to the Present*, ed. Paul Finkelman, vol. 1 (New York: Oxford University Press, 2009), 195.

10. Lawrence Mamiya, "The Black Church," in *Africana: The Encyclopedia of the African and African American Experience*, ed. Kwame Anthony Appiah and Henry Louis Gates Jr., 2nd ed. (New York: Oxford University Press, 2005), 490.

11. Carl F. Ellis Jr., "Evangelicals for Biblical Justice," lecture, Southwestern Baptist Theological Seminary, October 3, 2019.

12. Tony Evans, *Theology You Can Count On* (Chicago: Moody Publishers, 2008), 908.

13. Ernest Gray, "Contextual Considerations in a Tension-Filled New Testament Text," in *Say It! Celebrating Expository Preaching in the African American Tradition*, ed. Eric C. Redmond (Chicago: Moody Publishers, 2020), 78–79.

Chapter 6: The Nation of Islam

1. Noble Drew Ali, *The Holy Koran of the Moorish Holy Temple of Science* (1926; repr., Oakland, CA: Califa Media, 2014), 59.

2. Eric Lincoln, *The Black Muslims in America*, 3rd ed. (Grand Rapids: Eerdmans, 1994), 57.

3. Arthur Huff Fauset, *Black Gods of the Metropolis: Negro Religious Cults of the Urban North* (Philadelphia: University of Pennsylvania Press, 2002), 41–44.

4. Yvonne Yazbeck Haddad and Jane I. Smith, *Mission to America: Five Islamic Sectarian Communities in North America* (Gainesville: University Press of Florida, 1993).

5. C. Eric Lincoln, *Race, Religion, and the Continuing American Dilemma* (New York: Hill & Wang, 1984), 165.

6. Susan Nance, "Mystery of the Moorish Science Temple: Southern Blacks and American Alternative Spirituality in 1920s Chicago," *Religion and American Culture: A Journal of Interpretation* 12, no. 2 (2002): 123–66.

7. Eijah Muhammad, *Message to the Blackman in America* (Phoenix: Secretarius MEMPS, 1973), 17.

8. Nance, "Mystery of the Moorish Science Temple," 123.

9. Anthony B. Pinn, ed., *African American Religious Cultures*, vol. 1: A–R (Santa Barbara, CA: ABC-CLIO, 2009), 240.

10. Alex Haley, *The Autobiography of Malcolm X* (New York: Ballantine, 1992), 346.

11. Bruce Perry, *Malcolm X: The Last Speeches* (Atlanta: Pathfinder, 1989), 117.

12. A. Marshall, *Louis Farrakhan: Made In America* ([United States]: BSB, 1996), 38.

13. Marshall, *Louis Farrakhan*, 69–72.

14. Marshall, *Louis Farrakhan*, 100–106.

15. Judith Cuivinings, "Black Muslim Seeks to Change Movement," *New York Times*, March 19, 1978, https://www.nytimes.com/1978/03/19/archives/black-muslim-seeks -to-change-movement-farrakhan-says-he-will-bring.html.

16. Lincoln, *The Black Muslims in America*, 264.
17. *This Far by Faith*, documentary film, shown on PBS, 2003. See https://www.pbs.org/thisfarbyfaith/about/the_series.html.
18. *This Far by Faith*.
19. Cuivinings, "Black Muslim Seeks to Change Movement."
20. Marshall, *Louis Farrakhan*, 109–10.
21. Associated Press, "Farrakhan Again Describes Hitler as a 'Very Great Man,'" *New York Times*, July 17, 1984, https://www.nytimes.com/1984/07/17/us/farrakhan-again-describes-hitler-as-a-very-great-man.html.
22. Arthur J. Magida, *Prophet of Rage: A Life of Louis Farrakhan and His Nation* (New York: Basic, 1997), xvi.
23. Lincoln, *The Black Muslims in America*, 269; Frank Kelleter, *Con/Tradition: Louis Farrakhan's Nation of Islam, the Million Man March, and American Civil Religion* (Heidelberg, Germany: Universitätsverlag Winter, 2000), 10.
24. Kelleter, *Con/Tradition*, 35–53.
25. Lawrence A. Mamiya, "Louis Farrakhan," *Britannica* (online), updated August 27, 2020, https://www.britannica.com/biography/Louis-Farrakhan.
26. Mamiya, "Louis Farrakhan."
27. Marshall, *Louis Farrakhan*, 39–40.
28. Kelleter, *Con/Tradition*, 11.
29. Kelleter, *Con/Tradition*, 11.
30. "BEST Preaching EVER! Farrakhan Speaks at Fellowship Missionary Baptist Church," uploaded by Ahmad770, January 3, 2011, hosted by YouTube, https://www.youtube.com/watch?v=Claw_yRLF4M.
31. Mamiya, "Louis Farrakhan."
32. Eliza Gray, "Thetans and Bowties: The Mothership of All Alliances: Scientology and the Nation of Islam," *New Republic* (online), October 5, 2012, https://newrepublic.com/article/108205/scientology-joins-forces-with-nation-of-islam.
33. Elijah Muhammad, *Our Saviour Has Arrived* (Phoenix: Secretarius MEMPS, 1974), 39–41, 96–97, 146.
34. Muhammad, *Our Saviour Has Arrived*, 56–57.
35. Muhammad, *Our Saviour Has Arrived*, 96.
36. Muhammad, *Our Saviour Has Arrived*, 170.
37. Muhammad, *Message to the Blackman in America*, 27.
38. Muhammad, *Our Saviour Has Arrived*, 158.
39. Muhammad, *Our Saviour Has Arrived*, 157–58.
40. Muhammad, *Our Saviour Has Arrived*, 157.
41. Mattias Gardell, *In the Name of Elijah Muhammad: Louis Farrakhan and The Nation of Islam* (Durham, NC: Duke University Press, 1996), 235.
42. Muhammad, *Our Saviour Has Arrived*, 19.
43. Muhammad, *Our Saviour Has Arrived*, 20.
44. Elijah Muhammad, *The Supreme Wisdom: Solution to the So-Called Negroes' Problem* (Phoenix: Secretarius MEMPS, 1957), 2:80.
45. Muhammad, *Message to the Blackman in America*, 3.
46. *The True History of Jesus as Taught by the Honorable Elijah Muhammad*,

compiled by the Coalition for the Remembrance of Elijah (Chicago: Coalition for the Remembrance of Elijah, 1992), 13–14.

47. Elijah Muhammad, *The Fall of America* (Phoenix: Secretarius MEMPS, 2006), 205.

48. "The Crucifixion of Jesus; Easter Message '89," video, posted by IRONMUHAMMAD68, August 29, 2014, hosted on YouTube, https://www.youtube.com/watch?v=xQGaHwyVG74.

49. Muhammad, *Message to the Blackman in America*, 31.

50. Muhammad, *Message to the Blackman in America*, 11, 23, 51.

51. Muhammad, *Message to the Blackman in America*, 290.

52. "Pt 51 The Wheel Allah God's Calling Card The Time And What Must Be Done by Min Louis Farrakhan 1," video of lecture, posted by sighproductions, April 17, 2016, hosted by YouTube, https://www.youtube.com/watch?v=r30DboeRe7c.

53. William A. Maesen, "Watchtower Influences on Black Muslim Eschatology: An Exploratory Story," *Journal for the Scientific Study of Religion* 9, no. 4 (Winter 1970): 321–25.

54. For examples, look up the work of Abyssinian Baptist Church in Harlem, NY; the Rev. Floyd Flake, pastor of the Allen AME Church in Jamaica, NY, and the work that congregation has done in Queens, NY; the Rev. Wyatt Tee Walker, Chief Strategist for the Southern Christian Leadership Conference and former pastor of the Canaan Baptist Church in Harlem, NY, and the work that congregation has done in the historical Harlem community; Bishop Vaughn Mclaughlin, pastor of the Potter's House International Ministries in Jacksonville, Florida, and the work that this congregation is doing in the community to effect better housing, education, jobs, and career opportunities.

Chapter 7: Engaging Hebrew Israelites

1. We will explain this language in the next section. The Hebrew Israelite groups are not monolithic, but a few core commonalities pervade each group.

2. Aaron Earls, "African Americans Have Mixed Opinions and Often No Opinions on Israel," Lifeway Research, November 5, 2019, https://lifewayresearch.com/2019/11/05/african-americans-have-mixed-opinions-and-often-no-opinions-on-israel/.

3. "History of the Israelite Schools," Original Royalty, hosted by YouTube, uploaded on October 9, 2013, https://www.youtube.com/watch?v=RL9QyhkjF4k.

4. Arna Bontemps, introduction to *Black Thunder: Gabriel's Revolt: Virginia, 1800* (Boston: Beacon, 2010), Kindle.

5. "'For he who knoweth his Master's will, and doeth it not, shall be beaten with many stripes, and thus have I chastened you.' And the negroes found fault, and murmured against me, saying that if they had my sense they would not serve any master in the world. And about this time I had a vision—and I saw white spirits and black spirits engaged in battle, and the sun was darkened—the thunder rolled in the Heavens, and blood flowed in streams." Nat Turner, *The Confessions of Nat Turner The Leader of the Late Insurrections in Southampton, Va. As Fully and Voluntarily Made to Thomas R. Gray, in the Prison Where . . . Account of the Whole Insurrection* (Richmond: Gray, 1832), 8

6. "Among those leading the session was Arnold Josiah Ford, an immigrant from Barbados who considered himself an Ethiopian Hebrew and had helped to organize

the study group to persuade other Black Harlemites that they too were Hebrews. The group became formal in 1924 when Ford joined with colleagues Samuel Moshe Valentine and Mordecai Herman to organize a Hebrew congregation in Harlem." Judith Weisenfeld, *New World A-Coming: Black Religion and Racial Identity during the Great Migration* (New York: New York University Press, 2017), 29.

7. Eugene D. Genovese, *Roll, Jordan, Roll: The World the Slaves Made*, rev. ed. (New York: Vintage, 1976), 253.

8. Jacob S. Dorman, *Chosen People: The Rise of American Black Israelite Religions* (Oxford: Oxford University Press, 2013), 3.

9. Dorman, *Chosen People*, 37.

10. Dorman, *Chosen People*, 39.

11. In this belief, Crowdy differs from all current-day Hebrew Israelite groups, who identify themselves with the southern tribe of Judah.

12. However, circumstantial evidence, including the fact that Christian called his teachings "Free Mason religion," suggests that Crowdy had access to Masonic legends of the ancient Israelites. Older Masonic-Israelite ideas and African American traditions of Biblical exegesis probably both played a part in the formation of his identification as a Black Israelite. Dorman, *Chosen People*, 8.

13. Christopher M. Driscoll, Monica R. Miller, and Anthony B. Pinn, *Kendrick Lamar and the Making of Black Meaning*, Routledge Studies in Hip Hop and Religion (New York: Routledge, 2019), 277–78.

14. To be honest, it is difficult to find accurate details about this group, as there are many gaps in their history, including pieces of the story that are only known to older members of the group or former members. Some information is available in videos online, but not much is verifiable. There are conflicting accounts among members who have started their own camps and have their own version of how things began. We must rely on oral tradition and member testimonies as primary historical sources for this group from the 1970s through the 1990s. The few books that attempt to trace this history are not always reliable.

15. "Racist Black Hebrew Israelites Becoming More Militant," Southern Poverty Law Center (website), August 29, 2008, https://www.splcenter.org/fighting-hate /intelligence-report/2008/racist-black-hebrew-israelites-becoming-more-militant.

16. Interestingly, if that is the case, Jesus wasn't Jewish. Most members of 1West don't believe in the virgin birth anyway and argue that Jesus did have a human father.

17. Elder Nathanyel Ben Israel, "Welcome Home," new member orientation packet, the Israel United in Christ.

18. Ronald Dalton Jr., *Hebrews to Negroes: Wake Up Black America* (Detroit: G Publishing, 2014), chap. 3, Kindle.

19. God (Yahweh) never brought all of these curses on Israel at any one time, but rather some of the curses were brought on Israel at different points: when the Israelites disobey God and are defeated at Ai and Achan in Joshua 7, for example. These reflect the curse described in Deuteronomy 28:25. Similarly, the consequence for the Israelites' evil behavior in Judges 6:1–10 resembles the curse described in Deuteronomy 28:33, 51. The Assyrian captivity of the Northern tribes in 2 Kings 17:3–6 reflects Deuteronomy 28:36–37, as do the Babylonian and Persian captivities

described in Jeremiah 25 and 2 Chronicles 36. In the New Testament, Jesus foretells the destruction of the temple and Jerusalem (Matt. 24; Luke 21:20–24), and in AD 70 Jerusalem is destroyed because of the Jewish rejection of Jesus as the Messiah. In both of these passages, however, Jesus connects what he foretells to the end of an era, not to the curses in Deuteronomy 28.

20. Flavius Josephus, *The Works of Josephus: Complete and Unabridged*, trans. William Whiston (Peabody: Hendrickson, 1987), 748–49.

21. Jerome, *Zech.* ii. fol. 120, cited in Thomas Newton, *Dissertations on the Prophecies Which Have Been Remarkably Fulfilled* (Philadelphia: Martin, 1813), 11.

22. Michael S. Heiser and Vincent M. Setterholm, *Glossary of Morpho-Syntactic Database Terminology* (Bellingham, WA: Lexham, 2013).

23. Edward Lipiński, "קָנָה," in *Theological Dictionary of the Old Testament*, ed. G. Johannes Botterweck, Helmer Ringgren, and Heinz-Josef Fabry, trans. David E. Green (Grand Rapids: Eerdmans, 2004), 59.

24. Leonard J. Coppes, "קָנָה," in *Theological Wordbook of the Old Testament*, ed. R. Laird Harris, Gleason L. Archer Jr., and Bruce K. Waltke (Chicago: Moody Publishers, 1999), 803.

25. E. Ray Clendenen, "Hosea," in *CSB Study Bible*, ed. Edwin A. Blum and Trevin Wax (Nashville: Holman, 2017), 1352.

26. GOCC and GMS camps believe that gentiles may be saved based on passages such as Isaiah 60:3, but they also believe that there is an ethnic hierarchy that must be maintained.

27. Allen C. Myers, ed., *The Eerdmans Bible Dictionary* (Grand Rapids: Eerdmans, 1987), 393.

28. R. T. France, *The Gospel of Matthew* (Grand Rapids: Eerdmans, 2007), 181–83.

29. Simon Hornblower, Antony Spawforth, Esther Eidinow, *The Oxford Companion to Classical Civilization* (Oxford: Oxford University Press, 2014), 259.

30. Clinton E. Arnold, ed., *Zondervan Illustrated Bible Backgrounds Commentary: Romans to Philemon*, vol. 3 (Grand Rapids: Zondervan, 2002), 284.

Chapter 8: Kemeticism and the Gospel

1. Kyle Keefer, *The New Testament as Literature: A Very Short Introduction* (Oxford: Oxford University Press, 2008), 20.

2. Brian K. Blount, *Revelation: A Commentary* (Louisville: Westminster John Knox, 2009), 4–5; Richard A. Horsley, *Hearing the Whole Story: The Politics of Plot in Mark's Gospel* (Louisville: Westminster John Knox, 2001), 35.

3. Tatian the Syrian, "Oration Against the Greeks," in *The Ante-Nicene Fathers: Translations of the Writings of the Fathers down to AD 325*, ed. Philip Schaff, vol. 2 (New York: Christian Literature Company, 1885), 126.

4. Cicero, *De Provinciis Consularibus Oratio*, ed. Luca Grillo (Oxford: Oxford University Press, 2015), 57.

5. Plato, *Gorgias*, ed. James H. Nichols Jr. (Ithaca, NY: Cornell University Press, 1998), 74.

6. Juvenal, *Satire II: Moralists without Morals*, ed. G. G. Ramsay (London: William Heinemann, 1918), 19. Here I follow the racial, skin-color connotation of

Aethiopem as it was deployed in Latin (lit. "burnt-faced one") in favor of Ramsay's more confusing "blackamoor."

7. See 2 Kings 19:9; 1 Chron. 1:10; Jer. 13:23, 38:7–10; Pss. 68:31, 87:4; Song 1:5–6; Is. 11:11, 18:1–7; Amos 9:7; Zeph. 3:10; Acts 8:26–40.

8. C. Marvin Pate, *From Plato to Jesus: What Does Philosophy Have to Do with Theology?* (Grand Rapids: Kregel, 2011), 127. It should be pointed out, however, that both the Hebrew contextualization of the Canaanite name El and John's contextualization of *Yeshua* as the *logos* were not deployed exactly the same way as these concepts originally operated in their respective religious and philosophical traditions. This is an apt representation of the way in which the Bisrat both embraces and transforms all cultural forms according to the will and glory of *Nouda*.

9. Alberto R. W. Green, *The Storm-God in the Ancient Near East* (Winona Lake, IN: Eisenbrauns, 2003), 285.

10. See Lamin Sanneh, *Translating the Message: The Missionary Impact on Culture*, 2nd ed. (Maryknoll, NY: Orbis, 2009), 57.

11. "Ethiopian" simply meant a person with dark skin; the mention of "Kandake" (the Kushite title for queen) identifies this eunuch as a Nubian/Kushite.

12. Michael P. Weitzman, *The Syriac Version of the Old Testament: An Introduction* (Cambridge: Cambridge University Press, 1999), 2. The Syriac Old Testament was translated directly from the Hebrew instead of Greek since Syriac and Hebrew are linguistically related.

13. See *The Acts of Thomas*, ed. A. F. J. Klijn (Leiden: Brill, 2003).

14. See John of Ephesus, *Ecclesiastical History*, ed. Robert Payne Smith (New York: Oxford University Press, 1860), 224; Athanasius of Alexandria, *Apologia ad Constantium*, ed. A. Robertson, in *Nicene and Post-Nicene Fathers*, ser. 2, vol. 4 (New York: Scribner's, 1907), 251.

15. See King-Tsing, *The Nestorian Tablet*, in *The Sacred Books and Early Literature of the East*, ed. A. Wylie (London: Parke, Austin, and Lipscomb, 1917).

16. Malcolm X, *The Autobiography of Malcolm X* (New York, NY: Ballantine, 1964), 424.

17. Frederick Douglass, *Narrative of the Life of Frederick Douglass: An American Slave* (New York: Twelve, 2008), 71.

18. Alexander Heidel, ed., "Epic of Gilgamesh," in *Gilgamesh Epic and Old Testament Parallels* (Chicago: University of Chicago Press, 1946), 17.

19. Edward F. Wente, Jr., "The Contendings of Horus and Seth," in *The Literature of Ancient Egypt: An Anthology of Stories, Instructions, and Poetry*, edited by William Kelly Simpson, 3rd ed. (New Haven, CT: Yale University Press, 2003), 94.

20. Miroslav Verner, *Temple of the World: Sanctuaries, Cults, and Mysteries of Ancient Egypt* (Cairo: American University in Cairo Press, 2012), 331.

21. George Hart, *The Routledge Dictionary of Egyptian Gods and Goddesses*, 2nd ed. (New York, Routledge, 2005), 29.

22. Sarolta A. Takács, *Isis and Sarapis in the Roman World* (Leiden: Brill, 1995).

23. For an example of such theories, see D. M. Murdock, *Christ in Egypt: The Horus-Jesus Connection* (Seattle, WA: Stellar, 2009).

24. Various Kemetic funerary texts relate various aspects of the Horus story—see, E. A. Wallis Budge, ed. "Hymn to Osiris," in *The Book of the Dead: The Papyrus of Ani*, vol. 1 (New York: G. P. Putnam's Sons, 1913), 59–61; James P. Allen, ed., "The Offering Ritual of Unis," in *The Ancient Egyptian Pyramid Texts* (Atlanta: Society of Biblical Literature, 2005), 19–29; Wente Jr., ed., "The Contendings of Horus and Seth," 91–103; Nora E. Scott, "The Metternich Stela," in *The Metropolitan Museum of Art Bulletin* 9.8 (1951): 201–17.

25. Bart D. Ehrman, *Did Jesus Exist? The Historical Argument for Jesus of Nazareth* (New York, NY: HarperOne, 2012), 215.

26. G. Daressy, Statues de divinites, the French Institute for Oriental Archaeology in Cairo (Le Caire: Imprimerie de l'Inst. Français d'Archéologie Orientale, 1905–1906), pl LXI.

27. David P. Silverman, *Searching for Ancient Egypt: Art, Architecture, and Aftifacts from the University of Pennyslvania Museum of Arthaeology and Anthropology* (Ithaca, NY: Cornell University Press & Dallas Museum of Art, 1997), 71.

28. R. E. Witt, *Isis in the Ancient World* (Baltimore: Johns Hopkins University Press, 1971), 214.

29. Armand Veilleux, ed., *Life of Pachomius* (Kalamazoo, MI: Cistercian, 1980), 25.

30. Tensions between Christians and proponents of traditional religion, such as the riot in Alexandria in 485 CE, illustrate the degree to which Christians and traditional religion practitioners saw their faiths as mutually exclusive. On this riot, see Edward J. Watts, *Riot in Alexandria: Tradition and Group Dynamics in Late Antique Pagan and Christian Communities* (Berkeley, CA: The University of California Press, 2010).

31. There were some Kemetic people who attempted to fuse the Gospel with traditional Kemetic religion. A seventh-century healing charm invokes the name of "Jesus-Horus," David Frankfurter, *Christianizing Egypt: Syncretism and Local Worlds in Late Antiquity* (Princeton, NJ: Princeton University Press, 2018), 1. Such practice was very rare and condemned by most Kemetic Christians. If this type of syncretism had been common in Kemet, the gospel would likely not have been persecuted as it was.

32. For Kemetic Christian (*Nazrawi*) leaders resisting Roman Christian oppression, see Timothy Aelurus, "Extraits de Timothée Aelure," *Patrologia Orientalis* 13, 202–18 (1919), 215–216; Ignazio Guidi, ed., "Life of Daniel of Scetis," *Revue de l'Orient Chrétien* 5, 535–64 (1900), 547–49. For a secondary summary of Roman colonial oppression of Kemetic Christian (*Nazrawi*), see Stephen Davis, *The Early Coptic Papacy* (Cairo: American University in Cairo Press, 2004), 85–128.

33. See Athanasius of Alexandria, "Apologia ad Constantinum," *Patrologiæ Græcæ* 25, 593–642 (Paris: Imprimerie Catholique, 1857), 636; Pseudo-Peter of Alexandria, "A Letter Ascribed to Peter of Alexandria," *The Journal of Theological Studies* 24.2, 443–55 (1973), 451.

34. Shenoute of Atripe, *God Says Through Those Who Are His*, eds. David Brakke & Andrew Crislip, in *Selected Discourses of Shenoute the Great: Community, Theology, and Social Conflict in Late Antique Egypt*, 266–77 (Cambridge: Cambridge University Press, 2015), 266.

Chapter 9: Black Women and the Appeal of the Black Conscious Community and Feminism

1. Adam Coleman, "Introducing the Conscious Community: Part 2," True Id Apologetics, March 11, 2019, https://www.truidapologetics.com/home/introducing -the-conscious-community-part-2/.
2. "Baba" is the Swahili word for father, also used to honor an elder man who serves as a father figure in the community.
3. Oshun and Ogun are two gods (Orisha) in the Yoruba mythology. Oshun is the goddess of the sweet waters, rivers, love, creativity, fertility, sexuality, and sensuality (colors: yellow and gold). Ogun is the god of iron and war. Known for building, technology, and justice, he is the defender of the community who clears the path for others when it is blocked with his machete (colors: green and black). For further reading on the Orisha, see Phillip J. Neimark, *Way of the Orisha: Empowering Your Life through the Ancient African Religion of Ifa* (San Francisco: Harper, 1993).
4. Ife Jogunosimi, "The Role of Women in Ancient Egypt," in *Kemet and the African Worldview: Research, Rescue and Restoration*, ed. Maulana Karenga and Jacob Carruthers (Los Angeles: University of Sankore Press, 1986), 32.
5. Jogunosimi, "The Role of Women in Ancient Egypt," 33.
6. Joseph R. Gibson, *When God Was a Black Woman and Why She Isn't Now* (New York: KITABU, 2008), 98.
7. Daima Clark, "Similarites between Egyptian and Dogon Perception of Man, God and Nature" in *Kemet and the African Worldview*, 120.
8. Man and woman are created beings, but Jesus is creator (Gen. 1:26–27; Col. 1:15–19; John 1:3). The Bible testifies about Jesus's divinity (Isa. 7:14; 9:6; John 1:1, 14, 18; 5:18, 23; 8:24, 58; 14:6–7; 17:3–5; 20:31; Phil. 2:5–11; Col. 2:9; Titus 2:13; Heb. 1:2–3, 8; 1 John 5:20; Rev. 1:17–18; 22:13, etc.).
9. Christine Emba, "Black Women and Girls Deserve Better: A Famous Quote by Malcolm X Still Rings True More Than a Half a Century Later," The Lily, January 13, 2020, accessed May 13, 2020, https://www.thelily.com/black-women-and-girls -deserve-better/.
10. A portion of an article I wrote for the book *Woke Church*: "The black church was revolutionary in developing dignity through programs, awards, and celebrations for black girls. They created enrichment programs including but not limited to, black history studies, oratorical contests, fashion shows, drama productions, educational trips, mentoring, tutoring, youth retreats, Bible memorization competitions, inviting successful black women speakers, and volunteering. The black church did what the public school didn't do, and what poor parents couldn't afford to do." See Eric Mason, *Woke Church: An Urgent Call for Christians in America to Confront Racism and Injustice* (Chicago: Moody Publishers, 2018), 154.
11. Sigal Samuel, "The Witches of Baltimore: Young Black Women Are Leaving Christianity and Embracing African Witchcraft in Digital Covens," *The Atlantic*, November 5, 2018, https://www.theatlantic.com/international/archive/2018/11/black -millennials-african-witchcraft-christianity/574393/.
12. Luna Malbroux, "Why More Young Black People Are Trading in Church for African Spirituality," Splinter, December 18, 2017, https://splinternews.com/why -more-young-black-people-are-trading-in-church-for-a-1821316608.

13. Samuel, "The Witches of Baltimore."

14. Samuel, "The Witches of Baltimore."

15. MAAT is believed to be an ancient Kemetic deity influential in the life of the people in the Nile Valley. MAAT represents the principle ethic upon which the Kemetic culture was built. In MAAT, there are seven cardinal virtues, ten principles, and forty-two declarations of innocence. See Gbonde Ina Ma Wase, *MAAT: The American African Path of Sankofa* (Denver: Mbadu, 1998).

16. Michael Eli Dokosi, "A Look at the Rising Number of Black Women in the U.S. Leaving Churches for African 'Witchcraft,'" Face 2 Face Africa, September 12, 2019, accessed May 4, 2020, https://face2faceafrica.com/article/a-look-at-the-rising -number-of-black-women-in-the-u-s-leaving-churches-for-african-witchcraft.

17. Samuel, "The Witches of Baltimore."

18. Samuel, "The Witches of Baltimore."

19. Hannah Tooley, "Beyoncé Proclaims, 'God is God, Not Me' at VMAs," Premier Christian News, August 31, 2016, https://premierchristian.news/en/news/article /beyonce-proclaims-god-is-god-not-me-at-vmas.

20. Erykah Badu, vocalist, "On and On," by Erykah Badu and JaBorn Jaml, track 2 on *Baduizm*, Kedar Records, 1997.

21. Sigal Samuel, "The Witches of Baltimore."

22. Vince Bantu, *A Multitude of All Peoples: Engaging Ancient Christianity's Global Identity* (Downers Grove, IL: InterVarsity Press, 2020), 2.

23. Samuel, "The Witches of Baltimore."

24. Samuel, "The Witches of Baltimore."

25. Sarah Bessey, *Jesus Feminist: An Invitation to Revisit the Bible's View of Women; Exploring God's Radical Notion that Women Are People, Too* (New York: Howard Books, 2013), 11.

26. Bell Hooks, *Feminism is for Everybody: Passionate Politics* (New York: Routledge, 2015), xii.

27. Chimamanda Ngozi Adichie, *We Should All Be Feminists* (New York: Anchor, 2014).

28. Angela Y. Davis, *Women, Culture, and Politics* (New York: Vintage, 1990), 27.

29. For readings on Black feminism see Patricia Hill Collins, *Black Feminist Thought: Knowledge, Consciousness, and the Politics of Empowerment* (New York: Routledge, 2000).

30. Walker's four-part definition of "womanist" (1) validates femaleness that is characterized by an inquisitiveness that seeks to understand that which is essential to know oneself; (2) sees personhood as defying social constructions, such as perceptions of human sexuality that contradict our sense of unconditional acceptance; (3) encourages us to celebrate life in its totality, including genuine responses to life and death; and (4) demands a deeper, more intense critique relative to the multiple dimensions of Black women's lives, individually and collectively. See Katie G. Cannon, Emilie M. Townes, and Angela D. Sims, eds., *Womanist Theological Ethics: A Reader* (Louisville, KY: Westminster John Knox, 2011), xv–xvi.

31. Robert Longley, "Womanist: Alice Walker's Term for Black Feminist," ThoughtCo, updated July 16, 2019, 2020, https://www.thoughtco.com/womanist-feminism -definition-3528993.

32. Evangelical feminism or feminist theology critiques patriarchy and sexism in Christianity and interprets the Bible through a feminist lens. See Rosemary Radford Ruether, *Sexism and God-Talk: Toward a Feminist Theology* (Boston: Beacon, 1983). For a critique of evangelical feminism, see Wayne Grudem, *Evangelical Feminism: A New Path to Liberalism?* (Wheaton, IL: Crossway, 2006).

33. For readings on womanist theology, see Stephanie V. Mitchem, *Introducing Womanist Theology* (Maryknoll, NY: Orbis, 2002); Delores S. Williams, *Sisters in the Wilderness: The Challenge of Womanist God-Talk* (Maryknoll, NY: Orbis, 1993); and Cannon, Townes, and Sims, eds., *Womanist Theological Ethics*.

34. Rosemary Ruether, *Sexism and God-Talk*, chapter 2, "Sexism and God-Language: Male and Female Images of the Divine."

35. Bessey, *Jesus Feminist*, 11.

36. Mary A. Kassian, *The Feminist Mistake: The Radical Impact of Feminism on Church and Culture* (Wheaton, IL: Crossway, 2005), 7.

37. Kassain, *The Feminist Mistake*, 9.

38. Kassain, *The Feminist Mistake*, 9.

39. Both Christian ethics and feminist ideologies would likely agree that domestic violence is wrong, a form of oppression against women. On the other hand, feminist ideologies would disagree with a complementarian view of Scripture that sees a husband as called by God to be the head of his wife as Christ is the head of the church. Most feminists would consider the male headship teaching to be a form of oppressive patriarchy that must be rejected.

40. Nancy Tuana, *The Less Noble Sex: Scientific, Religious, and Philosophical Conceptions of Woman's Nature* (Bloomington: Indiana University Press, 1993), 56.

41. Merlin Stone, *When God was a Woman: The Landmark Exploration of the Ancient Worship of the Great Goddess and the Eventual Suppression of Women's Rites* (New York: Harcourt, 1976).

42. R. Kent Hughes, *Genesis: Beginning and Blessing* (Wheaton, IL: Crossway, 2004), 37.

43. Hannah Anderson, "Reflection: Made in God's Image," in *Identity Theft: Reclaiming the Truth of Who We Are in Christ*, ed. Melissa Kruger (Deerfield, IL: Gospel Coalition, 2018), 22–23.

44. Hughes, *Genesis*, 60.

45. Quoted in Hughes, *Genesis*, 60.

46. God is referred to as the helper of his people in Ex. 18:4; Deut. 33:7, 26, 29; Psa. 20:2; 33:20; 70:5; 89:19; 115:9–11; 121:1–2; 124:8; 146:5; Hos. 13:9.

47. "Influence," Lexico, accessed January 25, 2020, https://www.lexico.com/definition/influence.

48. Joyce Hollyday, *Clothed with the Sun: Biblical Women, Social Justice, and Us* (Louisville: Westminster John Knox, 1994), 3.

49. Hughes, *Genesis*, 61.

50. Hughes, *Genesis*, 61.

51. Both men and women are called to control their power; women do it by willingly submitting to men, and men do it by sacrificially serving women.

52. Eddie B. Lane, *The African American Christian Woman: The Village Gate Keeper* (Dallas: Black Family, 1999), 79.

53. Sarita T. Lyons, "The Woke Church in Action," in *Woke Church*, ed. Eric Mason (Chicago: Moody Publishers, 2018), 155.

Chapter 10: Intentionally Engaging Black Men

1. Note the command given to "the women" in verse 9.
2. Biblical Studies Press, The NET Bible First Edition; Bible. English. NET Bible.; The NET Bible (Biblical Studies Press, 2005).
3. Jawanza Kunjufu, *Adam! Where Are You?: Why Most Black Men Don't Go to Church* (Chicago: African American Images, 1997), 16.
4. C. Eric Lincoln and Lawrence H. Mamiya, *The Black Church in the African American Experience* (Durham: Duke University Press, 1990), 141. Figures are estimated averages; subgroups do not equal total. For the male population, if we combine the 70 adult men with the 29 male youth, the 99 men now represents 25 percent of the total population of 390. The combined female population of 291 represents 75 percent of the population of 390.
5. Kunjufu, *Adam! Where Are You?*, 16.
6. Craig S. Keener, *The IVP Bible Background Commentary: New Testament* (Downers Grove, IL: InterVarsity Press, 1993), 1 Cor. 4:15.
7. In my book *Manhood Restored*, I spend an entire chapter on this subject—it is *that* important.
8. Michael Battle, *Ubuntu: I in You and You in Me* (New York: Seabury, 2009), 1–2.
9. The NET Bible, "Proverbs 18: NET Notes," Biblical Studies Press, 2019, https://netbible.org/bible/Proverbs+18.
10. Carl Ellis Jr., "Thug Spirituality: From 'I Have a Dream' to 'Sagging Pants'; An Analysis of the Current African American Cultural Crisis" (PhD diss., Omega Graduate School, 2010), i–ii,.
11. Ellis, "Thug Spirituality," 19.
12. Elijah Anderson, *Code of the Street: Decency, Violence, and the Moral Life of the Inner City* (New York: W. W. Norton & Co., 1999), 134.

Chapter 11: Black Atheism

1. "U.S. Religious Landscape Study," Pew Forum on Religion & Public Life and Pew Research Center, 2014, https://www.pewforum.org/religious-landscape-study/racial-and-ethnic-composition/black/.
2. John Gray, *Seven Types of Atheism* (London: Picador, 2019), 2.
3. The term "Black atheism" is occasionally used in a more idiosyncratic way to denounce God as represented in the Abrahamic faiths. I do not use it in this way.
4. John Mbiti, *African Religions and Philosophy* (Jordan Hill, Oxford: Heinemann, 2010), 1, 7.
5. "U.S. Religious Landscape Study," Pew Forum and Research.
6. Isabel Wilkerson, *The Warmth of Other Suns: The Epic Story of America's Great Migration* (New York: Random House, 2010), 9.
7. Christopher Cameron, *Black Freethinkers: A History of African American Secularism* (Evanston, IL: Northwestern University Press, 2019), 43.
8. Cameron, *Black Freethinkers*, 42.

9. James Baldwin, *The Fire Next Time* (New York: Vintage, 1962), 47.

10. "Mark Hatcher - Extended Interview | African Americans for Humanism," uploaded by Center for Inquiry, January 29, 2012, hosted by Youtube, https://youtu.be/9jhpf8p3klI.

11. Ta-Nehisi Coates, "The Myth of Western Civilization," *The Atlantic*, December 31, 2013, https://www.theatlantic.com/international/archive/2013/12/the-myth-of-western-civilization/282704/.

12. Anthony B. Pinn, *Writing God's Obituary: How a Good Methodist Became a Better Atheist* (Amherst, NY: Prometheus, 2014), 218.

13. Teodros Kiros, *Zara Yacob: A Seventeenth Century Rationalist Philosopher of the Rationality of the Heart* (Lawrenceville, NJ: Red Sea, 2005), 108.

14. Claude Sumner, "The Significance of Zera Yacob's Philosophy," *Ultimate Reality and Meaning* 22, no. 3 (1999): 182.

15. Kiros, *Zara Yacob*, 39, 108.

16. Claude Sumner, *Classical Ethiopian Philosophy* (Los Angeles: Adey Publishing, 1994), 233.

17. Sumner, *Classical Ethiopian Philosophy*, 236.

18. William Lane Craig, *Reasonable Faith: Christian Truth and Apologetics* (Wheaton, IL: Crossway, 2008), 96.

19. Craig, *Reasonable Faith*, 107. Some philosophers have sought to strengthen the cosmological argument by appealing to a "restricted" form of the PSR. See Alexander R. Pruss, "A Restricted Principle of Sufficient Reason and the Cosmological Argument," *Religious Studies* 40, no. 2 (2004): 165-79.

20. William Lane Craig, *On Guard: Defending Your Faith with Reason and Precision* (Colorado Springs: David C. Cook, 2010), 55–56.

21. Joshua L. Rasmussen, *How Reason Can Lead to God: A Philosopher's Bridge to Faith* (Downers Grove, IL: InterVarsity Press, 2019), 30.

22. See Craig, *On Guard*; Craig, *Reasonable Faith*; and Joshua L. Rasmussen, *How Reason Can Lead to God: A Philosopher's Bridge to Faith* (Downers Grove, IL: InterVarsity Press, 2019).

23. Craig, *Reasonable Faith*, 57.

24. Craig, *Reasonable Faith*, 107–8.

25. Craig, *Reasonable Faith*, 108.

26. Craig, *On Guard*, 59.

27. Craig, *Reasonable Faith*, 154.

28. Sumner, *Classical Ethiopian Philosophy*, 246.

29. Sumner, *Classical Ethiopian Philosophy*, 233.

30. Rasmussen, *How Reason Can Lead to God*, 56.

31. Thomas Nagel, *Mind and Cosmos: Why the Materialist Neo-Darwinian Conception of Nature is Almost Certainly False* (Oxford: Oxford University Press, 2012), 35.

32. Sumner, *Classical Ethiopian Philosophy*, 235.

33. James Weldon Johnson and John Rosamond Johnson, "Lift Every Voice and Sing," song (New York: Edward B. Marks Music Corporation, 2020).

34. John S. Jacobs, "A True Tale of Slavery," in *The Leisure Hour: A Family Journal*

of Instruction and Recreation, 1861, Documenting the American South, page 85, https://docsouth.unc.edu/neh/jjacobs/jjacobs.html.

35. Robert Merrihew Adams, *Finite and Infinite Goods: A Framework for Ethics* (Oxford: Oxford University Press, 2010), 115–21. See also Robert Audi, ed., *The Cambridge Dictionary of Philosophy*, 2nd ed. (New York: Cambridge University Press, 1999).

36. Craig, *Reasonable Faith*, 173.

37. Craig, *On Guard*, 129.

38. Craig, *On Guard*, 131.

39. Craig, *On Guard*, 131.

40. Craig, *Reasonable Faith*, 126–28.

41. John Leslie Mackie, *Ethics: Inventing Right and Wrong* (Harmondsworth, UK: Penguin, 1983), 38.

42. Michael Ruse, "Evolutionary Theory and Christian Ethics," in *The Darwinian Paradigm Essays on Its History, Philosophy, and Religious Implications* (London: Routledge, 1989), 268–89.

43. Norman L. Geisler and Frank Turek, *I Don't Have Enough Faith to Be an Atheist* (Wheaton, IL: Crossway, 2007), 189–90.

44. Charles Darwin, *The Descent of Man and Selection in Relation to Sex*, 1871, Gutenberg Project, updated December 17, 2018, http://www.gutenberg.org/files/2300/2300-h/2300-h.htm.

45. Craig, *On Guard*, 137–38.

46. David Hume and Michael P. Levine, *A Treatise of Human Nature* (New York: Barnes & Noble, 2005), 362–63.

47. Craig, *Reasonable Faith*, 108.

48. Anne C. Bailey, *African Voices of the Atlantic Slave Trade: Beyond the Silence and the Shame* (Boston: Beacon, 2005), 131.

49. Michelle Faubert, *Granville Sharp's Uncovered Letter and the Zong Massacre* (Cham, Switzerland: Palgrave Macmillan, 2018), 12–24.

50. Albert Raboteau, introduction to *God Struck Me Dead: Voices of Ex-Slaves*, by Clifton H. Johnson (Cleveland, OH: Pilgrim, 1993), xxv.

51. James Daley, *Great Speeches by African Americans: Frederick Douglass, Sojourner Truth, Dr. Martin Luther King Jr., Barack Obama, and Others* (Mineola, NY: Dover, 2006).

52. Leonard Black, *The Life and Sufferings of Leonard Black: A Fugitive from Slavery* (New Bedford: Lindsey, 1847), 59.

53. Gary R. Habermas and Michael R. Licona, *The Case for the Resurrection of Jesus* (Grand Rapids: Kregel, 2004), 48.

54. Hamermas and Licona, *The Case for the Resurrection of Jesus*, 81–132.

Chapter 12: Philosophy and Worldviews

1. Garrett J. DeWeese and J. P. Moreland, *Philosophy Made Slightly Less Difficult: A Beginner's Guide to Life's Big Questions* (Downers Grove, IL: InterVarsity Press, 2005), 10; Mortimer J. Adler, *The Four Dimensions of Philosophy* (New York: Macmillan, 1993), ix.

2. J. P. Moreland and William Lane Craig, *Philosophical Foundations for a Christian Worldview*, 2nd ed. (Downers Grove, IL: IVP Academic, 2017), 14–16.

3. DeWeese and Moreland, *Philosophy Made Slightly Less Difficult*, 11.

4. DeWeese and Moreland, *Philosophy Made Slightly Less Difficult*, 11.

5. Harry Blamires, *The Christian Mind: How Should a Christian Think?* (Vancouver: Regent College Publishing, 2005), 3.

6. James W. Sire, *Habits of the Mind* (Downers Grove, IL: InterVarsity Press, 2000), 9.

7. DeWeese and Moreland, *Philosophy Made Slightly Less Difficult*, 10.

8. Sire, *Habits of the Mind*, 27–28, 205–6.

9. Moreland and Craig, *Philosophical Foundations*, 3–6; Christopher W. Brooks, *Urban Apologetics: Why the Gospel Is Good News for the City* (Grand Rapids: Kregel, 2014), 40–42; Ravi Zacharias, *The Real Face of Atheism* (Grand Rapids: Baker, 2004), 13; See Matt. 28:16–20; Blamires, *The Christian Mind*; J. P. Moreland, *Love Your God with All Your Mind: The Role of Reason in the Life of the Soul*, 2nd ed. (Colorado Springs: NavPress, 2012).

10. James W. Sire, *Naming the Elephant: Worldview as a Concept*, 2nd ed. (Downers Grove, IL: InterVarsity Press, 2015) 23–24.

11. James W. Sire, *The Universe Next Door: A Basic Worldview Catalog* (Downers Grove, IL: IVP Academic, 2009), 20; Ronald H. Nash, *Worldviews in Conflict: Choosing Christianity in a World of Ideas* (Grand Rapids: Zondervan, 1992), 16.

12. Sire, *The Universe Next Door*, 22–23; Glenn S. Sunshine, *Why You Think the Way You Do: The Story of Western Worldviews from Rome to Home* (Grand Rapids: Zondervan, 2009), 13.

13. Nash, *Worldviews in Conflict*, 16.

14. Os Guinness, *Fit Bodies, Fat Minds* (Grand Rapids: Baker, 1994), 9–21.

15. Nash, *Worldviews in Conflict*, 17.

16. Moreland and Craig, *Philosophical Foundations for a Christian Worldview*, 15.

17. Bernard L. Ramm, *A Christian Appeal to Reason* (Irving, TX: International Correspondence Institute, 1972), 13–19; DeWeese and Moreland, *Philosophy Made Slightly Less Difficult*, 25.

18. Douglas R. Groothuis, *Christian Apologetics: A Comprehensive Case for Biblical Faith* (Downers Grove, IL: IVP Academic, 2011), 52–60.

19. Groothuis, *Christian Apologetics*, 24.

20. According to Elijah Muhammad, Yakub was a geneticist who became disillusioned and bitter toward Allah. As an act of rebellion, Yakub learned to gradually breed the black "germ" out of human beings. The breeding process resulted in progressively fairer-skinned humans. Because virtue is somehow linked to darker skin, the fairer-skinned humans became progressively more evil and resulted in a white devil race. Elijah Muhammad, *Message to the Blackman in American* (Chicago: Muhammad's Temple No. 2, 1965), 103–22; Carl F. Ellis, *Free at Last? The Gospel in the African American Experience*, 2nd ed. (Downers Grove, IL: InterVarsity Press, 1996), 98–100.

21. Muhammad, *Message to the Blackman in American*, 103–24; Elijah Muhammad, *The Theology of Time: The Secret of Time* (Atlanta: Secretarius MEMPS, 1997), 60–77; Imam Benjamin Karim, ed., *The End of White World Supremacy: Four*

Speeches by Malcolm X (New York: Seaver Books, 1971), 49–66; Steven Tsoukalas, *The Nation of Islam: Understanding the 'Black Muslims'* (Phillipsburg, NJ: P&R, 2001), 113–24.

22. Jabril Muhammad, *This Is the One: The Most Honored Elijah Muhammad; We Need Not Look for Another*, vol. 1, 3rd ed. (Phoenix: Book Company, 1996), 17.

23. Muhammad, *This Is the One*, 121–22; Tsoukalas, *The Nation of Islam*, 39.

24. John Perkins, *Dream with Me: Race, Love, and the Struggle We Must Win* (Grand Rapids: Baker, 2017), 129–38.

25. Tsoukalas, *The Nation of Islam*, 113–24; William F. Buckley Jr., "Why the South Must Prevail," *National Review*, August 24, 1957, 148–49.

26. Buckley Jr., "Why the South Must Prevail," 148–49; Martin Luther King Jr., *Why We Can't Wait* (New York: Signet Classics, 2000), 85–112; Nicholas Buccola, *The Fire Is Upon Us: James Baldwin, William F. Buckley Jr., and the Debate Over Race in America* (Princeton: Princeton University Press, 2019), 82–96.

27. Tony Evans, *Kingdom Agenda: Life Under God* (Chicago: Moody, 2013), 27–46.

28. Paul Horich, "Truth," in *The Cambridge Dictionary of Philosophy*, ed. Robert Audi (Cambridge: Cambridge University Press, 1995), 812–13.

29. Douglas Groothuis, *Truth Decay: Defending Christianity against the Challenges of Postmodernism* (Downers Grove, IL: InterVarsity Press, 2000), 19–22.

30. Amy Wang, "'Post-Truth' Named 2016 Word of the Year by Oxford Dictionaries," *Washington Post*, November 16, 2016, https://www.washingtonpost.com/news/the-fix/wp/2016/11/16/post-truth-named-2016-word-of-the-year-by-oxford-dictionaries/.

31. Wang, "Post-Truth."

32. Harry G. Frankfurt, *On Truth* (New York: Knopf, 2006), 8–9.

33. Louis P. Pojman, "Relativism," in *The Cambridge Dictionary of Philosophy*, ed. Robert Audi (Cambridge: Cambridge University Press, 1995), 690.

34. Scott B. Rae, *Moral Choices: An Introduction to Ethics*, 3rd ed. (Grand Rapids: Zondervan, 2009), 15.

35. Mortimer J. Adler, *The Four Dimensions of Philosophy: Metaphysical, Moral, Objective, Categorical* (New York: Macmillan, 1993), 62–63.

36. J. Budziszewski, *What We Can't Not Know: A Guide* (San Francisco: Ignatius, 2011), 20–25.

37. Horich, "Truth," 812.

38. Horich, "Truth," 812.

39. Horich, "Truth," 812–13.

40. Pojman, "Relativism," 690.

41. Pojman, "Relativism," 690.

42. Frankfurt, *On Truth*, 8–9.

43. Moreland and Craig, *Philosophical Foundations for a Christian Worldview*, 63–64.

44. Moreland and Craig, *Philosophical Foundations for a Christian Worldview*, 63–64.

45. Moreland and Craig, *Philosophical Foundations for a Christian Worldview*, 16, 63–64.

46. Ramm, *A Christian Appeal to Reason*, 13–19.

47. William Lane Craig, *Reasonable Faith: Christian Truth and Apologetics* (Wheaton, IL: Crossway, 2008), 30–31.

48. Craig, *Reasonable Faith*, 19.

49. Moreland and Craig, *Philosophical Foundations for a Christian Worldview*, 18; DeWeese and Moreland, *Philosophy Made Slightly Less Difficult*, 10–11.

50. Mortimer J. Adler, *Truth in Religion: The Plurality of Religions and the Unity of Truth* (New York: Macmillan, 1990), 70–75.

51. Adler, *The 4 Dimensions of Philosophy*, 6–7.

52. J. P. Moreland, *Christianity and the Nature of Science* (Grand Rapids: Baker, 1989), 103–4; J. P. Moreland, *Scientism and Secularism: Learning to Respond to a Dangerous Ideology* (Wheaton, IL: Crossway, 2018), 26.

53. The scientific method is the process by which scientists, collectively and over time, endeavor to construct an accurate (i.e., reliable, consistent, and nonarbitrary) representation of the world. In general, the scientific method is presented as an airtight sequential process. Stephen S. Carey, *A Beginner's Guide to Scientific Method*, 4th ed. (Boston: Wadsworth Cengage Learning, 2012), 3–6.

54. Carey, *A Beginner's Guide to Scientific Method*, 3–6.

55. Douglas Groothuis, "The Logic of Theology," in *Convergence: Essays on the Intersection Between Philosophy and Theology*, ed. Daniel J. Fick and Jesse K. Mileo (Eugene, OR: Wipf and Stock, 2018), 11.

56. Groothuis, "The Logic of Theology," 48–49.

57. Irving M. Copi, Carl Cohen, and Victor Rodych, eds., *Introduction to Logic*, 15th ed. (New York: Routledge, 2018), 327.

58. Groothuis, "The Logic of Theology," 48–49.

59. Groothuis, "The Logic of Theology," 48.

60. Groothuis, "The Logic of Theology," 11.

61. Copi, Cohen, and Rodych, eds., *Introduction to Logic*, 327.

62. The phrase "religious pluralism" is used in many ways, which can result in ambiguity. However, Harold Netland defines it as the presumption "that salvation (or enlightenment or liberation) should be acknowledged as present and effective in its own way in each religion. No single religion can claim to be somehow normative and superior to all others, for all religions are in their own way complex historically and culturally conditioned human responses to the one divine reality." Harold A. Netland, *Encountering Religious Pluralism: The Challenge to Christian Faith and Mission* (Downers Grove, IL: InterVarsity Press, 2001), 53. See also Wm. Andrew Schwartz and John B. Cobb Jr., "All Worship the Same God: Religious Pluralist View" in *Do Christians, Muslims, and Jews Worship the Same God? Four Views*, ed. Ronnie P. Campbell Jr. and Christopher Gnanakan (Grand Rapids: Zondervan Academic, 2019), 23-43.

63. Harold Netland, *Dissonant Voices: Religious Pluralism and the Question of Truth* (Vancouver: Regent College Publishing, 1991), 112–150; Charles Gibson, "Bush on Religion and God," ABC News, January 6, 2006, http://abcnews.go.com/Politics /story?id=193746&page=1.

64. Douglas Groothuis, *Are All Religions One?* (Downers Grove, IL: InterVarsity Press, 1996), 4–5, 11–16.

65. Nabeel Qureshi, *No God but One: Allah or Jesus?* (Grand Rapids: Zondervan, 2016), 13, 30–38.

66. Tony Evans, *Theology You Can Count On* (Chicago: Moody Publishers, 2008),

193–197. Charles Octavius Boothe, *Plain Theology for Plain People* (Bellingham, WA: Lexham, 2017), 21–23.

67. Thabiti Anyabwile, *The Gospel for Muslims: An Encouragement to Share Christ with Confidence* (Chicago: Moody Publishers, 2018), 25.

68. Anyabwile, *The Gospel for Muslims*, 25–26.

69. Evans, *Theology You Can Count On*, 222–24.

70. Netland, *Dissonant Voices*, 33–35.

71. Groothuis, *Christian Apologetics*, 47.

72. Copi, Cohen, and Rodych, eds., *Introduction to Logic*, 327.

73. Groothuis, *Christian Apologetics*, 47.

74. Groothuis, *Christian Apologetics*, 47.

75. Groothuis, *Christian Apologetics*, 47.

76. Groothuis, *Christian Apologetics*, 47–48; Harry G. Frankfurt, *On Bullshit* (Princeton: Princeton University Press, 2005), 4, 8–16.

77. Thomas C. Oden, *How Africa Shaped the Christian Mind: Rediscovering the African Seedbed of Western Christianity* (Downers Grove: IVP Books, 2007).

78. William Dwight McKissic and Anthony T. Evans, *Beyond Roots II: If Anybody Ask You Who I Am; A Deeper Look at Blacks in the Bible* (Wenonah, NJ: Renaissance, 1994), 129–43; William Dwight McKissic, *Beyond Roots: In Search of Blacks in the Bible* (Wenonah, NJ: Renaissance, 1990), 38.

79. McKissic and Evans, *Beyond Roots II*, 141–42.

80. In a Christian worldview, God is both *transcendent* and *immanent*. To this point, Tony Evans writes, "God is transcendent. In other words, he is independent of the universe. He is our creator and sustainer. So, how can humans expect him to dwell in a temple? The answer is found in the reality that ours is not a god who is aloof from his creation and takes no interest in human affairs. He is not only transcendent, he is also immanent—that is, he is present within his creation while remaining distinct from it." Tony Evans, *The Tony Evans Bible Commentary* (Nashville: Holman Bible Publishers, 2019), 428. See also Reggie L. Williams, *Bonhoeffer's Black Jesus: Harlem Renaissance Theology and an Ethic of Resistance* (Waco: Baylor University Press, 2014), 78.

Chapter 13: Outreach as Apologetics

1. Julian. "Letter to Arsacius." *The Works of the Emperor Julian*, trans. Wilmer C. Wright, Loeb Classical Library 3 (Cambridge, MA: Harvard University Press, 1913).

2. Harvie Conn, *A Clarified Vision for Urban Mission* (Grand Rapids: Zondervan, 1987), 29.

3. Elmer Towns, "Understanding the Times, Lesson 1," pastor's Bible class lecture, Thomas Road Baptist Church, 2 January 2011, Lynchburg, VA.

4. Jonathan Leeman, "We Come in Peace." *Primer: Show and Tell*, issue 7, 2019.

Chapter 14: Knowing Your Bible

1. UNESCO Education Sector, "The Plurality of Literacy and Its Implications for Policies and Programs: Position Paper" (Paris: United Nationals Educational, Scientific and Cultural Organization, 2004).

Chapter 15: Apologetics as Spiritual Warfare

1. Bruce A. Demarest, *The Cross and Salvation: The Doctrine of Salvation*, Foundations of Evangelical Theology (Wheaton, IL: Crossway, 1997), 325.
2. Anthony A. Hoekema, *Saved by Grace* (Grand Rapids: Eerdmans, 1989), 57.
3. Demarest, *The Cross and Salvation*, 321.
4. See Michael S. Heiser, *The Unseen Realm: Recovering the Supernatural Worldview of the Bible* (Bellingham, WA: Lexham, 2015), 23–24; Clinton E. Arnold, *3 Crucial Questions about Spiritual Warfare* (Grand Rapids: Baker, 2011), Kindle.
5. Heiser, *The Unseen Realm*, 23–24.
6. Clinton E. Arnold, *3 Crucial Questions about Spiritual Warfare* (Grand Rapids: Baker Academic, 2011), 145.
7. Vince L. Bantu, *A Multitude of All Peoples: Engaging Ancient Christianity's Global Identity* (Downers Grove, IL: InterVarsity Press, 2020), 1–2.
8. Kristin Hickey, "Smudging 101: Burning Sage to Cleanse Your Space & Self of Negativity," MBG Mindfulness, updated July 15, 2020, https://www.mindbody green.com/0-17875/a-sage-smudging-ritual-to-cleanse-your-aura-clear-your-space .html.
9. FringePop321, "Lucid Dreaming, Astral Projection and the New Age: Steven Bancarz's Story," October 1, 2018, https://www.youtube.com/watch?v=DSEiAPXx5Xc.
10. Tinothy Friberg, Barbara Friberg, and Neva F. Miller, *Analytical Lexicon of the Greek New Testament*, vol. 4, Baker's Greek New Testament Library (Grand Rapids: Baker Books, 2000), 290.
11. Arnold, *3 Crucial Questions about Spiritual Warfare*, 55.

SUBJECT INDEX

SCRIPTURE INDEX

CPSIA information can be obtained
at www.ICGtesting.com
Printed in the USA
LVHW040129100421
684048LV00004B/4